Salesforce for Beginners

A step-by-step guide to creating, managing, and automating sales and marketing processes

Sharif Shaalan

BIRMINGHAM - MUMBAI

Salesforce for Beginners

Commissioning Editor: Kunal Chaudhari
Acquisition Editor: Alok Dhuri
Content Development Editor: Tiksha Lad
Senior Editor: Storm Mann
Technical Editor: Pradeep Sahu
Copy Editor: Safis Editing
Project Coordinator: Francy Puthiry
Proofreader: Safis Editing
Indexer: Pratik Shirodkar
Production Designer: Joshua Misquitta

First published: May 2020

Production reference: 1280520

Published by Packt Publishing Ltd.
Livery Place
35 Livery Street
Birmingham
B3 2PB, UK.

ISBN 978-1-83898-609-4

www.packt.com

To my wife, Zahira, and my daughter, Amal, for their love, support, and inspiration.

To my mother, Hayam, and my father, Adie, for their love and guidance.

Packt.com

Subscribe to our online digital library for full access to over 7,000 books and videos, as well as industry leading tools to help you plan your personal development and advance your career. For more information, please visit our website.

Why subscribe?

- Spend less time learning and more time coding with practical eBooks and Videos from over 4,000 industry professionals

- Improve your learning with Skill Plans built especially for you

- Get a free eBook or video every month

- Fully searchable for easy access to vital information

- Copy and paste, print, and bookmark content

Did you know that Packt offers eBook versions of every book published, with PDF and ePub files available? You can upgrade to the eBook version at www.packt.com and as a print book customer, you are entitled to a discount on the eBook copy. Get in touch with us at customercare@packtpub.com for more details.

At www.packt.com, you can also read a collection of free technical articles, sign up for a range of free newsletters, and receive exclusive discounts and offers on Packt books and eBooks.

Contributors

About the author

Sharif Shaalan was first introduced to Salesforce as an end user in 2007. His range of experience, from a sales rep to technical architect, helped him successfully lead more than 80 implementations including projects that were showcased on the main stage at Dreamforce. In 2013, Sharif was chosen as a Salesforce MVP, and in 2020 he was inducted into the Salesforce MVP Hall of Fame. Sharif is a regular speaker at Salesforce conferences and has obtained more than 10 Salesforce certifications. He is the founder and CEO of Agile Cloud Consulting and continues to be an active Salesforce community contributor.

I would like to thank Melih Abdulhayoglu, Thaddeus Ward, Suraj Nekram, Timothy Ay, Dan Reider, Najam Khawaja, Shivanath Devinarayanan, and Vinay Chaturvedi for their knowledge and support. I would also like to thank my Content Editor, Tiksha Lad; the Project Manager, Tanvi Bhatt; and the entire team at Packt.

About the reviewer

Adil Mohammed is a Salesforce Principal Architect with 12 years' experience in IT and 10 years' experience with Salesforce. Adil is a Salesforce Trailblazer, mentor, and community group leader. He has a master's degree in computer science from Governors State University, Chicago.

He is a certified system architect and application architect and holds 21 Salesforce certifications. He is also certified on Apttus Quote-to-Cash and Copado DevOps admin. He has worked with clients from different verticals, including healthcare and life sciences, real estate, non-profit, higher education, security, and technology.

He has integrated Salesforce with different legacy and middleware systems, such as MuleSoft, DataPower, and TIBCO.

I would like to thank Packt for giving me this opportunity. Additionally, I would like to thank my family, who were a constant support during this process. I want to acknowledge the Salesforce communities, Trailhead, and the user groups for the knowledge they have provided over the years.

Packt is searching for authors like you

If you're interested in becoming an author for Packt, please visit `authors.packtpub.com` and apply today. We have worked with thousands of developers and tech professionals, just like you, to help them share their insight with the global tech community. You can make a general application, apply for a specific hot topic that we are recruiting an author for, or submit your own idea.

Table of Contents

Section 3: Automating Business Processes Using Salesforce

Preface

This book will explain Salesforce's functionality within the context of business use cases for end users and admins. The book has been divided into three sections. The first section will take a deep dive into sales, services, and marketing and explains how users in these departments can utilize the Salesforce CRM to maximize efficiency and provide a 360-degree view of constituents.

Next, we will cover the basics of Salesforce administration as a starting point for any aspiring admin. Finally, we will take a deep dive into the automation features that are most frequently used by Salesforce admins on a day-to-day basis.

All of these together will help us understand the various tools and features of Salesforce and help us gain an overview of how it works.

Who this book is for

This book is for anyone interested in learning Salesforce as a user and/or as an admin. No prior knowledge of Salesforce is needed. We assume the reader has a basic understanding of sales, services, and marketing business processes.

What this book covers

Chapter 1, *Getting Started with Salesforce and CRM*, is the first look at the Salesforce CRM. It covers basic CRM concepts, the difference between Classic and Lightning, how to log into and navigate Salesforce, how to search for records, and how to maximize list views.

Chapter 2, *Understanding Salesforce Activities*, covers the basics of Salesforce activities. It explains what activities are, explores the different types of activities, and shows how to use activities across all objects.

Chapter 3, *Creating and Managing Leads*, covers the basics of Salesforce leads. It covers what leads are, how lead status helps you manage leads, what it means to convert a lead, and how to use web-to-lead.

Chapter 4, *Business Development with Accounts and Contacts*, explains the basics of Salesforce accounts and contacts. It explains what accounts are, what contacts are, what relationships are, and how these objects are used by the business.

Chapter 5, *Using Opportunities Effectively*, covers the basics of opportunities, including what opportunities are, how stages function, how sales paths help you visualize your workflow, how the contact roles function, how products and price books function, how quotes function, and how opportunities drive forecasting.

Chapter 6, *Achieving Business Goals Using Campaigns*, covers the basics of Salesforce Campaigns. It covers what Campaigns are, Campaign Members, the Campaign Hierarchy, and how Campaigns interact with third-party apps.

Chapter 7, *Enhancing Customer Service Using Cases*, covers the basics of cases and related case functionality. It also explains how cases help to provide various scenarios for our leads and contacts.

Chapter 8, *Business Analysis Using Reports and Dashboards*, covers the basics of reports and dashboards and explains how to work with them.

Chapter 9, *Setup and Configuration*, provides the basics of setup and configuration and their related sections.

Chapter 10, *An Overview of Sharing and Visibility*, covers the basics of sharing and visibility and how the different settings grant or restrict access.

Chapter 11, *Using Sandboxes and Change Sets*, covers the basics of sandboxes and change sets in Salesforce for various use cases.

Chapter 12, *Configuring Objects for Your Business*, covers the basics of page layouts, record types, custom fields, and custom objects.

Chapter 13, *Third-Party Applications and Salesforce Mobile*, covers the basics of third-party applications, managed packages, unmanaged packages, Salesforce AppExchange, and Salesforce Mobile.

Chapter 14, *Understanding the Workflow Rules*, covers the basics of workflow rules and how they influence our contacts and leads.

Chapter 15, *Implementing Process Builder*, covers the basics of process builder, which will help us understand how to implement it in our applications to automate them.

Chapter 16, *Approval Processes*, covers the basics of approvals, including how they work and how they are assigned to help provide the right approval assignments to admins.

Chapter 17, *Assignment Rules*, covers the basics of assignment rules and how they help assign contacts and leads with the right leads.

To get the most out of this book

To get the most out of this book, sign up for the developer edition of Salesforce here: `https://developer.salesforce.com/signup`.

Once you sign up, you will have a working Salesforce environment that you can use to build the examples presented in this book. No other software is needed for the purposes of this book.

Code in Action

Code in Action videos for this book can be viewed at `https://bit.ly/2ThY3S8`.

Download the color images

We also provide a PDF file that has color images of the screenshots/diagrams used in this book. You can download it here: `https://static.packt-cdn.com/downloads/9781838986094_ColorImages.pdf`

Conventions used

There are a number of text conventions used throughout this book.

`CodeInText`: Indicates code words in text, database table names, folder names, filenames, file extensions, pathnames, dummy URLs, user input, and Twitter handles. Here is an example: "Any new case with a state/province of `New York` will be assigned to the New York Cases queue."

Bold: Indicates a new term, an important word, or words that you see onscreen. For example, words in menus or dialog boxes appear in the text like this. Here is an example: "Clicking on **Setup** in the preceding screenshot brings you to the administration section of Salesforce."

Warnings or important notes appear like this.

Tips and tricks appear like this.

Get in touch

Feedback from our readers is always welcome.

General feedback: If you have questions about any aspect of this book, mention the book title in the subject of your message and email us at customercare@packtpub.com.

Errata: Although we have taken every care to ensure the accuracy of our content, mistakes do happen. If you have found a mistake in this book, we would be grateful if you would report this to us. Please visit www.packtpub.com/support/errata, selecting your book, clicking on the Errata Submission Form link, and entering the details.

Piracy: If you come across any illegal copies of our works in any form on the Internet, we would be grateful if you would provide us with the location address or website name. Please contact us at copyright@packt.com with a link to the material.

If you are interested in becoming an author: If there is a topic that you have expertise in and you are interested in either writing or contributing to a book, please visit authors.packtpub.com.

Reviews

Please leave a review. Once you have read and used this book, why not leave a review on the site that you purchased it from? Potential readers can then see and use your unbiased opinion to make purchase decisions, we at Packt can understand what you think about our products, and our authors can see your feedback on their book. Thank you!

For more information about Packt, please visit packt.com.

Section 1: Salesforce for Sales, Marketing, and Customer Relationship Management

1

In this section, we will cover the Salesforce standard objects and how they interact across the sales, service, and marketing business units.

We will look at the following chapters in this section:

- Chapter 1, *Getting Started with Salesforce and CRM*
- Chapter 2, *Understanding Salesforce Activities*
- Chapter 3, *Creating and Managing Leads*
- Chapter 4, *Business Development with Accounts and Contacts*
- Chapter 5, *Using Opportunities Effectively*
- Chapter 6, *Achieving Business Goals Using Campaigns*
- Chapter 7, *Enhancing Customer Service Using Cases*
- Chapter 8, *Business Analysis Using Reports and Dashboards*

Getting Started with Salesforce and CRM

1

Once upon a time, before Facebook and iPhones, businesses ran their operations using on-premises software. These operations included managing customers and their interactions with the sales, customer service, and marketing departments of the organization. On-premises meant that the servers that ran this software were within the physical infrastructure of the business. Having the servers onsite meant huge maintenance and upkeep costs, as well as long deployment times for the smallest of changes. In 1999, Marc Benioff and his co-founders started Salesforce.com. As Benioff states in his book, *Behind the Cloud*, the idea was to make software easier to purchase, simpler to use, and more democratic, without the complexities of installation, maintenance, and constant upgrades. Salesforce was at the forefront of **Software as a Service** (**SaaS**) and cloud computing.

Fast-forward to 2019, when Salesforce.com reported $13.3 billion in total revenue in FY 2018 and is now constantly expanding the platform and acquiring new companies. This led to the Salesforce economy, which Salesforce projects to have created 3.3 million jobs by 2022. How did Salesforce get to this point? It started as a **Customer Relationship Management** (**CRM**) tool; then, over the years, it morphed into a powerful business platform with various clouds, including Sales Cloud, Service Cloud, Marketing Cloud, Analytics Cloud, Community Cloud, and many more.

In this book, we will focus on Sales Cloud and Service Cloud. These two clouds contain all of the core CRM functionality, which is the foundation of all the other clouds and sets up the path for you as the end user or aspiring admin to continue learning.

Salesforce is a platform to build your entire business on. Don't let the word *sales* mislead you. The platform supports the ability to manage all aspects of a business, including sales, customer service, marketing, finance, and much more, through out-of-the-box functionality and customization.

In this chapter, we will cover the following topics:

- Understanding the core concepts of CRM
- Understanding the difference between Salesforce Lightning and Salesforce Classic
- Learning how to navigate Salesforce
- Learning about the different search options
- Learning how to use list views across all objects
- Learning what Salesforce Chatter is and how to use it in your organization
- Learning the personal settings options available to end users

What is CRM?

CRM includes all interactions with an organization's constituents. This includes prospecting, the sales process, retention, marketing efforts, and customer service. The core of Salesforce is the out-of-the-box CRM functionality that is provided when you sign up for the platform. There are various editions provided by Salesforce; each edition provides different features and per-user price points. The four editions of the core CRM product are as follows:

- Salesforce Essentials: A small-business CRM for up to 10 users
- Salesforce Professional: A complete CRM for any size of team
- Salesforce Enterprise: A deeply customizable sales CRM for your business
- Salesforce Unlimited: Unlimited CRM power and support

Salesforce uses the concept of different clouds to bring together specific features. For example, all of the core features of running a sales operation, such as lead and opportunity management, are included in Sales Cloud. Features such as cases and knowledge bases fall under Service Cloud. There are also other clouds, such as Marketing Cloud, Analytics Cloud, and so on. The preceding editions in the bullet list focus on Sales Cloud and/or Service Cloud.

There is also a developer edition. The developer edition is one of the most valuable training tools when starting to learn how to use Salesforce, especially if you don't have access to a Salesforce environment of your own to practice what you are learning. Developer edition orgs are free, full-featured enterprise orgs with less storage and a limit of two licenses. These orgs are made for you to try out and develop features in an environment that is not directly tied to a paid production org. You can sign up for unlimited developer orgs. Regardless of the edition, the core objects are the same; we will cover them in detail in the following chapters of this book.

 In this book, we will use the terms environment, org, and instance interchangeably. These three words mean the same thing—the configuration that you see when you log in to a unique version of Salesforce. This can be a development org, a client's production org, or a sandbox. We will cover sandboxes in `Chapter 11`, *Using Sandboxes and Change Sets*.

Now is a good time to go to `https://developer.salesforce.com/signup` and sign up for your own developer edition.

As we walk you through the concepts of this book, you can follow along on your own org. As you sign up, you will be asked to enter a company name. If you don't belong to a company, don't worry—just re-enter your name for the company name since it is a required field.

Classic versus Lightning

Over the years, Salesforce has had a few UI makeovers to keep up with the latest trends in usability and design. The latest, and by far the biggest, UI change Salesforce has carried out is the introduction of Salesforce Lightning in 2015. This was a fundamental change to the look and feel that Salesforce users were used to and brought with it many new features that are only available on Lightning. Some of these features include the following:

- A modern UI
- The Lightning Component framework, which allows developers to build responsive applications for any device with less effort

Many organizations that have used Salesforce for a long time either plan to migrate, or have already migrated to Lightning. When Lightning was released, the older Salesforce UI was renamed to Salesforce Classic to differentiate between the two. The following screenshots show the exact same page in Salesforce Classic and Salesforce Lightning. Notice the option to toggle between the two interfaces. This means any user you grant this permission to switch back and forth between Classic and Lightning. This feature helps with adoption when you first bring users on to Lightning.

This is the UI for Salesforce Classic. Although there is great functionality in Classic, the UI is not modern:

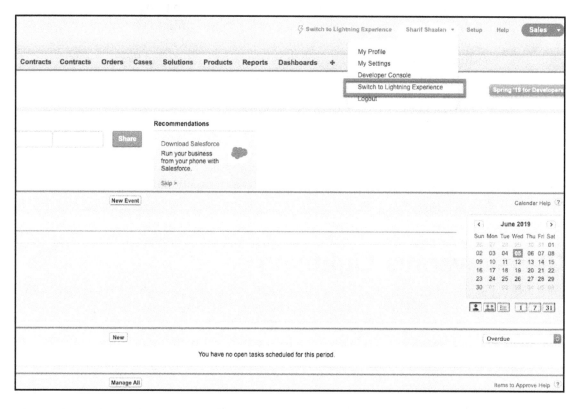

This is the UI for Lightning Experience. As you can see, the UI is more modern and you get a sense of the component-based framework from the home page items, on the left-side of the page:

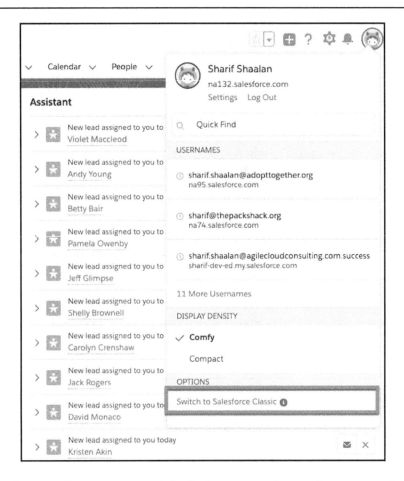

 As an end user or potential admin, you need to make sure you learn how to use Lightning as it is the future of Salesforce. At the same time, you need to be familiar with Classic since many organizations still use Classic or have a hybrid system set up, where some users use Classic and some use Lightning. In this book, we will show all of our examples in Lightning, but I recommend you toggle back and forth to see how the concepts work in Classic as well.

Now that we know what the difference between Salesforce Classic and Salesforce Lightning is, let's take a look at how to log in to Salesforce and navigate to various useful sections.

Login and navigation

Once you get access to your development org, it's time to log in. To log in to Salesforce, you need to go to `https://login.salesforce.com/`. This is important, as we'll see later when we discuss sandboxes—you have to go to `https://test.salesforce.com/` to log in to a sandbox. Your Salesforce username has to be in the format of an email, but not an actual email address. This is a key point since you may have access to multiple Salesforce orgs and the username has to be unique. So, when you set up your account, there is a requirement for an email address, which does have to be a real email address since you will receive your verification confirmation for the first-time login there. The username can be anything that takes the form of an email: so, for instance, my email might be `sharif@me.com`, but my username could be `sharif@me.com.myneworg`.

Once you log in, you will notice all of the tabs at the top of the page:

These tabs will help you navigate to the various objects in Salesforce. Objects can be considered as buckets of information or tables in a database. The **Account** object holds the various account records, the **Contact** object holds the various contact records, and so on. We will cover these objects in more detail in the upcoming chapters. You will also see tabs for things such as reports, dashboards, and Chatter. So, tabs are a mix of objects, as well as items you may want to easily access. When you log in, you will always land on the home page, which can be customized with various items that can make your job easier. The home page has components such as quarterly performance and Einstein Voice Assistant, which can be customized as needed. The quarterly performance component allows the logged-in user to see their sales statistics for the current quarter. The Einstein Voice Assistant is an artificial intelligence module that lets you know which customers or potential customers to follow up with using a phone call or an email based on data points, such as the last activity.

In the following sections, we will cover App Launcher, the search functionality, list views, Chatter, and the personal settings that can be applied.

App Launcher

On the upper left-hand side of the page, you will notice a few tiles under the cloud icon. These tiles take you to **App Launcher**, where you can access various apps in your Salesforce instance:

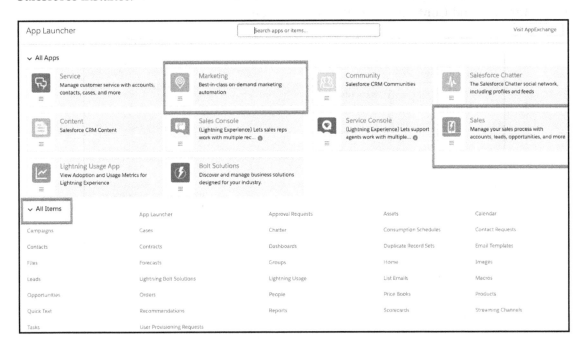

Apps are a collection of tabs that can be customized. Changing the apps will change the tabs you see in your navigation. Some good examples of things you will see when you click on this tile are the **Sales** and **Marketing** apps. The **Sales** app has things such as **Leads**, **Contacts**, **Opportunities**, and other tabs that are used for the sales process. The **Marketing** app has these same tabs, along with the **Campaign** tab, which is heavily used in marketing. You will also see **All Items**, which shows you all the objects in case you need to access one of them and it is not a part of the specific app you have chosen.

Search

At the top of the page, you will notice the global search bar. This search bar allows you to enter any search term and returns any object where that term is included. In the following example, I searched for `grand hotels`. Notice that Salesforce returns the **Accounts**, **Opportunities**, and **Contacts** where this term is present:

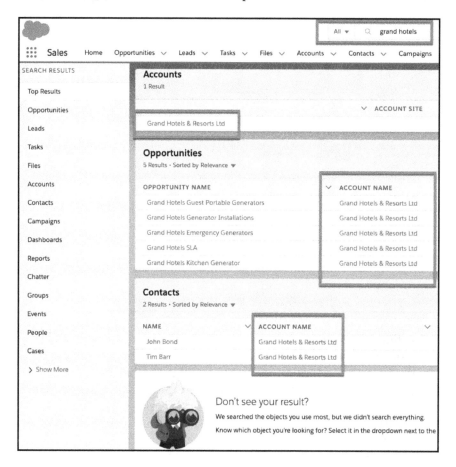

Once you have looked at the top results, you can narrow the search down to a specific object and refine the search further, if needed:

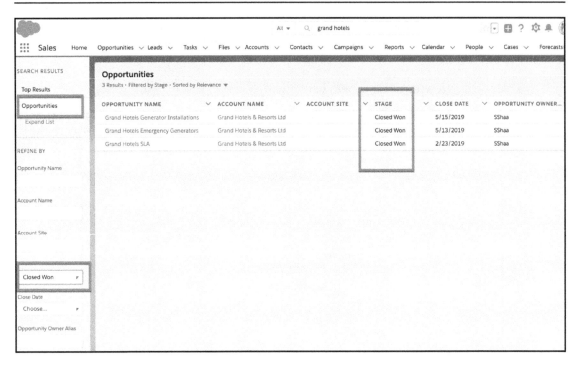

In the preceding example, I narrowed the search down to the **Opportunity** object and further refined the search by setting the **Stage** filter under **Opportunities** to **Closed Won**.

List views

List views are one of the most useful tools available to Salesforce end users. They allow you to sort, prioritize, and analyze records that are important to you within a given object using filter criteria. You will notice that whenever you click on a tab that is connected to an object, you will always land on a default view called **Recently Viewed**. This view shows any records you have recently worked on:

You can create as many list views as you need to help facilitate your work. For example, let's say you are an account manager and you only work with accounts in California. Let us see how to build this:

1. Click on **New** to create a new list view:

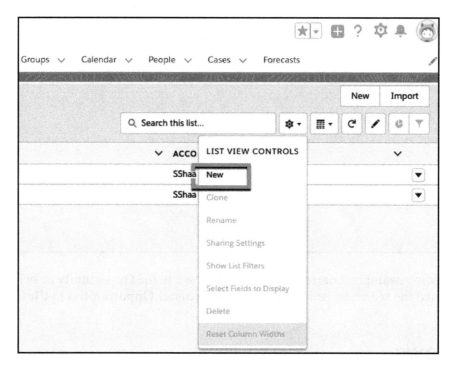

2. On the next screen, enter the list view name, California Accounts. The API name is the name used for development/coding purposes; this name is automatically set based on your list view name. As you will notice, the API name cannot have any spaces, so underscores are automatically entered in place of any spaces in the name.
3. Here, you can also set the sharing settings for this list view. The view can be private, shared with all users, or shared with a subset of users:

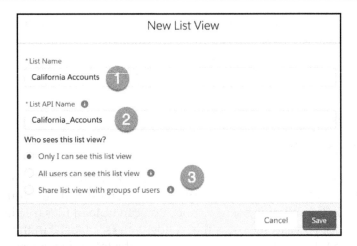

4. Next, you can choose your filters. You can filter by the accounts you own or all accounts and you can add multiple filters. For our example, we want any account where the billing state or the shipping state is **CA**. The filter logic allows you to set the AND/OR logic. In this case, we set it to 1 OR 2 since we want any records with the billing or the shipping state set to **CA** as shown in the following screenshot:

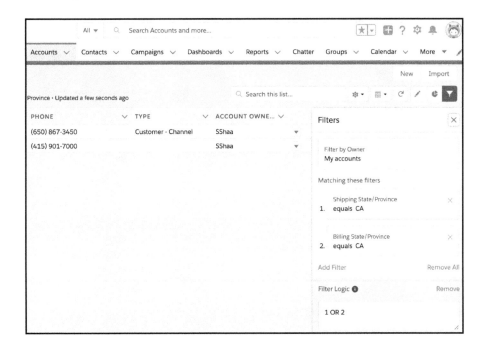

Create a few list views in your development org (organization) to get the hang of using this feature. As you do this, use different objects to see the different field options you have within a specific object and think about the use cases where you may need list views in a business context. Now that we have learned about login and navigation, let's take a look at Salesforce Chatter.

Salesforce Chatter

Chatter is a real-time collaboration tool within Salesforce. Think of it as Facebook within your organization. You have your own profile, you can share updates, you can create groups (see label 1 in the following screenshot), you can upload files (see label 2 in the following screenshot), you can see users that follow you (see label 3 in the following screenshot), you can follow other users (see label 4 in the following screenshot), and much more! You can access your profile by clicking on the icon at the upper-right side of the page or by clicking on the **People** tab. Your profile will show the groups you belong to, the files you have shared, people you follow, and people that follow you:

If you scroll down on your profile, you will see your feed:

The feed includes any posts you have made, any posts you follow, or updates to tracked fields on records you follow. The actions can be customized to include more than the post, poll, and question action.

If you click on the **Chatter** tab, you get an expanded view of the feed:

This view allows you to further refine your feed (see label 1 in the preceding screenshot), post new updates (see label 2 in the preceding screenshot), and view recommendations from Einstein (see label 3 in the preceding screenshot). Now that we have looked at Salesforce Chatter, let's look at some of the personal settings options.

 Salesforce Einstein is the artificial intelligence offering of Salesforce. Some limited Einstein functionality comes out of the box and is included in features such as the Chatter recommendations you see in the preceding screenshot.

Personal settings

To round out our general overview, let's take a look at some personal settings:

1. To access your personal settings options, click on the profile picture at the upper-right corner of your screen, then click on **Settings**:

On this page, you will see all of your options under a set of categories on the left-hand side:

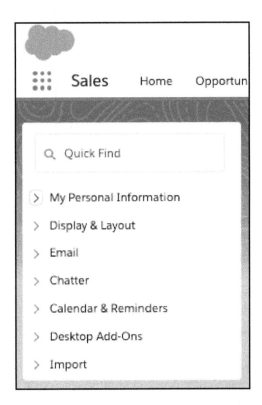

2. Under each one of these categories, you will find some personal customization options. Under **My Personal Information**, you have the option to add the following information:

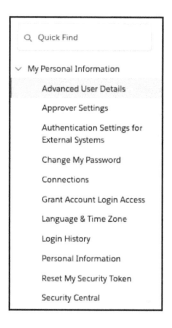

These are the following features in it:

- **Advanced User Details**: This page contains the fields on your user record that you can edit.
- **Approver Settings**: This page allows you to set a delegated approver—your manager—and approval email settings.
- **Authentication Settings for External Systems**: If you are connected to external systems, you can adjust the settings here.
- **Change My Password**: This page allows you to change your Salesforce password.
- **Connections**: This page shows any OAuth connections or third-party account links.
- **Grant Account Login Access**: This page allows you to grant login access to Salesforce customer service or a third-party app provider as needed.
- **Language & Time Zone**: This page allows you to set your time zone, locale, language, and email encoding.

- **Login History**: This provides an itemized list of all of the times you have logged in.
- **Personal Information**: This provides basic information from your user records, such as your email address and phone number.
- **Reset My Security Token**: This allows you to reset your security token, which is needed to access certain tools.
- **Security Central**: This shows the detailed account activity, which displays all of your sessions.

3. Next is **Display & Layout:**

Here you have the following options:

- **Customize My Pages**: This allows you to choose what related items show up for you for each object.
- **My Social Accounts and Contacts**: This allows you to adjust the settings to enable your social accounts and contacts, as well as Twitter and YouTube videos related to leads, accounts, and contacts.

4. Then we have **Email**:

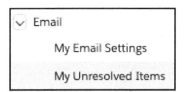

Here you have the following options:

- **My Email Settings**: This page contains the options for setting your email name, your email address, automatic BCC as an option, your email signature, and your email subscription settings, which allows you to opt in and out of things such as Chatter email digests.
- **My Unresolved Items**: This page has the settings for items that had no match when synced through third-party email integration. We will cover this page further in later chapters.

5. Next is **Chatter**:

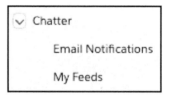

Here you have the following options:

- **Email Notifications**: This page allows you to set your email options related to Chatter.
- **My Feeds**: This page has an option to automatically follow any records you create.

6. **Next is Calendar & Reminders**:

Here you have the following option:

- **Activity Reminders**: This allows you to set defaults for reminders related to tasks and events. We will cover reminders in detail in Chapter 2, *Understanding Salesforce Activities*.

7. Then we have **Desktop Add-Ons**:

Here you have the following options:

- **Files Connect Offline**: This page has a direct installation link for Files Connect.
- **Salesforce for Outlook**: This page offers a step-by-step guide to setting up Salesforce for Outlook.

8. Next is **Import**:

Here you have the following option:

- **Data Import Wizard**: If you have permission to import data, this page will take you to the launch wizard.

 This overview is meant to give you a quick look into some very useful functionality. Make sure you review these items in your development org to get a feel for how they look and function in the Salesforce environment!

Now that we have looked at some of the personal settings, let's summarize what we have learned so far.

Summary

By now, you should understand the core concepts of CRM and the difference between Salesforce Lightning and Salesforce Classic. You should also now know how to navigate Salesforce and understand the different search options available to you. You should know how to build a list view, what Chatter is and how to use it, and what personal settings are available to you.

This is a good time to review what you have learned in your development org and see whether you can answer some questions.

This chapter will help us review all that we have learned in the development org and will help us answer all such related questions.

Now that we have an overview of Salesforce, we will start our deep dive into the application, starting with activities in the next chapter!

Questions

This is a good time to review what you have learned in your development org and see whether you can answer some questions:

1. What is the Salesforce economy?
2. What does CRM stand for?
3. What are two advantages of using Salesforce Lightning?
4. Are all tabs objects?
5. What is an app in Salesforce?
6. What does a global search return?
7. What is the default list view that appears when you go to a tab for the first time?
8. What is Salesforce Einstein?
9. Which personal setting allows you to grant login access to Salesforce customer service?

Further reading

Check out the *Learn CRM Fundamentals for Lightning Experience* Trailhead module at `https://trailhead.salesforce.com/en/content/learn/trails/crm-essentials-lightning-experience`.

2
Understanding Salesforce Activities

Now that we've had an overview of the basics of CRM, let's start digging into some core functionality. This chapter covers activities. Activities are at the core of CRM because they help you manage the relationship you have with your constituents, that is, the people you are doing business with. Activities include all the touchpoints you go through with your constituents. We will cover the main types of activities in this chapter, which are tasks, events, and emails, and how they affect the user's workflow.

The following topics will be covered in this chapter:

- Navigating to what Salesforce defines as activities
- Creating entries for events and calendars
- Sending emails from Salesforce and exploring the email integration options

By the end of this chapter, you will have learned about tasks, events, calendar integration, and emails in Salesforce.

Technical requirements

For this chapter, log into your development organization and follow along as we learn how to create activities.

Navigating to activities

In Salesforce, activities include tasks, events, and calendars. Activities help you prioritize your time and keep up with any object. The main objects that you will use with activities are **Accounts**, **Campaigns**, **Contacts**, **Leads**, and **Opportunities**. Emails are another type of activity that you may use to stay in touch with your contacts and leads. Having all the touchpoints logged in Salesforce will give you a 360-degree view of your contacts and let you look at any person related to a specific Account, Contact, Opportunity, Lead, or Campaign that you may be working with. Out of the box, you will see that these main objects have a connection to activities. You can also view your activities on the home page, depending on your home page's layout. This gives you a shortcut to all of your activities. Let's see what activities look like when they're connected to objects. The following screenshot shows the **GenePoint** account:

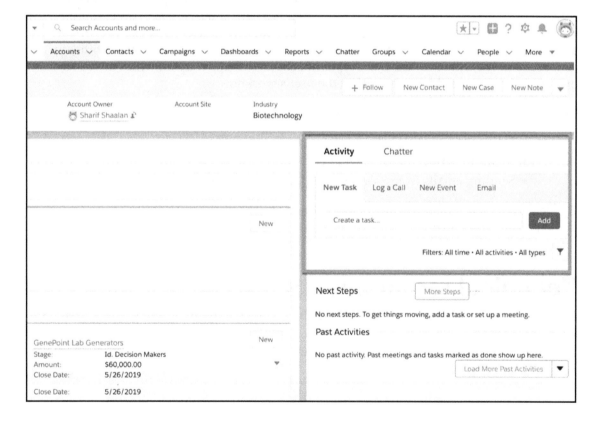

Here, I have navigated to the **Accounts** tab and then to the **GenePoint** Account. On the right-hand side, you can see that there is an **Activity** section, which allows us to create a task, log a call, create an event, or send an email. If you navigate to any of the other tabs, you will see that the same **Activity** section exists.

Let's cover each of these activity types in detail.

Tasks

Tasks are objects on your to-do list. They help you stay on top of things that you need to do and are related to the accounts you manage, deals you are working on, or marketing campaigns you may be managing.

Business use case

You are a sales representative at XYZ Widgets. **Mr. Jack Rogers** is a contact that is interested in buying your product. You call Jack and have a good conversation with him. After the conversation, you decide to set up a follow-up task so that you can call Jack again so that you can gather more information on the next steps to take. Let's see how this is done.

Creating tasks

To create a task, navigate to any object that you want to log a task for and go to the **Activity** section. Take a look at the following screenshot:

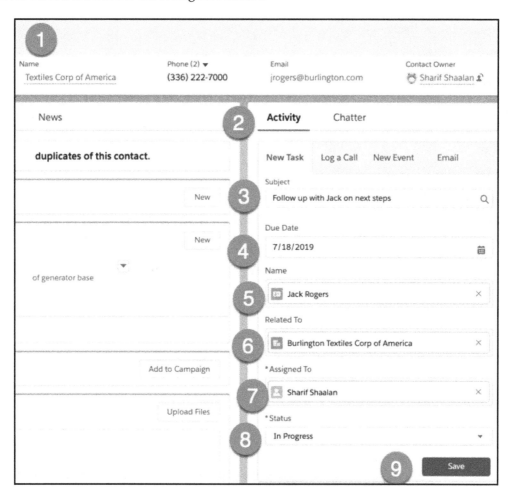

From the preceding screenshot, we can see the following (the following nine points coincide with the numbers shown in the preceding screenshot):

1. I navigated to **Mr. Jack Rogers.**
2. Then, I navigated to the **Activity** section.
3. I filled in the subject of the task.
4. Then, I filled in the due date for when I wish to perform this task.
5. The name of the contact is pre-populated since I am on the contact record.
6. Then, I added the account that Jack is related to.
7. The task is assigned to me since I am the logged-in user.
8. I set the task to **In Progress.**
9. I saved the record.

After performing these steps, we can see that the task shows up in the **Next Steps** section, as shown in the following screenshot:

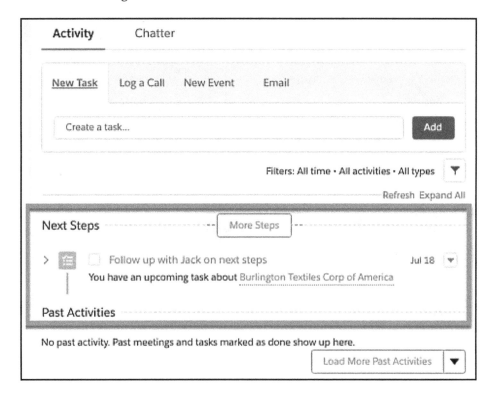

Once the task has been completed, you can check the **Next Steps** box to mark it as completed. This is highlighted as (1) in the following screenshot. You can then set up a follow-up task if needed (highlighted as 2 in the following screenshot):

Notice that the task now shows up in **Past Activities**, as shown here:

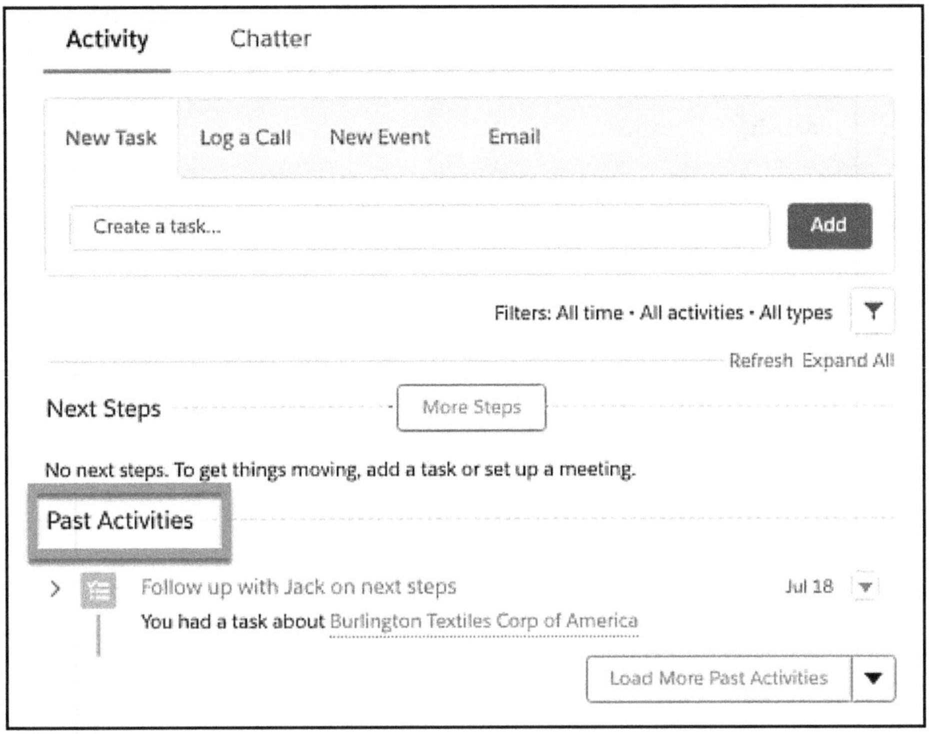

Now that we have learned how to create a task, let's take a look at how to log a call.

Logging a call

Logging a call is a type of task. It works exactly as a task does, except for two things: first, the due date always defaults to today; second, the status is always set to **Completed**.

Business use case

As a sales representative for XYZ Widgets, Jack Rogers calls in with a question. After the call, you want to update Salesforce with details of the call that took place.

Logging a call

In the following screenshot, I navigated to the **Log a Call** sub-tab in order to log a call. You will notice no options for **Due Date** or **Status**:

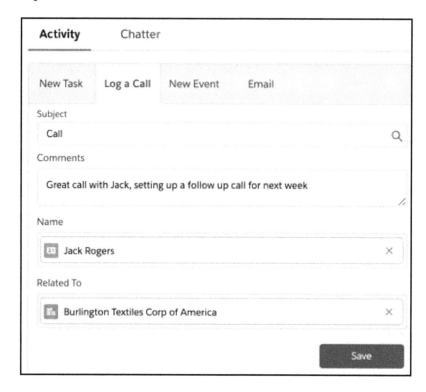

This is because the **Log a Call** functionality is built only logs calls you've just completed with a client.

In this case, the due date is set to the current day and the status is automatically set to completed, as shown in the following screenshot:

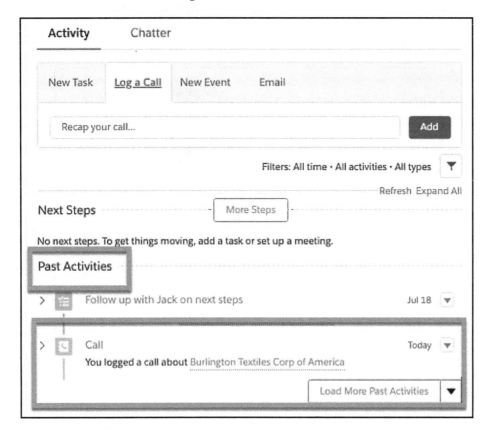

As you can see, when you save the call, the task automatically shows up under **Past Activities**.

Task List View

There are times where we'll have a few pending tasks that need to be performed during the course of the day. To see all such outstanding tasks, navigate to the **Tasks** tab, where you can keep track of them. The following screenshot shows this:

As you can see, you can filter by the following options:

- **Delegated Tasks** (these are tasks someone else has assigned to you)
- **Open Tasks**
- **Overdue Tasks**
- **Recently Completed Tasks**
- **Recently Viewed Tasks**
- **Today's Tasks**
- **Unscheduled Tasks** (tasks with no due date)

These list views will help you organize your day and view the lists of **Tasks** you wish to work on.

Viewing tasks on the home page

Another place where you can easily access your tasks and events is your home page. The default home page layout contains two components that show activities.

The following screenshot shows these components:

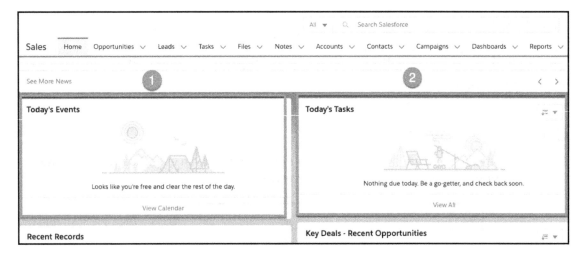

As you can see, the two components are called **Today's Events** (1) and **Today's Tasks** (2). Now that we have covered tasks, let's take a look at events.

Creating events and calendar entries

Events are activities that require a start date/time and an end date/time and are used to log actual meetings. An event activity is different from a task in a couple of ways:

- Events have a start date/time and an end date/time rather than a due date. This means that when the end date and time passes, the event automatically moves to **Past Activities** without you needing to take action. For ongoing tasks, you have to mark them as complete since only a date is provided – not a specific time.
- Events show up on your Salesforce calendar and will sync to Outlook or Gmail if you have the connector set up. We will cover connectors later in this chapter.

Now, let's take a look at events in more detail.

Understanding Events

Events are meetings that have a start date and a start time, as well as an end date and an end time. They let you set up meetings related to the accounts you manage, the deals you are working on, or the marketing campaigns you may be managing.

Business use case

As a sales representative for XYZ Widgets, you close a sale with Jack Rogers and want to schedule a kick-off meeting for the next steps. You enter this event in Salesforce so that it shows up on your calendar.

Creating an event

To create an event, navigate to any object that you want to log an event for and go to the **Activity** section, as shown in the following screenshot:

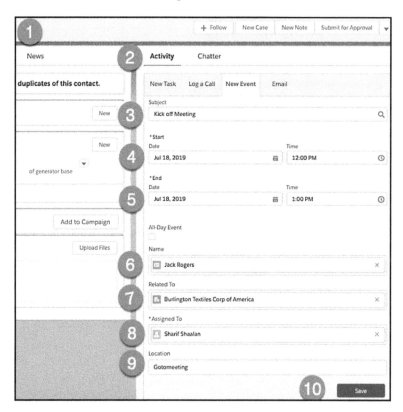

Here, we have to do the following (the following 10 bullet points coincide with the numbers shown in the preceding screenshot):

1. Navigate to **Mr. Jack Rogers.**
2. Go to the **Activity** section.
3. Fill in the subject of the event.
4. Fill in the start date/time of the event.
5. Fill in the end date/time of the event.
6. Ensure that the name of the contact is pre-populated if the user is on the contact record.
7. Add the account that Jack is related to.
8. Ensure that the task has been assigned to the user (this is me since I am the logged-in user).
9. Enter the location of the meeting.
10. Save the record.

After doing this, you'll see that the event now shows up in the **Next Steps** section, as shown in the following screenshot:

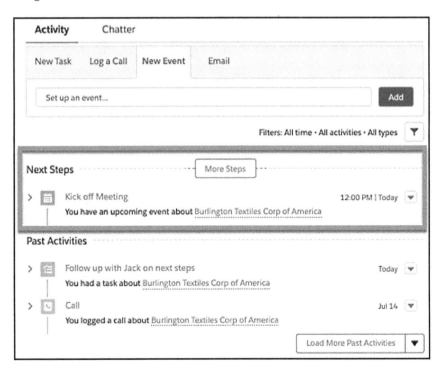

Once the date for the meeting has passed, the event will automatically move to the **Past Activities** section.

This is how events work. In the next section, we'll learn how the Salesforce calendar is aligned with these events.

Salesforce calendar

Once an event has been created, it will show up on your Salesforce **calendar**, as shown in the following screenshot:

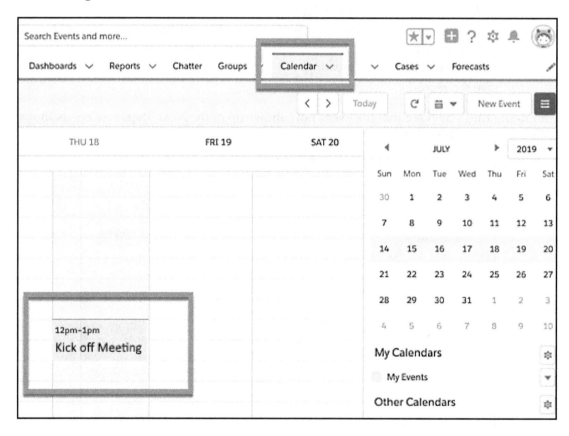

To navigate to your calendar, click on the **Calendar** tab. Here, you will see all of your events. If you have the Lightning Sync feature enabled and configured for Gmail or Outlook, your events will sync from Salesforce to those services.

Now, you are familiar with how events can be set up, how to follow up on them, and how such events can be synced to Salesforce calendars or with Gmail or Outlook. In the next section, we will learn how emails and email integration options work.

Sending emails and email integration options

Salesforce allows you to send emails directly from any standard or custom object. This takes place from the same **Activity** section that we used to log tasks and events.

Business use case

As a sales representative for XYZ Widgets, you want to send Jack Rogers a follow-up email after your initial conversation. You can do this directly from Salesforce as an activity! Let's see how this is done.

Sending an email

As shown in the following screenshot, I navigated to the **Activity** section under the **Jack Rogers** contact and clicked on **Email**:

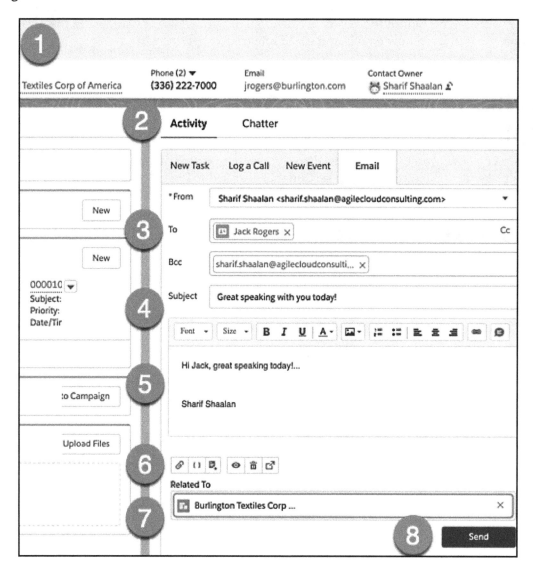

From the preceding screenshot, we can see the following (the following eight bullet points coincide with the numbers shown in the preceding screenshot):

1. Navigate to **Mr. Jack Rogers.**
2. Go to the **Activity** section.
3. Fill in the **To** information. This can be a contact on the system or a free text email address.
4. Add the subject.
5. Add the body of the email.
6. Here, you have the option to choose a template, add quick text, and attach a file.
7. The activity is assigned to the user.
8. Save the record, shown as follows:

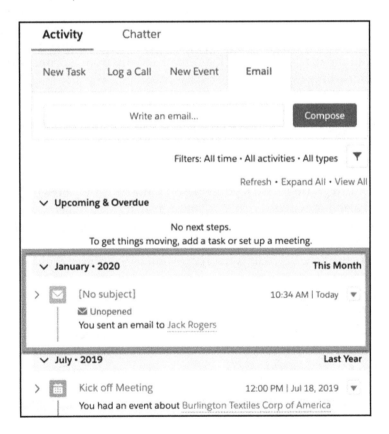

Once the email has been sent, it will show up in the **Past Activities** section.

Using Gmail integration options

Calendar integration helps you sync specific events and emails to Salesforce. This is useful so that you don't create double entries in your email/calendar client and Salesforce. The following options are available for Gmail:

- **Send through Gmail**: This is for representatives who spend most of their time in Salesforce but want to use a Gmail account to send emails. Emails are composed in Salesforce but are sent through a connected Gmail account and appear in the Gmail **Sent** folder. When **Send through Gmail** is enabled, the activity history for leads and contacts includes a **Compose Gmail** button. Emails are logged to the records the email was sent from.
- **Gmail Integration**: This is for representatives who spend most of their time on their Gmail account. When emails are sent, they can select which Salesforce records to log the emails to.
- **Einstein Activity Capture**: This option is for users who prefer to have emails logged automatically. Einstein logs email activity from a connected client or device, including Gmail.

Using Outlook integration options

The following options are available for Outlook:

- **Outlook Integration**: When you work in Outlook, you can sync your emails and/or calendar events directly to Salesforce and vice versa.
- **Outlook Integration with Inbox and Einstein Activity Capture**: Einstein Activity Capture lets you automatically log emails and events if you have this feature turned on. Einstein is the AI portion of Salesforce that auto-suggests useful steps to take as you work.
- **Lightning Sync for Microsoft Exchange**: Salesforce admins can set up Lightning Sync so that users can sync contacts and emails with your exchange server.
- **Salesforce for Outlook**: This option syncs contacts, events, and tasks between Outlook and Salesforce.
- **Email to Salesforce**: This option lets users add emails to Salesforce records by copying a unique BCC email to all emails you send out.

Sending emails is a primary activity in any business. Using the preceding tools ensures that you are not entering information in multiple systems. It does this by allowing you to sync your emails and/or events with your email and calendar client. Now, let's review what we have learned in this chapter.

Summary

Activities are at the core of CRM, so it is very important that you understand how to log your interactions with constituents.

In this chapter, we learned about the use cases for tasks and how to create and work with tasks. Then, we learned how we create use cases for events and how to create and work with them, as well as how to create use cases for sending emails from Salesforce and the options we have if we wish to extend this functionality to Outlook or Gmail. All of these skills will help us in our daily interactions, which will lead to more sales!

This is a good time to review what we have learned in our development organization and see if we can answer some questions. In the next chapter, we will tackle Leads!

Questions

1. What type of activity should be used to set up a reminder to research an account?
2. Which activity type should be used to set up an onsite meeting with a client?
3. Is it possible to send an email to a client and copy someone not in the system as a contact?
4. Do tasks appear on your Salesforce calendar?
5. Which tab shows all of your open tasks?
6. If you use Gmail but spend most of your time in Salesforce, which integration option should you use?
7. Can we log activities regarding Opportunities?

Further reading

- **Trailhead Module: Manage Your tasks, events, and emails**: `https://trailhead.salesforce.com/en/content/learn/modules/lightning-experience-productivity/manage-your-tasks-events-and-email`
- **Send Through Gmail**: `https://help.salesforce.com/articleView?id=email_send_through_external.htmtype=5language=en_US`
- **Gmail Integration**: `https://help.salesforce.com/articleView?id=email_int_user_overview.htmtype=5language=en_US`
- **Einstein Activity Capture**: `https://help.salesforce.com/articleView?id=einstein_sales_aac.htmtype=5language=en_US`
- **Outlook Integration**: `https://help.salesforce.com/articleView?id=app_for_outlook_overview.htmtype=0`
- **Outlook Integration with Inbox and Einstein Activity Capture**: `https://help.salesforce.com/articleView?id=inbox.htmtype=0`
- **Lightning Sync for Microsoft Exchange**: `https://help.salesforce.com/articleView?id=exchange_sync_admin_implement_ex_sync.htmtype=0`
- **Salesforce for Outlook**: `https://help.salesforce.com/articleView?id=outlookcrm_sfo_about.htmtype=5%20%C2%A0`
- **Email to Salesforce**: `https://help.salesforce.com/articleView?id=emailadmin_email2salesforce.htmtype=0`

Creating and Managing Leads

3

Leads are the first step of the sales and marketing cycle—they keep opportunities flowing into our sales funnel. Leads are prospects or people that may be interested in your product or service. The goal of working with them is to move them through the sales cycle and assess them as either **unqualified** or **qualified** for workable opportunities. Understanding how leads work is beneficial as it familiarizes you with how a lead starts off the sales cycle and how to move from a lead to the next step in the sales cycle. This is what we will explore in this chapter.

The following topics are covered in this chapter:

- What are leads and what are they used for?
- What is Lead Status and how is it used in the sales cycle?
- What is lead conversion and what happens when you convert a lead?
- What is web-to-lead and how is this feature used?
- What are lead auto-response rules and how do you set them up?
- Lead settings and lead processes

In this chapter, we will learn the skills needed to create a lead, as well as learning what a lead record contains. We will also learn how to move a lead through the initial sales cycle, how to convert a qualified lead into an opportunity in order to move to the next step of the sales cycle, and how to create web-to-lead forms.

Technical requirements

For this chapter, log in to your development org and follow along as we create and convert a lead.

Understanding leads

Converting leads into opportunities is the key to a successful business. Managing your leads effectively allows you to convert more leads into opportunities, which ultimately results in more business. Leads can be captured in many different ways, such as through conferences, websites, purchasing lists, and any other way you may come into contact with potential customers. Let's look at a business use case where a lead may need to be created, then we'll walk through the steps for creating a lead.

A business use case

You are a sales representative for your company, XYZ Widgets, and have been sent to a conference to talk to potential customers. While at the conference, you have a great conversation with Brenda Mcclure, the CFO of Cardinal Inc. Brenda is interested in potentially purchasing 1,000 widgets for Cardinal and gives you her card. This is a hot lead! Let's see how you work this lead in Salesforce.

Creating leads

After this conversation, you take the business card and decide to enter the information into Salesforce right away. Usually, you would wait until after the conference and enter all of the leads' information together, but this is a big deal and you want to make sure you get it into Salesforce ASAP. Your manager always says "*If it doesn't exist in Salesforce, it doesn't exist!*" Let's see how the lead is created in Salesforce.

The following screenshot is the main navigation page on your development org. This is where we will start:

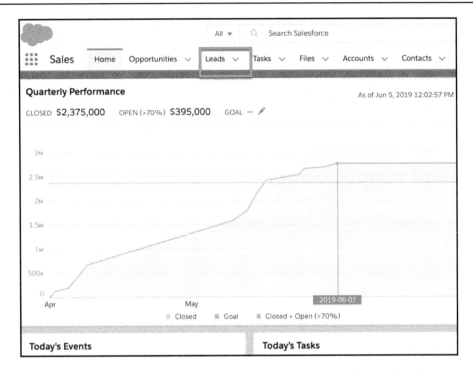

Let's start creating our lead by clicking on **Leads**, as in the preceding screenshot.

From here, you will land on the following page:

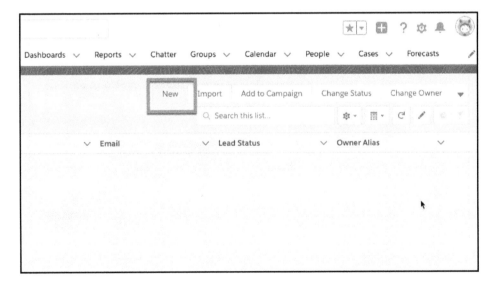

In the preceding screenshot, you can see the **Recently Viewed** view, as discussed in Chapter 1, *Getting Started with Salesforce and CRM*. Here, click on the **New** button to create a new lead.

In the following screenshot, you can see the popup to create a lead. You should fill this out with the information on Brenda's business card:

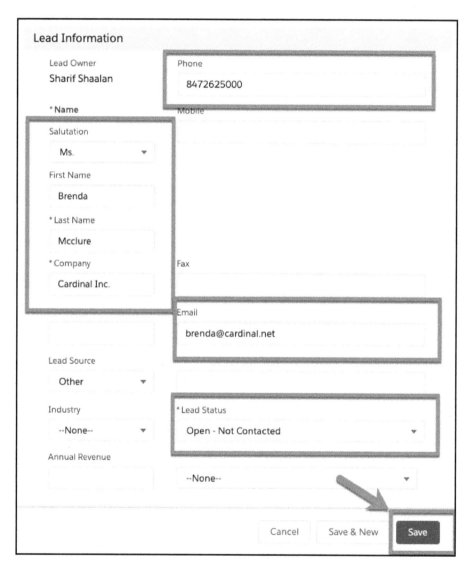

As you can see in the preceding screenshot, we have entered the details for the **Salutation**, **First Name**, **Last Name**, **Company**, **Phone**, **Email**, and **Lead Status** fields. The **Lead Source** field is set to **Other** by default; we will need to add `Conference` as a **Lead Source** value to this field. We will take a look at how to do this in the *Salesforce Administration* section of this book. Click on **Save** and you have now created your lead!

Let's take a look at the newly created lead in the following screenshot:

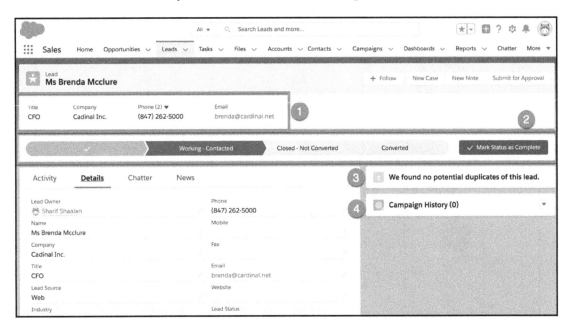

As indicated in the preceding screenshot, when you first land on a lead, there are a few important sections:

1. This section shows your summary fields. These fields include the title, company name, phone number, and email address of the lead. These are important for logging your activities, as discussed in `Chapter 2`, *Understanding Salesforce Activities*.

2. In this section, you will notice a path with all of your lead status values, which we will discuss in more detail in the *Exploring the Lead Status field* section of this chapter.

3. This section shows you any potential duplicates, which works by checking the email address of this lead against other lead email addresses to see whether it has already been logged.

4. You will also see a **Campaign History** section that shows you whether this lead is associated with any marketing campaigns (we will cover campaigns in more detail in Chapter 6, *Achieving Business Goals Using Campaigns*).

Note that there is an **Activity** tab on the lead as well. This is where you log all calls, tasks, events, and emails, as discussed in Chapter 2, *Understanding Salesforce Activities*.

Now, we will look at the **Details** section of the lead by navigating to the **Details** sub-heading on the lead's page:

Looking at the **Details** section, you will see a few very important fields:

1. **Lead Owner**: Who the lead is assigned to, which is the person working the lead.
2. **Name**: The first and last name of the person you are contacting.
3. **Company**: The name of the company that this person works for.
4. **Lead Source**: Where this lead came from.
5. **Phone**: The lead's phone number.
6. **Email**: The email address of the lead.
7. **Lead Status**: Where you are in the process of this lead.
8. **Rating**: This can be set to **Cold**, **Warm**, or **Hot** and can be used by reps to tag leads for a quick reference on how the interaction is going.
9. **Created By**: This is a system field used for auditing purposes that is automatically set and displays the user that created the lead.
10. **Last Modified By**: This is a system field used for auditing purposes that is automatically set and displays the user that last edited the lead.

There are also a few other fields in the **Details** section that are optional but used by many organizations. These include the following:

- **Industry**: This is a picklist with different customer industries.
- **Annual Revenue**: This helps you determine the size of the prospect if you have this information.
- **Number of Employees**: This helps you determine the size of the prospect as well.

As you can see, the **Details** section shows you the primary fields on the lead's record. One of the most important fields in this section is **Lead Status**. Let's take a look at **Lead Status** in more detail.

Exploring the Lead Status field

The **Lead Status** field shows you where you are in the life cycle of working this lead. The lead life cycle is important as this is the beginning of the sales process for any organization. The following flowchart simplifies this process a bit:

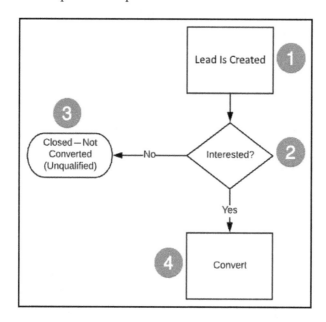

From the preceding flowchart diagram, we can understand the following:

1. Once the lead is created, it can be dispositioned in two ways.
2. You will contact the lead to present your product or service and the lead will either be interested in speaking further or not.
3. If not, the lead status is changed to **Closed - Not Converted**, or in some cases, this status is called **Unqualified**.
4. If the lead is interested, the status reads **Convert**.

We will cover conversion in more detail in the next section.

Let's take a look at how these status values appear in Salesforce and what happens when each lead status is chosen. Take a look at the following screenshot:

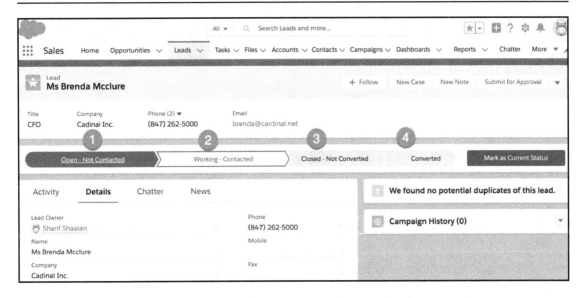

From the preceding screenshot, we learn the following:

1. **Open - Not Contacted**: This is the default status when the lead is created and means that you have not logged any activities to this lead.
2. **Working - Contacted**: This status means that you have reached out and logged activities but you have not received a definitive answer about whether the lead is interested.
3. **Closed - Not Converted**: This is the status used if you make contact and the lead does not want to speak further. Typically, you would use this value to filter these leads out of the open leads list view that you are working with. Setting this status marks it as a dead lead, which you would want to keep in the system for reporting purposes, but would not want to see in the list view of the open leads that have a chance of being converted.
4. **Converted**: This status means the lead is interested and would like to speak further.

In this section, we have learned about the importance of the **Lead Status** field and how the values in this field contribute to the sales process. Let's take a look at what actually happens when a lead is interested in your services and you actually convert a lead.

Understanding how lead conversion takes place

When you call Brenda, she seems very interested, which is a good sign! You decide to convert the lead.

When a lead is converted, something very important happens. The lead disappears from the system (on the frontend, it is still available for reporting) and it turns into three records. It becomes an account, an opportunity, and a contact. All the information about the company goes to the account, the information about the person goes to the contact, and the information about the actual sale goes to the opportunity. This is an important step in the sales process since this is the point where you stop working with a lead and instead start working with an opportunity.

Let's look at how to convert a lead:

1. To convert a lead, navigate to the lead record you created and click on **Converted** (see label **1** in the following screenshot), then click on **Select Converted Status** (see label **2** in the following screenshot). (Optionally, you can click on the arrow next to the **Submit for Approval** button and use the **Convert** button (see label **3** in the following screenshot):)

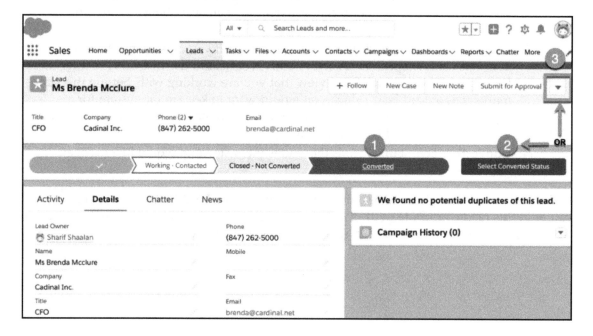

2. After performing the previous step, a pop-up page will appear on your screen:

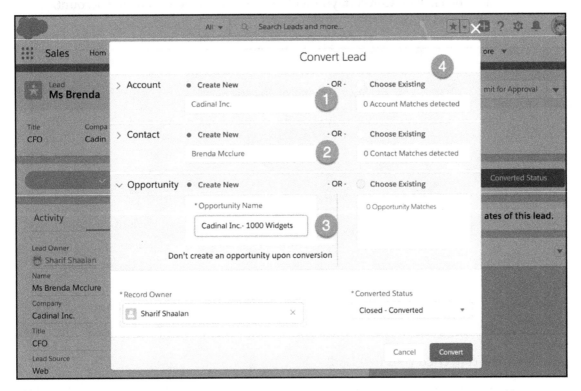

This is the page where you can update the **Account** name (see label **1** in the preceding screenshot), the **Contact** name (see label **2** in the preceding screenshot), and the **Opportunity** name (see label **3** in the preceding screenshot). Notice how everything on the left is used to create new records. If Salesforce detects possible duplicates, they show up on the right, where you can attach the lead to an existing account, contact, or opportunity (see label **4** in the preceding screenshot).

3. After filling in the fields shown in the preceding screenshot, click on **Convert**. Once you click on **Convert**, you will see links to the newly created account, contact, and opportunity, as follows:

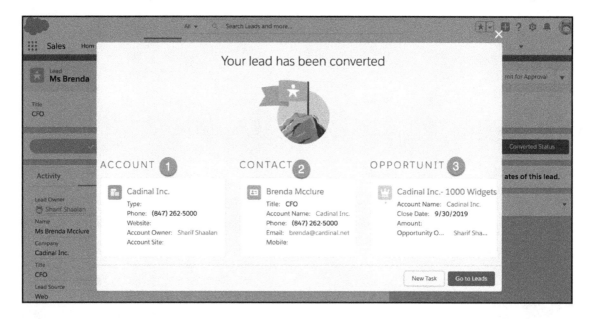

You have now converted your first lead!

In this section, we learned how to convert a lead. Converting a lead is the *happy path* goal of the sales process. The more leads you convert into opportunities, the more chance it will lead to sales. More about the **Account**, **Contact**, and **Opportunity** objects is covered in greater detail in later chapters of this book. Next, let's see how web-to-lead helps with lead capturing.

Working on forms with web-to-lead

Using web-to-lead is an easy way to generate HTML code that you can drop into your website to create a lead capture form. A lead capture form is generated outside of Salesforce but creates a lead directly in Salesforce when the form is saved. This can take the form of a **Contact Us** page on your website or any other form where you would want the information to be automatically added to Salesforce. Let's see how this is done:

1. Click on the gear at the top of the page (see label **1** in the following screenshot) and choose **Setup** (see label **2** in the following screenshot):

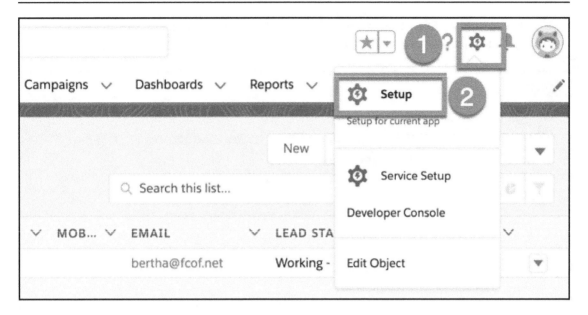

Clicking on **Setup** in the preceding screenshot brings you to the administration section of Salesforce.

2. Next, type web in the quick-find box (see label **1** in the following screenshot). This will bring up **Web-to-Lead**. Click on the link (see label **2** in the following screenshot), as in the following screenshot:

3. Clicking on **Web-to-Lead** brings you to the **Web-to-Lead** settings page. On this page, click on **Create Web-to-Lead Form**:

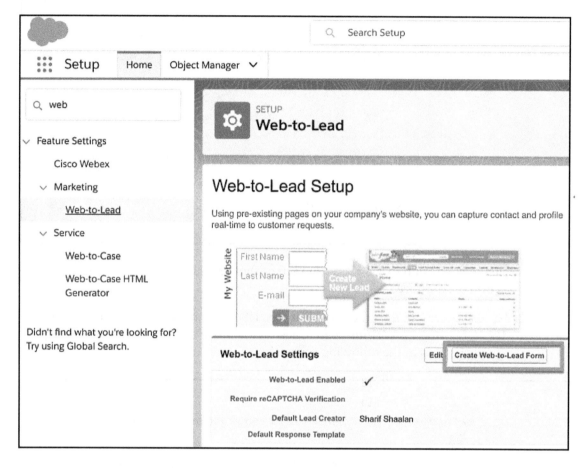

4. This brings you to the web-to-lead creation section. There are a few options on the next page to be filled in before you generate the code:

- **Available Fields**: These are all of the fields available on the leads object. You can pull any of them into your form.
- **Selected Fields**: These are the fields that are included in the form once you generate the HTML code.

- **Return URL**: This is where the user lands after submitting the form.
- **Include reCAPTCHA in HTML**: This is optional—you can add a reCAPTCHA to the form.

After this, click on **Generate**. The following screenshot shows the preceding steps:

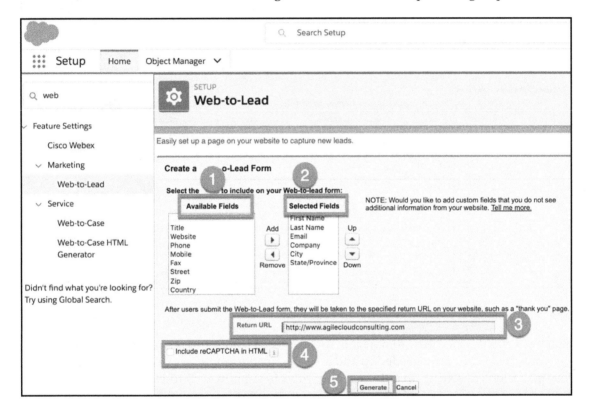

5. Clicking on **Generate** is the final step that will generate the HTML code for you. Now, you have your HTML code! You can copy and paste this right into your website and start capturing leads:

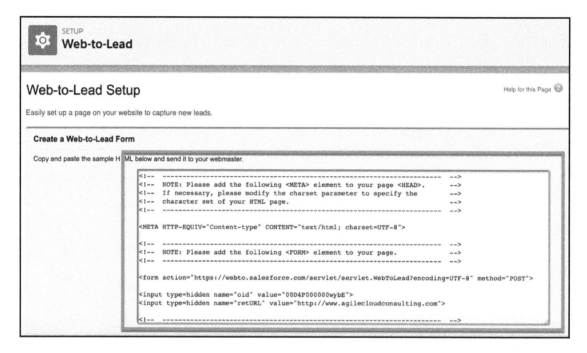

The preceding screenshot shows the final output.

You have now learned how to navigate to the web-to-lead setup section and how to generate the HTML code needed to add a web-to-lead form to an external website. Next, let's take a look at setting up auto-response rules to support web-to-lead submissions.

Setting up auto-response rules

Now that we have set up the web-to-lead, an important function to support the submission of a form is auto-response rules. Auto-response rules allow you to automate the email that a user receives when a lead is submitted via a web-to-lead form based on specific criteria on the lead record, such as the lead source. Let's see how auto-response rules are created:

1. First, navigate to the **Home** tab of the **Setup** page (see label **1** in the following screenshot):

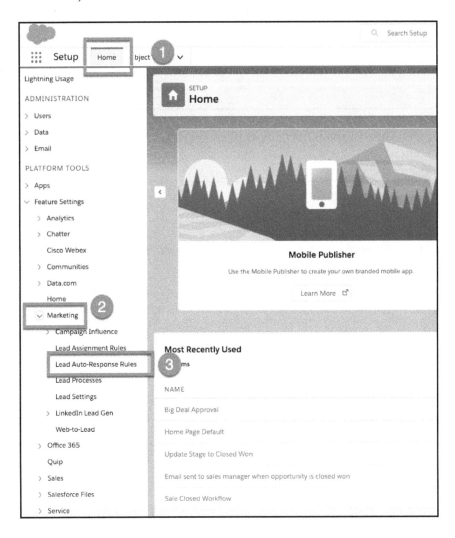

2. From here, we move to **Marketing** (see label **2** in the preceding screenshot), then click on **Lead Auto-Response Rules** (see label **3** in the preceding screenshot). The following screenshot shows the auto-response rules creation page:

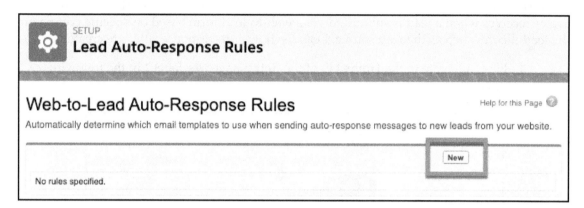

3. On the **Auto-Response** screen, click on **New**, which leads you to the following screen:

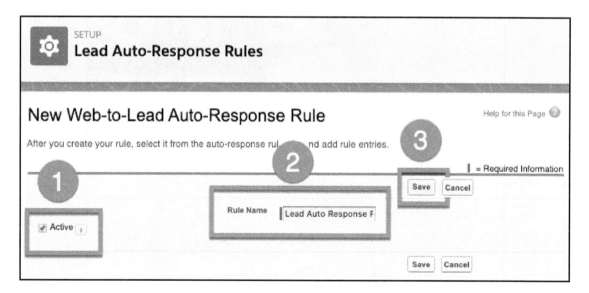

4. We then move to the **Active** checkbox (see label **1** in the preceding screenshot), enter the rule name (see label **2** in the preceding screenshot), and click on **Save** (see label **3** in the preceding screenshot) to lead you to the following screen:

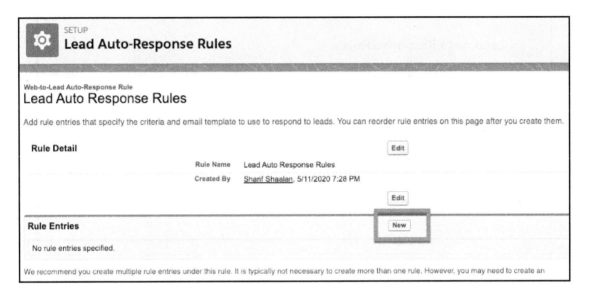

5. The preceding screenshot shows you the created auto-response rule. Next, let's click on **New** to create a rule entry. Clicking on **New** leads to the following rule entry creation screen:

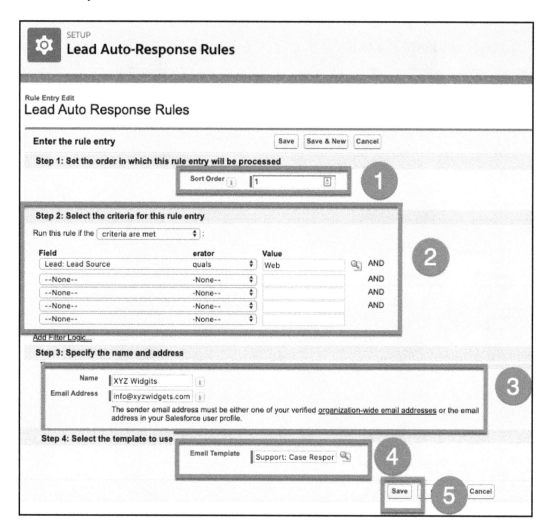

The preceding screenshot shows you the steps to add a rule entry:

1. **Sort Order**: Salesforce evaluates all of the entries on an auto-response rule with this option. Once a match is found, the response is sent and the evaluation stops. This field allows you to determine the order that the rule entries are evaluated.
2. **Select the criteria for this rule entry**: For our business use case, the criteria for this rule is any lead where the **Lead Source** field is set to **Web**. Any leads created through the web meets these criteria and triggers this auto-response rule.
3. **Name** and **Email Address**: This is the name and email address that shows up on the response email.
4. **Email Template**: This is the email template used for the auto-response rule.
5. **Save**: Clicking on **Save** completes the rule entry creation.

You can create many rule entries based on the complexity of your business use case. Next, let's take a look at the lead settings and lead processes.

Lead settings and lead processes

In this section, we will cover some of the configuration options for leads.

Using the lead settings

The lead settings allow you to configure some options for your leads and convert leads into opportunities. Let's take a look at these options.

First, we will navigate to **Home** (see label **1** in the following screenshot) | **Marketing** (see label **2** in the following screenshot) | **Lead Settings** (see label **3** in the following screenshot) from the **Setup** page, as shown:

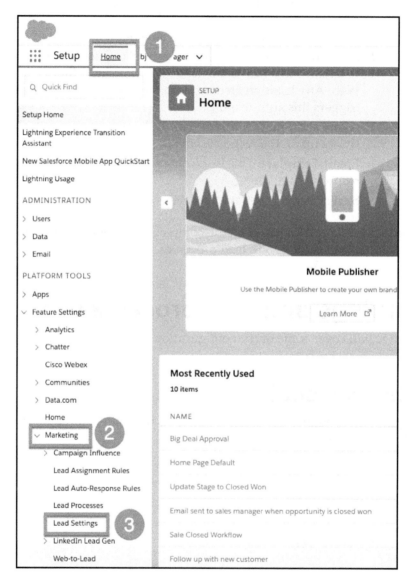

This brings us to the following screen:

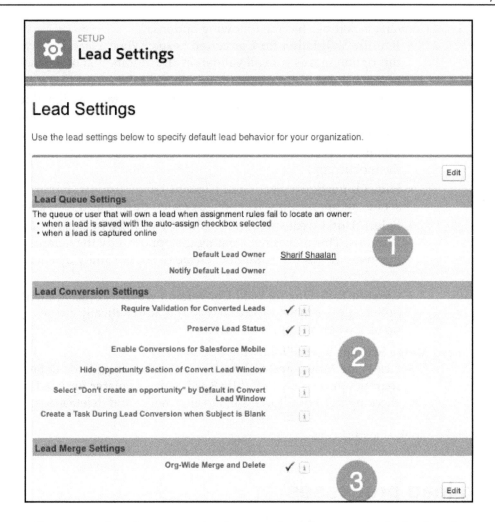

The preceding screenshot shows you the three sections that contain the lead settings options:

1. **Lead Queue Settings** has the following two options:
   - **Default Lead Owner**: This is the user that owns all the new leads created through the web-to-lead feature and that are not assigned to another user based on criteria.
   - **Notify Default Lead Owner**: This sends an email to the default lead owner when a lead is assigned to them.

2. Lead Conversion Settings has the following options:

- **Require Validation for Converted Leads**: When a lead is converted, this option makes sure all validation and automation on the new account, contact, and opportunity is enforced.
- **Preserve Lead Status**: This preserves the lead status assigned to the original lead owner when converting the lead, rather than updating the new owner's default lead status on conversion.
- **Enable Conversions for Salesforce Mobile**: Allows conversion using the mobile app.
- **Hide Opportunity Section of Convert Lead Window**: If this option is set up, an opportunity will not be created during lead conversion.
- **Select "Don't create an opportunity" by Default in Convert Lead Window**: This makes not creating the opportunity the default option but gives the user the option to create the opportunity by checking a checkbox.
- **Create a Task During Lead Conversion when Subject is Blank**: This option applies to Salesforce Classic and automatically creates a follow-up task when a lead is converted.

3. **Lead Merge Settings** has the following options:

- **Org-Wide Merge and Delete**: If your organization-wide default sharing option is set to **Public Read/Write/Transfer for Leads**, checking this box allows users to also merge and delete leads.

Next, let's take a look at lead processes.

Using lead processes

Lead processes allow you to assign different lead status values to different lead record types. We will cover record types in Chapter 12, *Configuring Objects for Your Business*. Let's take a look at lead processes.

First, we will navigate to **Home** (see label **1** in the following screenshot) | **Marketing** (see label **2** in the following screenshot) | **Lead Processes** (see label **3** in the following screenshot) from the **Setup** page, as shown:

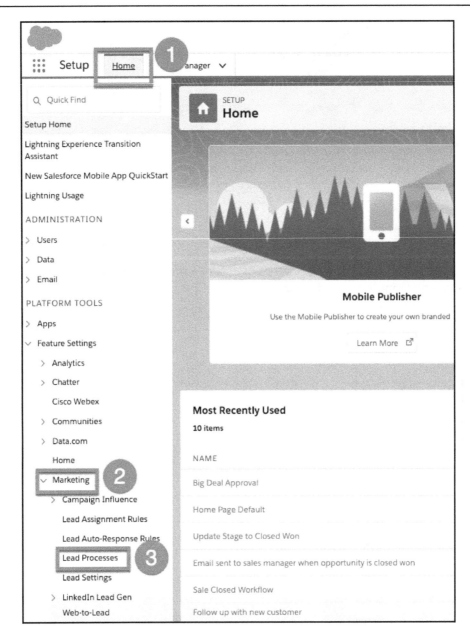

This leads us to the following screen:

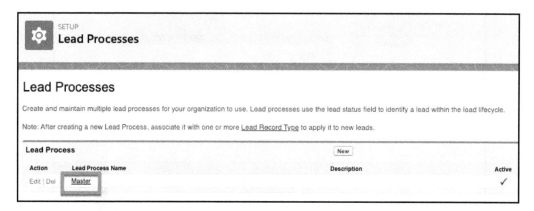

As you can see in the preceding screenshot, we have a master lead process and you have the option to create multiple lead processes. Let's take a look at what the **Master** process contains by clicking on **Master**, as shown:

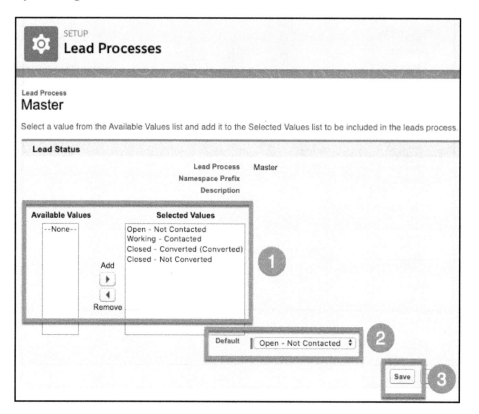

As you can see in the preceding screenshot, there are several steps to review:

1. Here, you can see all of the values in the **Lead Status** field. A lead process allows you to add and remove values as needed for a specific process, which is then assigned to a specific lead record type.
2. You have the option to add a default lead status for this specific process.
3. Click on **Save** to finish editing the lead process.

Now that we have seen the lead configuration options, let's review what we have learned in this chapter.

Summary

In this chapter, we learned what a lead is and how it is used to start the sales cycle. We understood what the **Lead Status** field is used for and how the values drive the process. We also understood how to convert a lead into an opportunity and that we can convert a lead when we think there is further potential for a sale. We saw the use case for web-to-lead and how to generate web-to-lead code in order to capture leads online, as well as setting up auto-response rules for these leads. Finally, we learned about the lead settings and lead processes, as well as how these configuration options can help us optimize the use of leads. These skills will help you organize and work your leads, as well as convert them into opportunities to continue the sales cycle. Understanding this process will result in efficiently working leads, which leads to more sales!

In the next chapter, we will look at accounts and contacts and why these objects are used in Salesforce in more detail.

Questions

1. What are some ways that leads can be captured?
2. What determines whether a lead should be converted into an opportunity?
3. What happens to a **Closed-Not Converted (Unqualified)** lead?
4. What happens to a converted lead? Where does it go?
5. Where does the company information go when a lead is converted?
6. What is web-to-lead used for?
7. Once you have generated the HTML code, what do you do with it?
8. What does the **Org-Wide Merge and Delete** lead setting allow you to do?

Further reading

- The *Working with Leads and Opportunities* Trailhead module can be found at `https://trailhead.salesforce.com/en/content/learn/modules/lex_salesforce_tour/lex_salesforce_tour_sales`.
- The *Convert and Assign Leads* Trailhead module can be found at `https://trailhead.salesforce.com/en/content/learn/modules/admin_intro_opptys_leads/admin_intro_opptys_leads_leads`.
- The *Generate Leads from Your Website for Your Sales Teams* article can be found at `https://help.salesforce.com/articleView?id=setting_up_web-to-lead.htmtype=5`.
- Check out `https://help.salesforce.com/articleView?id=creating_auto-response_rules.htmtype=5` for more information on setting up auto-response rules.
- Check out `https://help.salesforce.com/articleView?id=customize_leadmgmt.htmtype=5` for more information on configuring lead management.

Business Development with Accounts and Contacts

4

Accounts and contacts are the foundation of a **Customer Relationship Management (CRM)** approach. Accounts are typically organizations that you already do business with or organizations that contain opportunities that have been converted from leads and are in the sales cycle. Contacts are people within these organizations that you have already contacted for various purposes, such as sales, marketing, or billing.

The following topics are covered in this chapter:

- What are accounts and what are they used for?
- What are contacts and what are they used for?
- What are relationships and what are they used for?

With the help of these topics, we will gain skills in creating an account and we will see what an account record contains. We will also learn how to create a contact and learn what a contact record contains. Lastly, we will look at how to create a relationship and what a relationship record contains.

Technical requirements

For this chapter, make sure you log in to your development org and follow along with the examples. You will need to enable **Contacts to Multiple Accounts** for the relationships feature to work:

```
https://trailhead.salesforce.com/en/content/learn/modules/admin_intro_accounts_
contacts/admin_intro_accounts_contacts_relationships
```

Understanding how accounts work

Accounts are the organizations you have saved in Salesforce. These can be customers, partners, vendors, or any other company you would want to keep track of in your system.

A business use case

You are a sales rep for XYZ Widgets. There is a customer in a legacy system that you wish to add to Salesforce. Since this customer is not a new lead, you have to enter the customer directly as an account. Let's see how this is done.

Creating an account

In this section, we will focus on accounts as customers or potential customers. There are two ways of creating accounts:

- Creating an account by converting a lead
- Creating an account by navigating to the **Accounts** tab

We covered creating an account by converting a lead in Chapter 3, *Creating and Managing Leads*. Let's now see how we can create an account by navigating to the **Accounts** tab, as well as what is contained in an account record. The following screenshot shows the main navigation page in your development org, which is where we will start:

Let's look at our first account by clicking on the **Accounts** tab, highlighted in the following screenshot. Once you click on the **Accounts** tab, you will land on the page in the following screenshot:

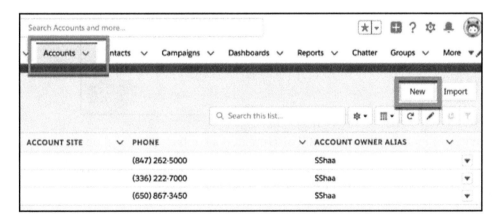

As we discussed in Chapter 1, *Getting Started with Salesforce and CRM*, you will be taken to the **Recently Viewed** page. Click on the **New** button.

As you can see in the following screenshot, I entered all of the information for the new account:

Click **Save** after creating the account. I also created a contact, case, and opportunity in order to show you how these related items look in the next section. Creating a contact will be covered later on in this chapter and creating an opportunity and case will be covered in more detail in *Salesforce for Sales, Marketing and Customer Relationship Management* section of this book.

When you click on the newly created **GenePoint** account, you see a page similar to the one in the following screenshot:

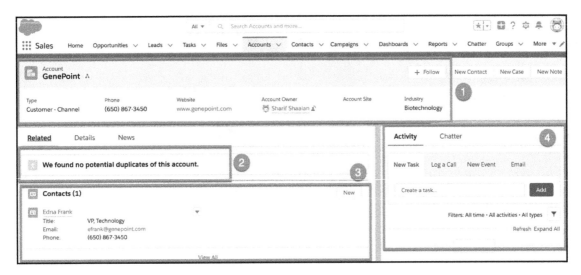

In the preceding screenshot, you can see that when you first open an account, you land on the **Related** sub-tab, where you will see a few important sections:

- The highlighted section **1** shows your summary fields. These fields include **Type**, **Phone**, **Website**, **Account Owner**, **Account Site**, and **Industry**.
- In section **2**, you will notice that Salesforce automatically checks for duplicates based on the account name and lets you know whether there are any potential duplicate records.
- In section **3**, you can see all the related contacts.
- In section **4**, you can also see the section for logging activities, as discussed in Chapter 2, *Understanding Salesforce Activities*.

The following screenshot shows you the rest of this section:

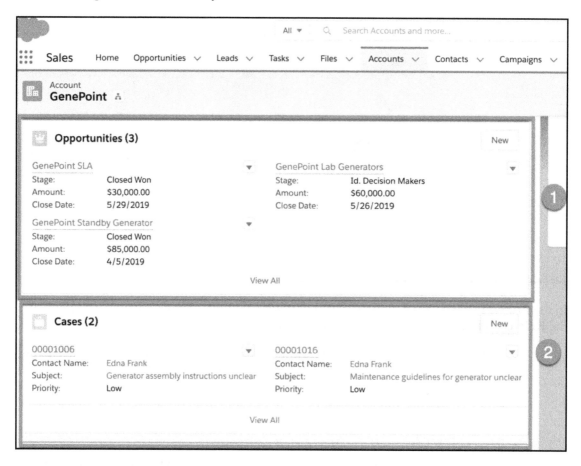

In the preceding screenshot, you can see two more important sections in the **Related** sub-tab:

- The highlighted section **1** shows all the opportunities related to this account. This is very important as these are both closed opportunities (sales) and open opportunities (potential sales that the sales rep is currently working on).
- In section **2**, you can see all the cases related to this account. Cases are related to customer service and will be covered in Chapter 7, *Enhancing Customer Service Using Cases*.

The **Related** section is very important as it shows all of the non-account records, such as opportunities, contacts, and cases, that are directly related to this organization. Let's take a look at the **Details** sub-tab in the following screenshot:

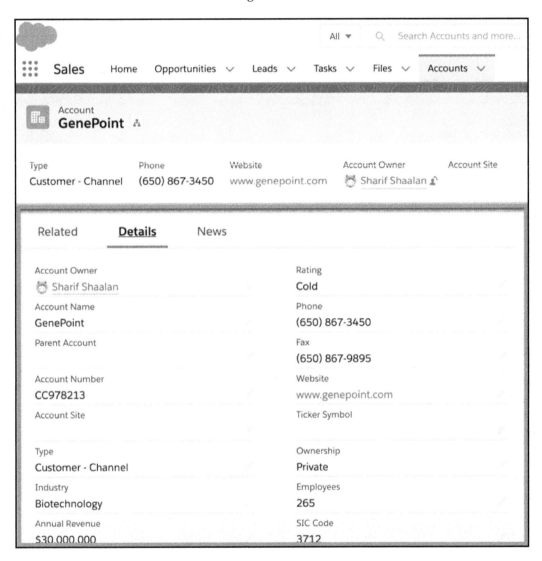

Looking at the **Details** section, you will see all the fields that are directly related to the organization, such as **Type**, **Industry**, **Employees**, **Annual Revenue**, and **Website**, as well as the information to directly contact this organization. The following screenshot shows what the **News** sub-tab contains:

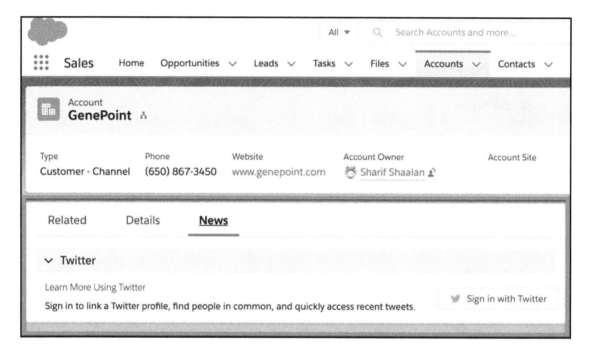

In the preceding screenshot, we can see that there is an option for the Salesforce user to log in with their Twitter account to connect directly with this company. Once this is done, it shows all of the tweets that relate to this company and gives the Salesforce user a look at the latest Twitter news of this company.

There is also a way for administrators to add a **News** section here that directly searches the company name on Google News and shows any related articles. This is covered in more detail in Section 2, *Salesforce Administration*.

In this section, we learned how to navigate to an account and what an account record contains. This is important as accounts are the organizations you do business with and are the central point of interaction within the CRM. Now that we have seen what companies look like in Salesforce, let's take a look at how the people within these companies show up in Salesforce.

Moving toward creating contacts

Contacts are the people connected to Salesforce accounts. These can be customers, partners, vendors, or any other contacts related to the accounts you want to keep track of in your system.

A business use case

You are a sales rep for XYZ Widgets. We created an account for GenePoint in the previous section. You now have to create a contact record for the person you will be directly interacting with from GenePoint.

Creating a contact

In this section, we will focus on contacts as customers or potential customers. There are two ways of creating contacts:

- By converting a lead
- By navigating to a specific account and creating a contact related to that account

We covered creating contact by converting a lead in Chapter 3, *Creating and Managing Leads*. Let's now see how to create a contact by navigating to an account and creating a contact related to that account. The following screenshot shows the main navigation page in your development org, which is where we will start:

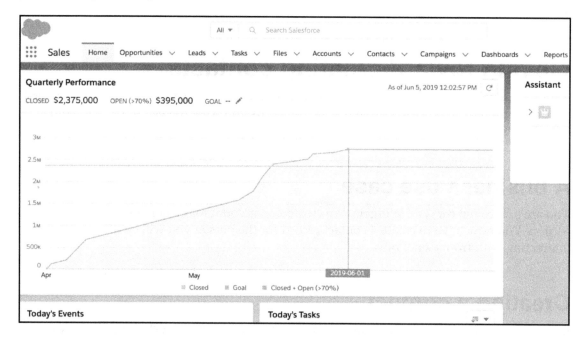

Let's now look at how we create a contact from the **Accounts** tab:

1. First, click on the **Accounts** tab, which takes you to the following page:

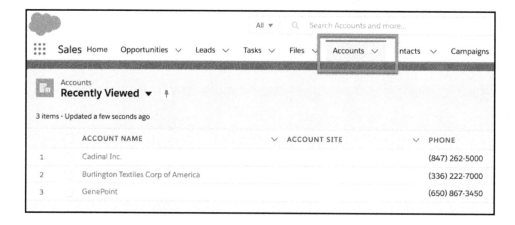

You will be taken to the **Recently Viewed** view, as we discussed in Chapter 1, *Getting Started with Salesforce and CRM*.

2. Click on **GenePoint** to navigate to the account we looked at in the *Understanding how accounts work* section of this chapter, where you will see the following:

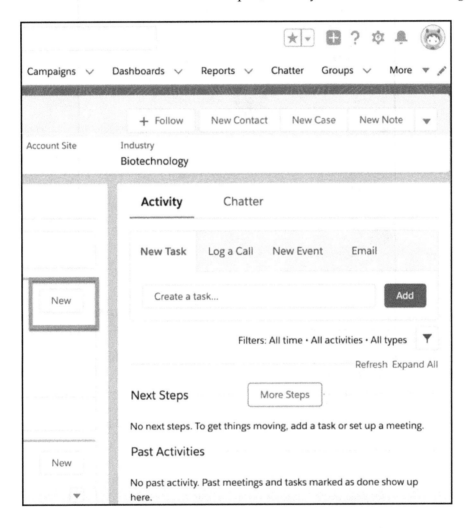

3. Under the **Contacts** section of the **GenePoint** account, you have the option to create a new contact. When you click on **New**, you will see a popup, as in the following screenshot:

In the preceding screenshot, we can see that clicking on **New** brings up the following important fields:

1. The first field is the **Salutation** field.
2. This is the **First Name** field of the contact you are dealing with.
3. The third field is the **Last Name** field of the contact you are dealing with.
4. The fourth field is the account that the contact is related to. This field is prepopulated since you are creating the contact directly from this account.
5. The fifth field is the **Title** field, which shows the position of the contact in the company.
6. The sixth field is the **Phone** field. This will usually copy over the phone number from the account **Phone** field.

7. The seventh field is the **Home Phone** field for the contact's home phone number.

8. The eighth field is the **Mobile** field for the mobile number of the contact.

4. The following screenshot shows the rest of the **Contact** creation screen:

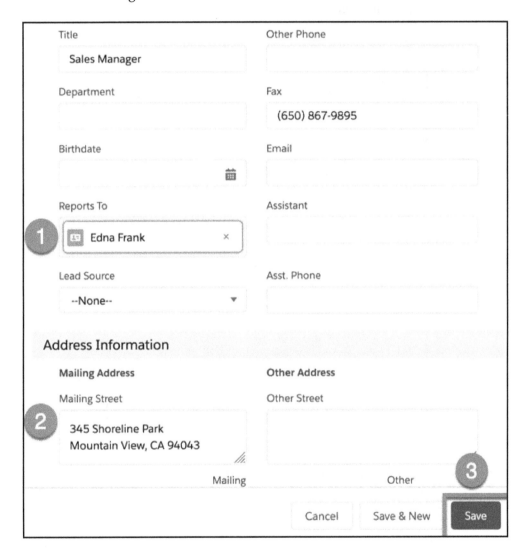

In the preceding screenshot, you can see a few more important fields:

1. The first field is the person that this contact reports to. This is typically another contact that exists on this account.
2. This is the **Mailing Address** field of the user.
3. When you click **Save**, this saves the contact and you will see the following screen:

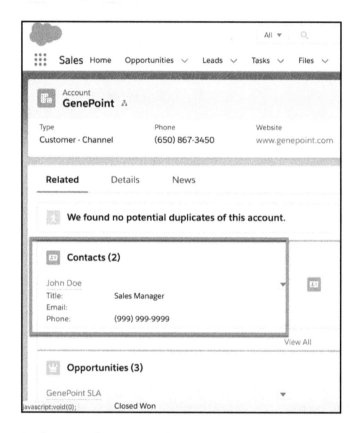

In the preceding screenshot, you can see that the contact is now created on the **GenePoint** account and shows up in the **Contacts** section alongside the contact that was already on the account.

5. Click on **John Doe**. The following screenshot shows you what the new contact record contains:

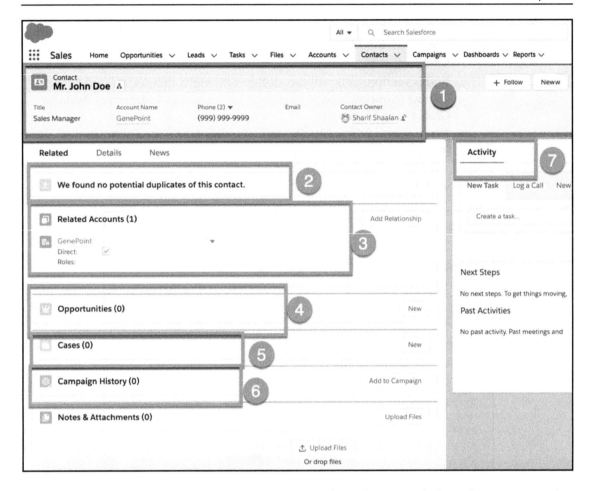

In the preceding screenshot, you can see that when you click on this contact and go to the **Related** sub-tab, there are a few important sections:

1. This section shows your summary fields. These fields include **Title**, **Account Name**, **Phone**, **Email**, and **Contact Owner**.

2. In this section, you will notice that Salesforce automatically checks for duplicate entries based on the contact's name and email address and lets you know whether there are any potential duplicate records.

3. In this section, you will see all the related accounts. We will cover these relationships in the next section.

4. In this section, you will see all the opportunities that are related to the contact (opportunities will be covered in Chapter 5, *Using Opportunities Effectively*).

5. In this section, you will see all the cases that are related to the contact (cases will be covered in `Chapter 7`, *Enhancing Customer Service Using Cases*).

6. In this section, you will see all the campaigns that are related to the contact (campaigns will be covered in `Chapter 6`, *Achieving Business Goals Using Campaigns*).

7. In this section, you will also see a section for logging activities, as discussed in `Chapter 2`, *Understanding Salesforce Activities*.

When you click on the **Details** sub-tab, you will see the following details:

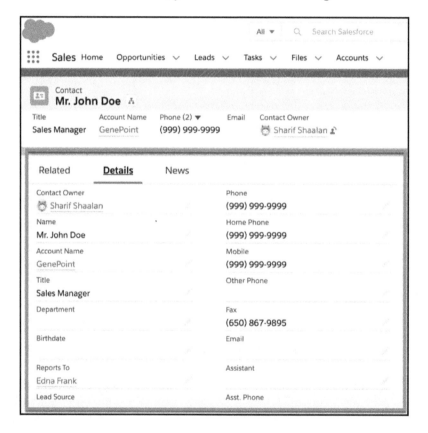

In the preceding screenshot, you can see all of the fields you added when you created the contact. Then, click on the **News** sub-tab. The following screenshot shows the **News** section:

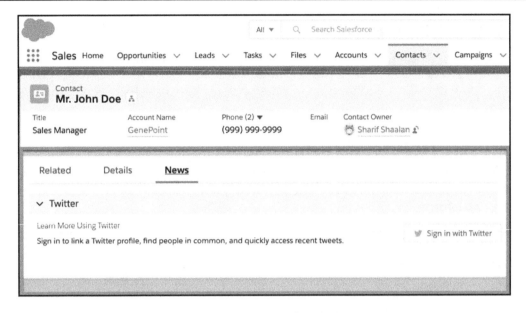

In the preceding screenshot, we can see that there is an option for the Salesforce user to log in with their Twitter account to connect directly with this contact. If this is done, this section will show all the tweets related to this contact and give the Salesforce user a look at the latest Twitter news for this contact. There is also a way for administrators to add a **News** section here that directly searches for the contact's name on Google News and shows any related articles here. This will be covered in the *Salesforce Administration* section of this book.

In this section, we learned how to create a new contact and what a contact record contains. This is important as contacts are the people you communicate with from the organizations that you do business with. Contacts, along with accounts, are the central point of interaction in the CRM. Now that we have seen how contacts and accounts work in Salesforce, let's take a look at a business use case where a contact may be related to multiple accounts. These connections are called **relationships**.

Understanding relationships

Relationships are the connections between contacts and multiple accounts in Salesforce. A contact is always connected to the account (organization) that the user works for. There are some cases where these contacts are connected to other accounts in the system, such as contractors, board members, or any other role that the contact could be connected to. Let's see how this works.

A business use case

For our example here, let's assume that John Doe is the sales manager at GenePoint but also sits on the board of another one of our accounts, Cardinal Inc.. As the sales rep for XYZ Widgets, you will make the connection in Salesforce. Let's see how to go about this.

Enabling relationships

The first step is to enable the **Allow users to relate a contact to multiple accounts** feature. As you can see in the following screenshot, I navigated to the setup and configuration section of Salesforce:

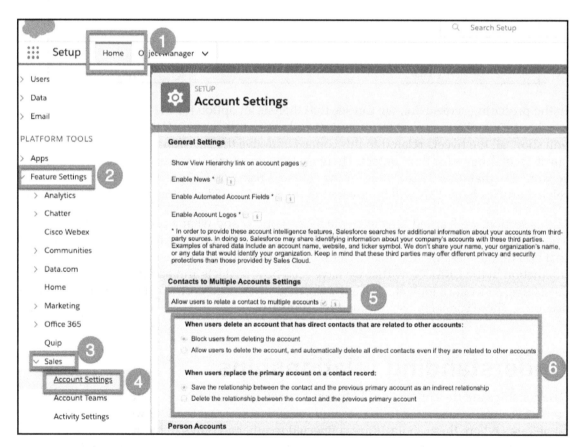

There are several steps, which are shown in the preceding screenshot, to activate this feature:

1. Navigate to the **Home** tab under the setup and configuration page.
2. Click on **Feature Settings**.
3. Click on **Sales**.
4. Click on **Account Settings**.
5. Set **Allow users to relate a contact to multiple accounts** to **True**.
6. I chose to block the option to delete an account that has contacts with relationships to other accounts, rather than allow these contacts to be deleted with the account, breaking the other relationships. I also chose to save the relationship as an indirect relationship if a primary relationship is removed from a contact, rather than delete the relationship altogether.

The next step is to add the **Related Contacts** list to the page layout so that we can use the relationships. As you can see in the following screenshot, I navigated to the setup and configuration section of Salesforce:

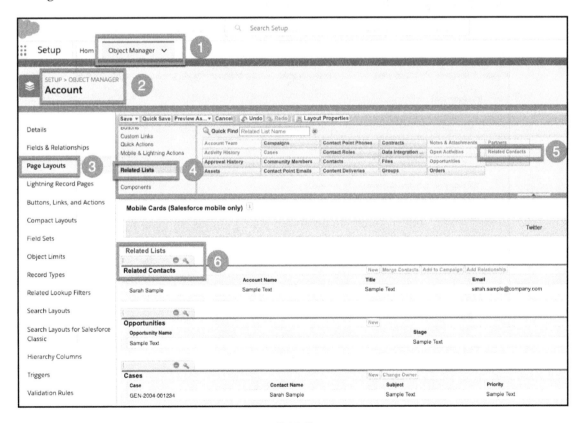

The preceding screenshot shows the steps to adding this related list:

1. Navigate to the **Object Manager** tab under the setup and configuration page.
2. Choose the **Account** object.
3. Click on **Page Layouts**.
4. In the appropriate layout, click on **Related Lists**.
5. You will see the **Related Contacts** list in the available lists section.
6. Drag the **Related Contacts** list to the **Related Lists** section of the layout.

Now that the feature is active and the list is added to the required layout, let's look at how to add a relationship.

Adding relationships

Let's see how this connection is made:

1. Start by navigating to the **John Doe** contact record:

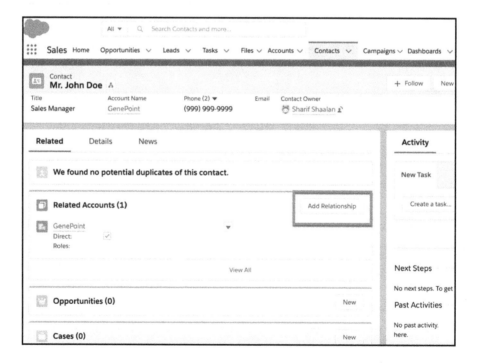

In the preceding screenshot, we can see that in the **John Doe** contact record under the **Related Accounts** section, there is an option to add a relationship.

2. Clicking on this option takes us to the following screen:

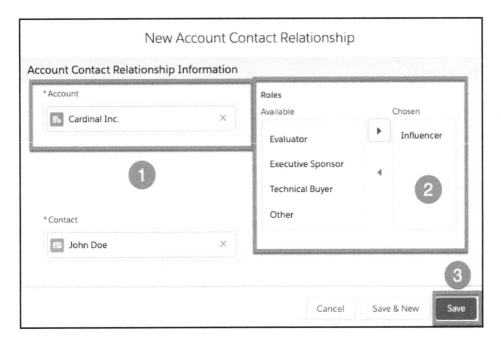

In the preceding screenshot, you can see a few important sections:

1. The first field is for setting the account that you want to connect this contact to.
2. The second field is the role that this contact plays in the organization; for our example, we will pick **Influencer** since John Doe is a board member of this organization.

3. When you click **Save**, this saves the relationship and you will see the following updated **Contact** screen:

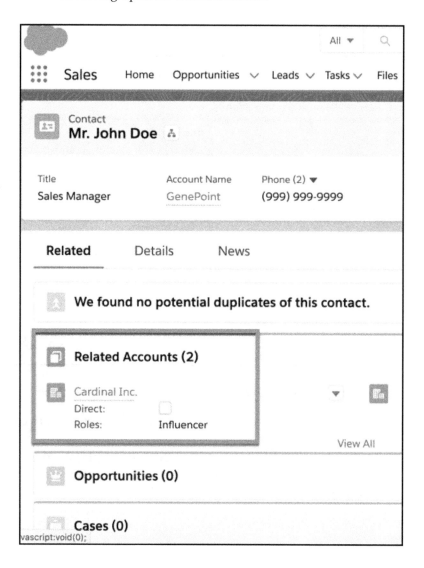

In the preceding screenshot, you can see that John Doe is now related to both GenePoint as the sales manager and **Cardinal Inc.** as an influencer. The following screenshot shows you how this relationship shows up on the **Cardinal Inc.** account:

As you can see in the preceding screenshot, **Cardinal Inc.** has a **Related Contacts** section that shows **John Doe** as an influencer, along with Brenda Mcclure who works for Cardinal Inc.. Let's take a look at how to remove a relationship if needed.

Removing relationships

In the following screenshot, you can see that I navigated back to the **Cardinal Inc.** account:

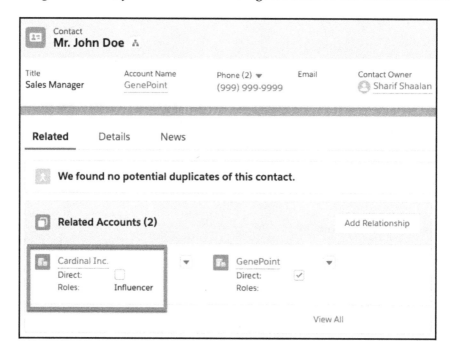

As you can see in the preceding screenshot, I clicked on **Remove Relationship** next to the John Doe contact, which led to the following popup:

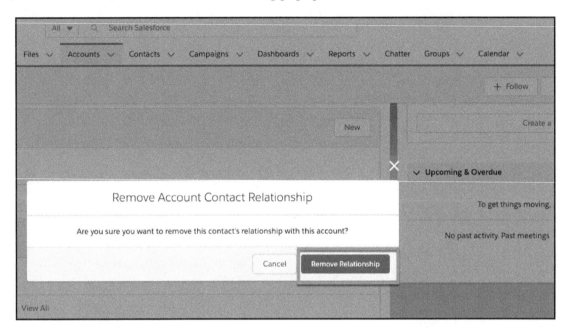

This popup asks for confirmation that you want to delete the relationship. Clicking on **Remove Relationship** brings you back to the following screen:

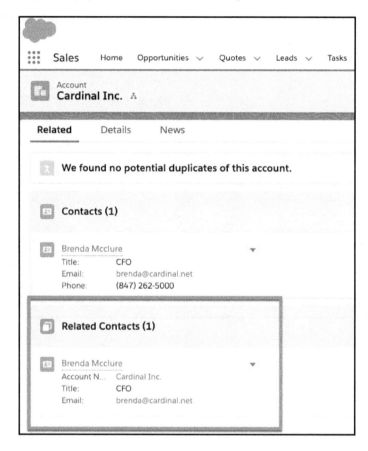

As you can see in the preceding screenshot, the relationship with John Doe is now gone.

In this section, we learned what a relationship is, how to activate the feature, how to add the **Related Contacts** list, how to create a relationship, how to remove a relationship, and what this relationship looks like on both the contact and account records. Let's go over what we learned in this chapter.

Summary

After finishing this chapter, we now know what an account is and how to create and view an account. We learned about the important sections of an account's record, including the **Related Items**, **Details**, and **News** sections. We then learned what a contact is and how to create a new contact on an account record. We also learned about the important sections in a contact's record, including the **Related Items**, **Details**, and **News** sections.

Finally, we learned about when to use a relationship and how to create a relationship between a contact and an account.

In the next chapter, we will look at opportunities—the most important part of the sales cycle in Salesforce!

Questions

1. What are some use cases for the types of accounts that an organization may want to keep track of in Salesforce?
2. Why would you want to create contacts related to accounts you are doing business with?
3. When would you create a relationship from a contact to an account that the contact does not directly work for?
4. How can you enable the **Relationships** feature?
5. How do you remove a relationship?

Further reading

- Accounts and contacts for the Lightning experience: `https://trailhead.salesforce.com/en/content/learn/modules/accounts_contacts_lightning_experience`

Using Opportunities Effectively

Opportunities are the foundation of sales and drive growth for any business. Working on an opportunity involves moving from one stage to the next as you get closer to closing a deal. This is referred to as a **pipeline** or **funnel** in some organizations. The reason it is called a pipeline or funnel is that you usually have more opportunities in the earlier stages of a deal—the top of the funnel—and fewer opportunities in the later stages—the bottom of the funnel. Each stage is tied to a percentage of the likelihood of closing the opportunity. These percentages tie into the forecasting of future sales.

The following topics are discussed in this chapter:

- Using opportunities and understanding their creation
- Understanding the opportunity stages and their contribution to the sales process, as well as the sales path and how it ties into the opportunity stages
- Understanding the contact roles for opportunities
- What opportunity products are and how they are created to drive an opportunity
- What quotes are and how they are created and used with opportunities
- Using forecasting and seeing how opportunities drive your forecast

With the help of these topics, you will be able to develop the required skills to create an opportunity and see what an opportunity record contains. You will be able to create contact roles, opportunity products, and quotes and be able to see how the opportunity stages drive the sales path and forecasting. These skills will allow you to get a full picture of the sales cycle that we started in Chapter 3, *Creating and Managing Leads*.

Technical requirements

To follow along with this chapter, make sure you log in to your development org. You will need to enable **Quotes** from the **Setup** menu in order to generate quotes for the *Using quotes* section of this chapter, and also enable **Forecasts** from the **Setup** menu in order to view forecasts for the *Using forecasting* section.

Using opportunities

Opportunities are the main component of your sales pipeline. Within the sales cycle, once you convert a lead—as we saw in Chapter 3, *Creating and Managing Leads*—all of your interactions for the sale take place in the opportunity section.

There are many components to opportunities that drive the overall sales cycle, starting with working the opportunity, to forecasting future sales for the management of your sales. We will see how opportunities work by using a business use case.

Business use case

As a sales rep for XYZ Widgets, you have been corresponding with GenePoint, the account you created in Chapter 4, *Business Development with Accounts and Contacts*. Your conversations have been going well and the customer asks you to send a quote. You now have to create an opportunity, add products, and create and send a quote. After this, you will see the opportunity in your sales forecast for the month and will finally be able to close the deal! Let's see how this all comes together.

Creating an opportunity

There are two ways of creating opportunities:

- **For a new customer**: We saw how this works in Chapter 3, *Creating and Managing Leads*, where an opportunity is created upon lead conversion. Since leads are potential clients, this is how you create an opportunity and work it until you close the first sale.
- **For an existing customer**: If you already have an account created for an organization, navigate to that organization and create the opportunity for a potential sale.

Let's see how the second option works.

Navigate to the existing GenePoint account and scroll down to the related **Opportunities** section. Click on **New** to create a new opportunity. This is shown in the following screenshot:

Clicking on this button takes you to the opportunity creation screen, as you can see in the following screenshot:

As you can see in the preceding screenshot, there are several important fields to fill out:

1. **Opportunity Name**: You should include a name that lets you know what you are selling.
2. **Account Name**: The account name automatically populates from the account that the opportunity relates to.
3. **Type**: This can be a new or existing customer.
4. **Lead Source**: Where this lead originated.
5. **Amount**: How much the sale is worth. This is updated when you add products in the next step.
6. **Close Date**: When you expect the deal to close.
7. **Stage**: What stage this opportunity is in. We will cover the different stages in detail in the next section.
8. **Probability**: This is auto-populated and ties into forecasting, which we will cover later on in this chapter in the *Using forecasting* section.

There is also a campaign field—which is optional—here to tie the opportunity to a marketing campaign. This is to show the campaign source for this opportunity if there is one. Clicking **Save** creates the opportunity.

In this section, we learned how to create an opportunity. Next, we will look at the opportunity stages and the sales path, as well as how they contribute to working an opportunity.

Using the opportunity stages and the sales path

Once an opportunity is created, the user can track the activities that relate to the opportunity, as we covered in Chapter 2, *Understanding Salesforce Activities*. One of the most important aspects of an opportunity is marking the correct stage that the opportunity is in. Stages mark the progress of an opportunity and are customizable for each Salesforce instance. Salesforce offers a feature that allows you to visualize the stages of an opportunity. This feature is called the **sales path**. Let's see how to enable this feature.

In the following screenshot, I navigated to the setup and configuration section of Salesforce:

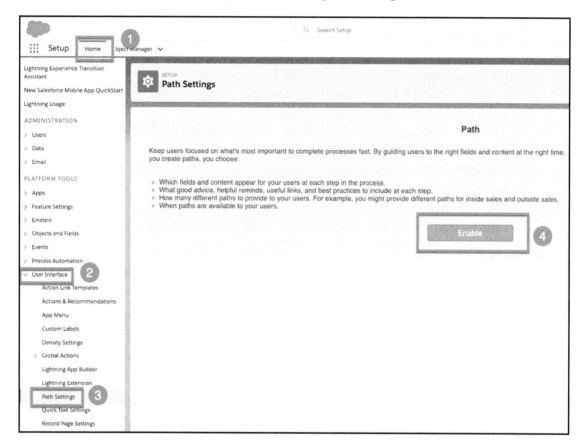

As you can see in the preceding screenshot, I took a couple of steps:

1. Go to **Home (1)** | **User Interface (2)** | **Path Settings (3)** to enable the path settings for the case.
2. Click on the **Enable (4)** button, which brings you to the following screen:

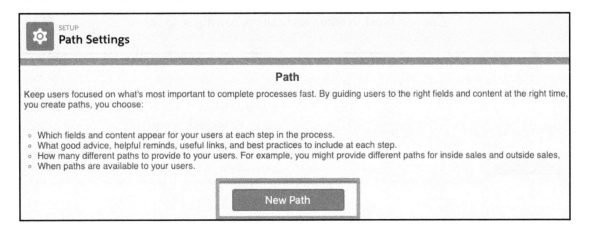

3. Here, click on **New Path**, which brings us to the following screen:

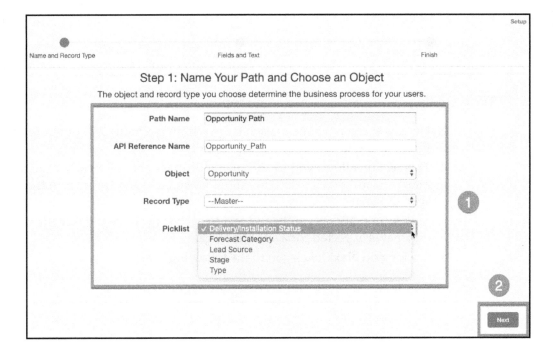

As you can see here, we took a couple of steps:

1. Fill in the path name, API name, object, and record type (if there are no record types, it will default to **Master**), as well as the picklist you want to use for the path. In our case, we want to choose the **Stage** field.

2. Click on **Next** to take you to the following screen:

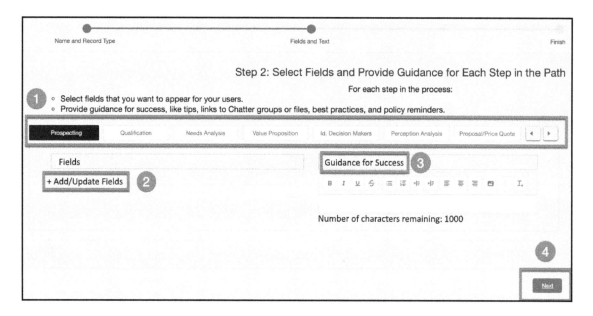

The preceding screenshot shows us some important sections:

1. Here, you can navigate to each stage within the path and configure the **Fields** and **Guidance for Success** options.

2. This section allows you to add the fields that appear for each stage for reference and may need to be edited when the opportunity is in that specific stage.

3. This section allows you to add text to each stage to help guide the user on what is expected for a specific stage.

4. Clicking on **Next** takes you to the following screen:

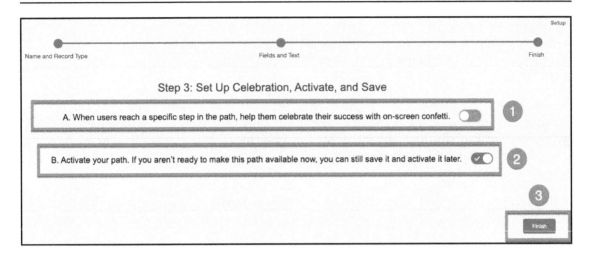

In the preceding screenshot, you can see the following options:

1. There is an option to add visual confetti when a certain stage is reached as a celebration. An example would be confetti coming down on the screen when a sale is closed and the stage changes to **Closed Won**.
2. This is where the path is activated.
3. Clicking on **Finish** completes the path setup.

Let's navigate back to our opportunity. In the following screenshot, we can see that the out-of-the-box stages that come with Salesforce are the default stages that can be changed by the admin to match your organization's sales process:

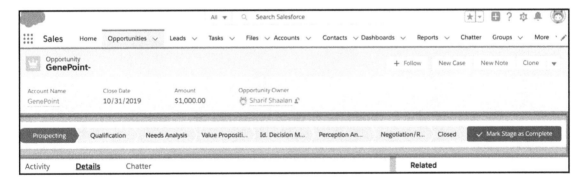

As you can see in the preceding screenshot, there is a sales path. The sales path is the visual representation of the opportunity stages and you, as the user, can click on any of the stages and then click on **Mark Stage as Complete** to indicate that the opportunity is in a specific stage.

Stages are also important as they represent the probability of closing a deal. The further along you are in a stage, the higher the probability of closing the deal. In the preceding screenshot, the **Probability (%)** value is only at **10%** since this opportunity is in the first stage. These probabilities relate to forecasting, which we will cover at the end of this chapter.

In this section, we learned what stages are and how to move to different stages using the sales path. Next, let's look at what contact roles are and how to add them to an opportunity.

Understanding contact roles

Contact roles are the people you communicate with to close a specific deal. You could have one or more contact roles, depending on the opportunity. First, let's look at how to add new contact roles that may not be in the default list. First, navigate to the setup and configuration section of Salesforce:

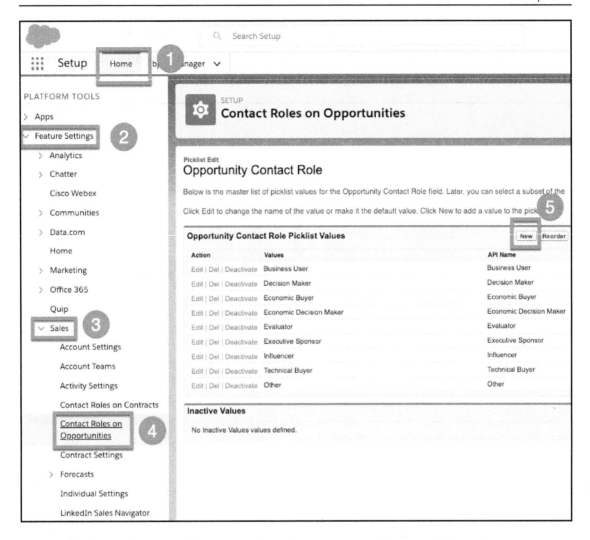

As you can see in the preceding screenshot, there are several steps to follow if you want to add or edit the roles that come up when adding a contact role:

1. Go to **Home** (1) | **Feature Settings** (2) | **Sales** (3) | **Contact Roles on Opportunities** (4).
2. On this page, click on **New** (5) to add a new contact role or edit any existing roles.

Now that we have seen how to add roles as needed, let's add an actual role:

1. Navigate to the **Contact Roles** section of the opportunity to add a contact role, as in the following screenshot:

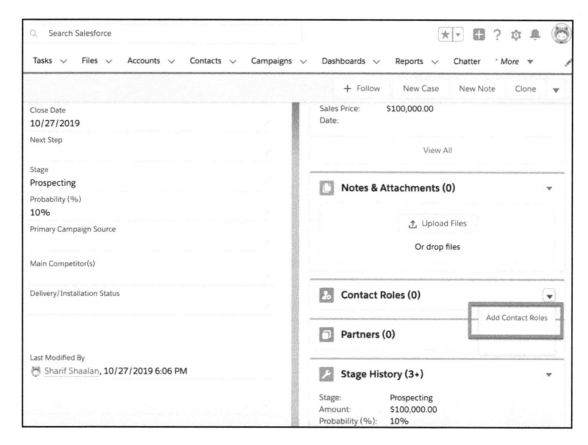

2. After that, click on **Add Contact Roles**, highlighted in the preceding screenshot. The following screenshot shows the first page that shows up when you do so:

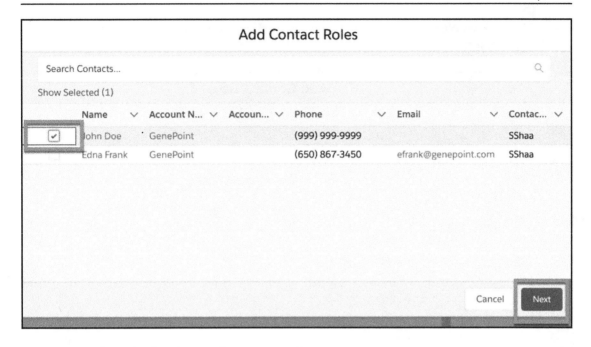

I selected **John Doe** as the contact role.

3. Click on **Next**. The following screenshot shows you how to add the role of the contact:

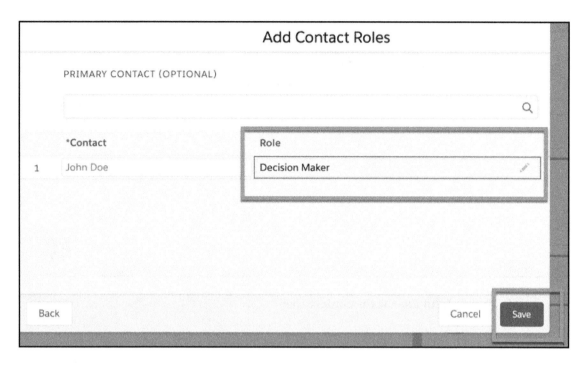

I added the role of **Decision Maker** to **John Doe**. This is the person I will interact with and add activities for as I work to close this deal.

4. Click on **Save**. The contact role will save to the opportunity.

Let's see how we can edit the contact role if needed. In the following screenshot, I navigated back to the opportunity:

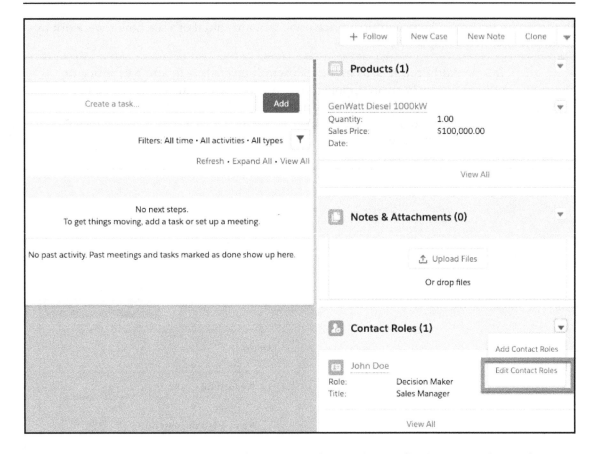

As you can see, to edit the contact roles, you need to click on **Edit Contact Roles** in the **Contact Roles** section.

In this section, we learned how to add a contact role to an opportunity to close a deal. Next, let's look at products and price books.

Using products and price books

Price books are a collection of products that can be added to an opportunity to show what is purchased. An opportunity can only be tied to one price book. Price books are created by administrators and assigned to specific teams that sell a specific product line. Salesforce automatically creates a **Standard** price book as a master list of all the products and default prices. It is best practice to create multiple **Custom** price books that contain the list prices if you offer products at different prices to different market segments.

Products are the actual items within a price book that are sold. Let's see how they work by taking the following steps:

1. Click on **Add Products**, as in the following screenshot, to add a product, or multiple products, to an opportunity. Notice that you also have the option here to choose a price book for this particular opportunity if you have access to more than one price book. If you only have access to one price book, it is chosen by default, as is the case in our example:

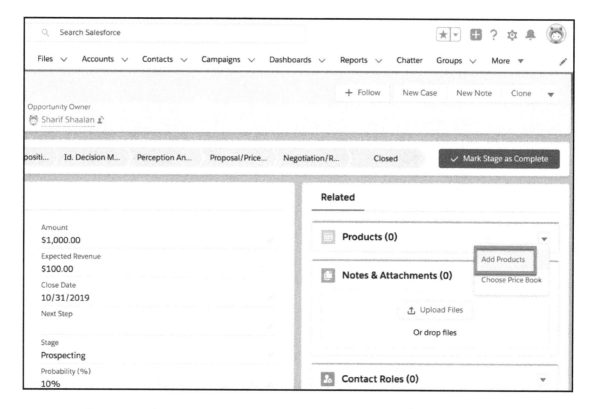

We can see the initial stage of the **Add Products** page in the following screenshot:

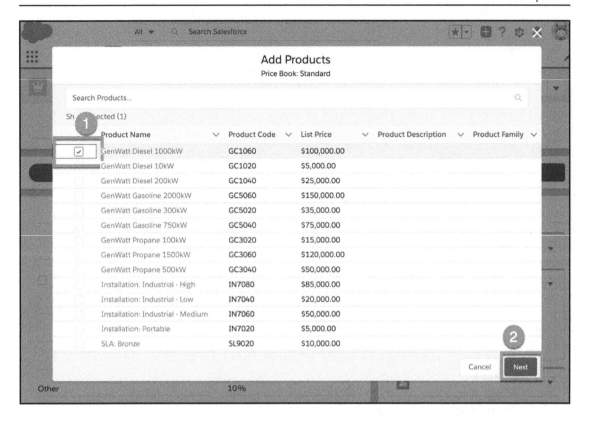

2. You have the option to add one or more products. For this example, I added one product.

Now, let's see the options. The following screenshot shows the options for the product:

3. As you can see in the preceding screenshot, you can add the quantity, adjust the sales price if there is a discount on offer, set a date, and add a line description.

4. Once you have added these data points, click on **Save** to add the product to the opportunity. The following screenshot shows the product added to the opportunity:

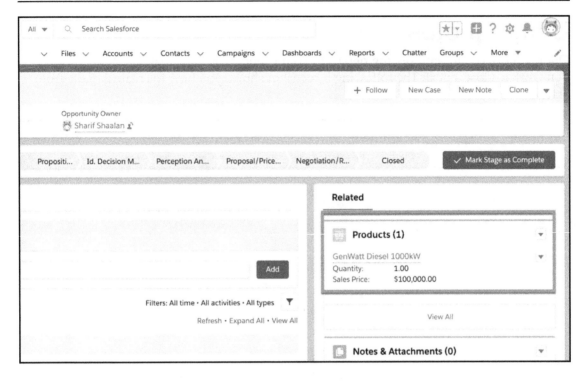

In the preceding screenshot, you can see that the product is now added to the opportunity. Notice that the opportunity account automatically inherits the sales price amount from the product.

In this section, we learned what products and price books are and how to add products to an opportunity. Next, let's take a look at how to add and send a quote to the decision-maker.

Using quotes

Quotes allow you to send pricing details to your clients. You can create multiple quotes as you work to close a deal. The following screenshot shows you how to create a quote from an opportunity:

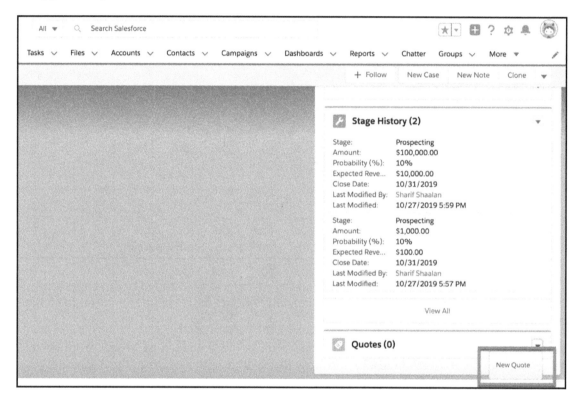

Navigate to the **Quotes** section of the Opportunity and click on **New Quote**. The following screenshot shows the quote creation page:

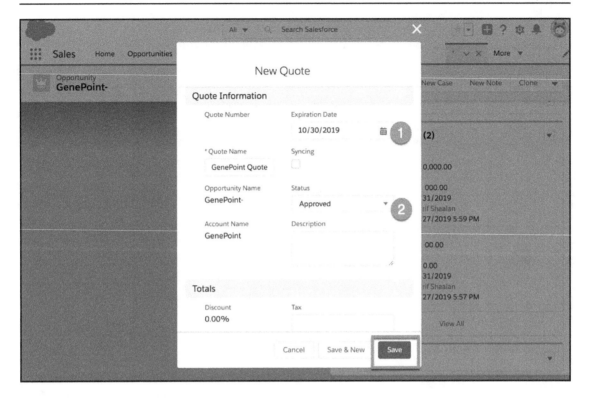

Then, fill in the **Expiration Date** field for the quote and set **Status** to **Approved** so that the quote can be used.

The following screenshot shows you how to generate a PDF of the quote by choosing **Create PDF** from the drop-down menu. Creating a PDF of the quote makes it easy to share the quote with a client:

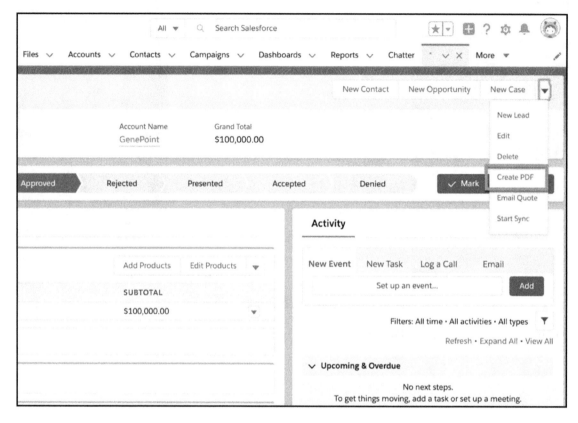

The following screenshot shows you how to send the quote out once the PDF is generated:

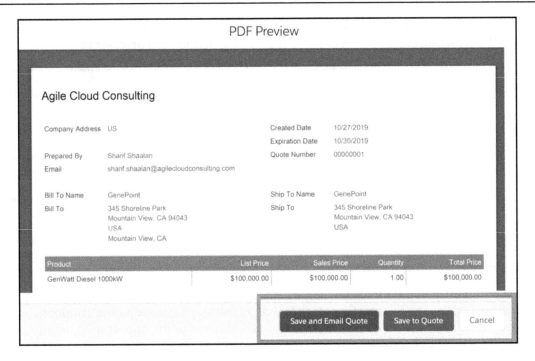

Once you review the quote, you can save and email it or save the PDF to the quote to send it at a later time. The quote will be saved to the files associated with the opportunity.

In this section, we learned what a quote is and how to send a quote from an opportunity. Next, we will look at how opportunities tie into forecasting.

Using forecasting

Forecasting allows sales managers to predict how much income is projected for a specific time period. Each opportunity stage has a probability that ties into the forecast categories. Salesforce defines the forecast categories as follows:

- **Best Case** includes the amount you are likely to close, closed-won opportunities, and opportunities in the **Commit** category.
- **Closed** includes the total for closed-won opportunities.
- **Commit** includes the amount you are fairly sure you will close.
- **Omitted** means the opportunity does not contribute to your forecast.
- **Pipeline** includes all open opportunities.

The following screenshot shows you how the forecast looks for the GenePoint deal, which is in the **Prospecting** stage. To get to this page, I navigated to the **Forecasts** tab:

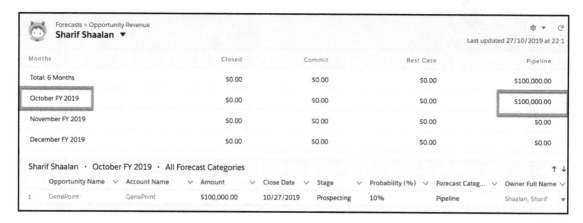

The deal shows up in the **Pipeline** category since it is not yet closed and is in a lower **Prospecting** stage. The **Prospecting** stage is the default stage when an opportunity is created. Now that we have added all the required elements to the opportunity, let's close it and see how this opportunity will show up in the forecast.

The following screenshot shows you how we mark an opportunity as Closed Won, which means you got the sale:

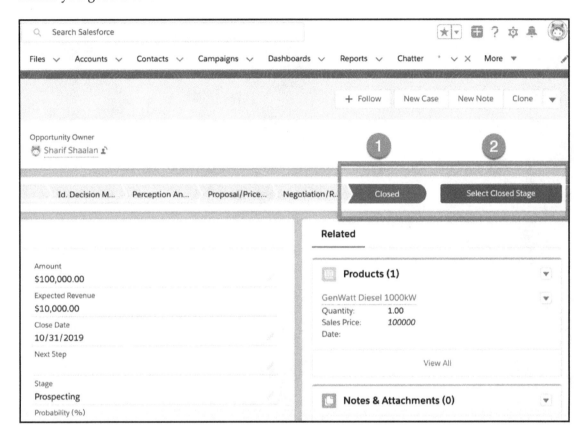

Click on **Closed** (1) in the sales path, then click on **Select Closed Stage** (2) The following screenshot shows the popup that will appear on your screen:

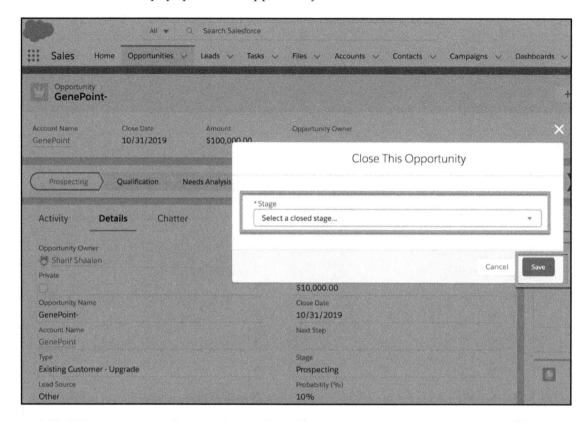

The preceding screenshot shows the closed stage options. You can choose **Closed Won**, which means you won the deal, or **Closed Lost**, which means you lost the deal. The following screenshot shows what happens when the deal is set to **Closed Won**:

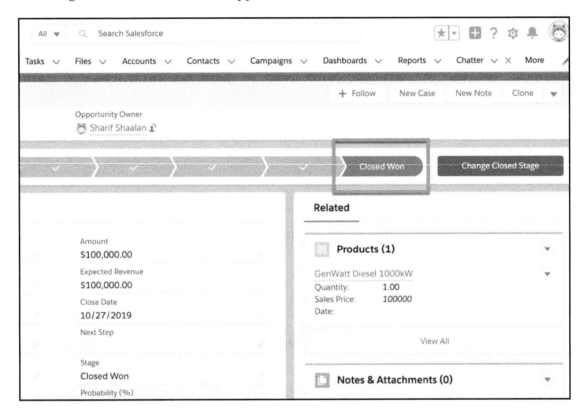

In the preceding screenshot, we can see that the sales path has turned entirely green and the deal is set to **Closed Won**. The following screenshot shows you how the forecast looks when the deal is won:

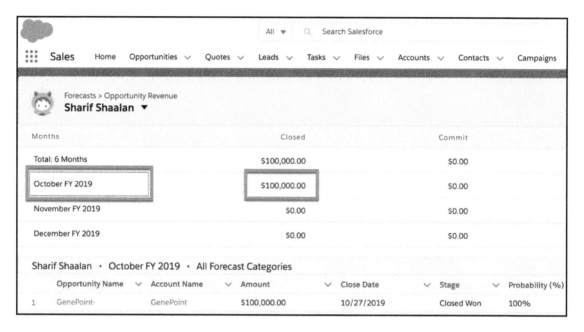

In the preceding screenshot, you can see that the deal now shows up in the **Closed** category in the forecasting section.

In this section, we learned what forecasts are and how an opportunity contributes to forecasts.

Summary

In this chapter, we learned what opportunities are and how to create them. We learned about opportunity stages and how they are used with the sales path to record the progress of an opportunity. We learned what contact roles are and how to add them to an opportunity. We learned what products and price books are and how to add products to an opportunity to show what is being sold. We learned how to create and generate a quote PDF. Finally, we learned what forecasts are and how opportunities tie into forecasting.

In the next chapter, we will cover campaigns—the foundation of marketing functionality in Salesforce.

Questions

1. How many opportunities can you have on an account?
2. What is the difference between the opportunity stages and the sales path?
3. How many **Contact Role** instances can be added to an opportunity?
4. What happens to the **Amount** field on an opportunity when you add products?
5. Who do you send quotes to in an opportunity?
6. What are the two types of **Closed** stages in an opportunity?
7. What is included under the **Best Case** forecast category?

Further reading

- Salesforce opportunities: `https://help.salesforce.com/articleView?id=opportunities.htmtype=5`
- Salesforce forecasting: `https://help.salesforce.com/articleView?id=forecasts3_overview.htmtype=5`

6
Achieving Business Goals Using Campaigns

Campaigns are outbound marketing initiatives that target leads and contacts. They can take the form of direct mail, events, print ads, emails, or any other marketing outreach where you are trying to get a response from the recipients. This response can take the form of interest in a product, attending an event such as a seminar or a webinar, or clicking on an ad. Campaigns tie marketing and sales together as they help generate leads and track those leads as they convert into opportunities and, finally, into opportunity closure. This closure can either be **Closed Won**—a sale—or **Closed Lost**—a lost sale. Campaigns use campaign members to track who is associated with a campaign. Campaign members can be leads or contacts that have been contacted for a specific marketing campaign. Campaigns can also be nested in a hierarchy. This means that you may have an overall campaign, such as `2020 Email Campaigns`, and underneath it resides all the email marketing campaigns of that year. This is very useful as all the campaign statistics come under the parent, showing the overall performance of all the sub-campaigns. Many third-party apps, such as email providers or event management tools, also integrate with Salesforce and tie into campaigns.

In this chapter, we will cover the following topics:

- Using campaigns and understanding how to create them
- Using campaign members and seeing how to add them to campaigns and view their campaign history
- Using campaign hierarchies and how they are helpful for marketing
- Using third-party apps to extend campaign functionality

With the help of these topics, we will gain the required skills to create a campaign and see what a campaign record contains. We will learn how to create campaign members associated with a campaign and see how this looks on a lead and a contact record. We will also be able to create a campaign hierarchy and see how this helps with the reports. Finally, we will see how integrating third-party apps can make using campaigns more powerful by automating aspects of responses to a campaign.

Technical requirements

For this chapter, make sure you log in to your development org and follow along.

Using campaigns

Campaigns are outbound marketing initiatives used by marketers. The reason campaigns are so important is that they are a primary means of obtaining leads and starting the sales cycle. You can look at campaigns as buckets that bring together leads, contacts, and opportunities.

A business use case

You are a marketing rep at XYZ Widgets. You have been tasked with delivering a webinar and you need to create the webinar campaign in Salesforce, as well as inviting attendees and tracking their progress. Let's see how this is done.

Creating a campaign

Let's take a look at how to create a campaign in Salesforce and go through the various fields to include when creating a campaign:

1. Go to the **Campaigns** tab (see label **1** in the following screenshot) to start the process, then click on **New** (see label **2** in the following screenshot):

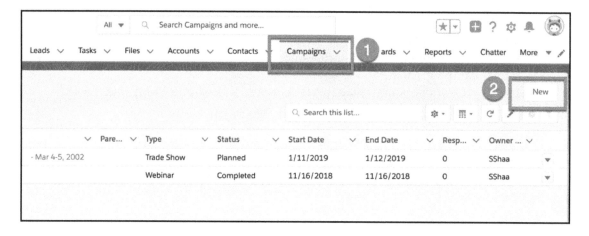

In the following screenshot, you can see part of the campaign creation screen:

As you can see in the preceding screenshot, there are several fields on this page:

- **Campaign Owner** (**1**): This is the name of the person that created the campaign and so owns it in Salesforce.
- **Campaign Name** (**2**): This is the unique name that you need to include to indicate what the campaign is used for. In this example, we used `Agile Cloud Consulting January 2020 Webinar`.
- **Active** (**3**): This checkbox is used to set the campaign as **Active**, which means it is currently being worked on.
- **Type** (**4**): This field defines the type of the campaign. This can be **Email**, **Direct mail**, **Webinar**, and so on. In this example, we will set it to **Webinar**.
- **Status** (**5**): This field lets us know what the current status of the campaign is. This can be **Planned**, **In Progress**, or **Complete**.
- **Start Date** (**6**): This field lets us know when the campaign is set to start.
- **End Date** (**7**): This field lets us know when the campaign is set to end.

In the following screenshot, you can see the rest of the fields on the campaign creation screen:

As you can see in the preceding screenshot, there are several more important fields to fill in:

- **Expected Revenue in Campaign** (**1**): This is how much revenue—closed opportunities—you expect to come by from this campaign.
- **Budgeted Cost in Campaign** (**2**): This is how much the campaign costs. In our example, it would be the budget you have to put on the webinar.
- **Actual Cost in Campaign** (**3**): This is filled in after the campaign is complete. It should note how much it actually cost to put on the webinar.

- **Expected Response (%) (4)**: This is how many responses from leads and contacts we expect to receive out of all of the invitations we send out.
- **Num Sent in Campaign (5)**: This is how many leads and contacts are included in the campaign. This number is automatically calculated once we add campaign members in the next section.
- **Parent Campaign (6)**: This is how to set up the campaign hierarchy, which we will cover in further detail in the *Using Campaign Hierarchies* section of this chapter. This allows the numbers from the webinar campaign to come under the parent campaign.
- **Save (7)**: When all the fields are filled in, you can save the campaign to create it.

The following screenshot shows you what the created campaign looks like:

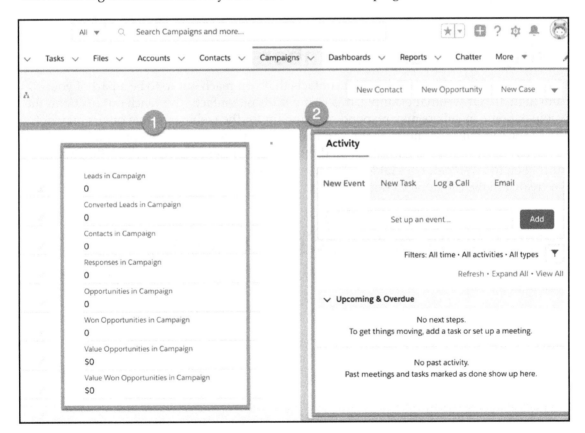

As you can see in the preceding screenshot, the campaign is now created. There are two important sections to note here:

- **The campaign roll-up fields** (**1**): These fields auto-calculate based on the leads and contacts that are added, the leads that are converted into opportunities, and the opportunities that are turned into sales. These fields are important in analyzing the **Return on Investment** (**ROI**) for a specific campaign. They allow you to see how many responses or leads you had and how many of those leads were converted into opportunities. You can then see how many of the opportunities were closed, giving you a lead-to-opportunity-to-sale ratio that indicates whether the campaign was a success or not.
- **Activities** (**2**): Note that you can add activities to campaigns as you could with leads, contacts, accounts, and opportunities.

Now that we have created the campaign, let's see how we can add campaign members in the following section.

Using campaign members

Campaign members are the leads and contacts that you reach out to to be a part of your campaign. In our webinar example, this is any leads or contacts you reach out to attend the webinar. Some members may respond and sign up for the webinar, while others may not. Out of the campaign members that respond, some may go on to make a purchase as a result of the webinar—these sales would be tied directly to the campaign and show the ROI of putting on the webinar. Let's take a look at how to add leads and contacts to the campaign we created in the previous section.

Adding leads as campaign members

As you can see in the following screenshot, you first need to navigate to the **Campaign Members** section:

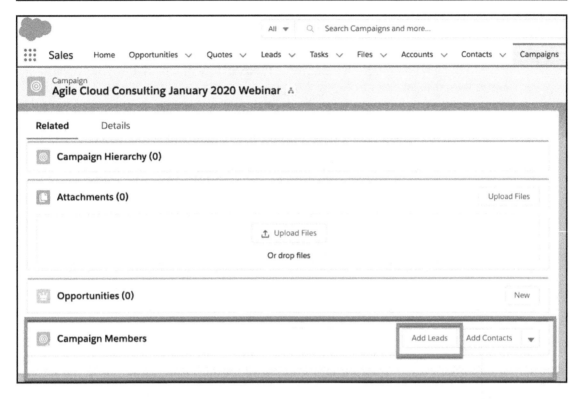

After navigating to the **Campaign Members** section, click on **Add Leads**.

In the following screenshot, you can see the **Add Leads to Campaign** page:

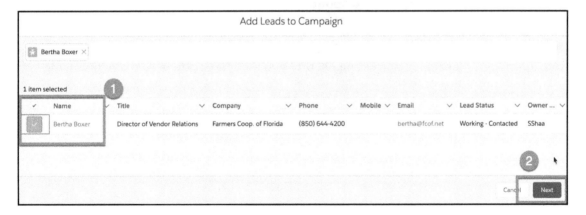

As you can see in the preceding screenshot, there are two actions to be taken:

- Choose the leads you want to add (**1**). This is done by clicking on the checkbox next to the lead name. In this example, there is only one lead, but you can add more than one lead at once.
- Click on **Next** (**2**) to move on to the final step of adding a campaign member.

In the following screenshot, you can see the popup that will appear on your screen:

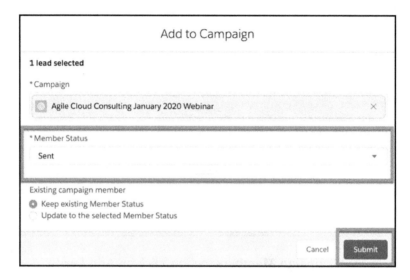

As you can see in the preceding screenshot, the default status is **Sent**. If the lead signs up for the webinar, this is updated to **Responded**. Clicking on **Submit** creates the campaign member record.

There is also an option to mass import leads if, for example, you have a list in a CSV file from a conference or from a marketing list that you may have purchased. The following screenshot shows this option:

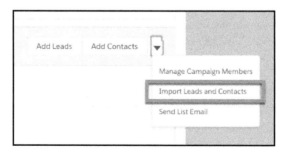

As you can see in the preceding screenshot, if you click on the drop-down arrow next to **Add Leads** and **Add Contacts**, you will find the **Import Leads and Contacts** link. This takes you to an import wizard that allows you to mass-import leads or contacts as needed.

Next, let's take a look at how to add a contact as a campaign member.

Adding contacts as campaign members

In the following screenshot, we can see what the **Campaign Members** list looks like now that a lead has been added:

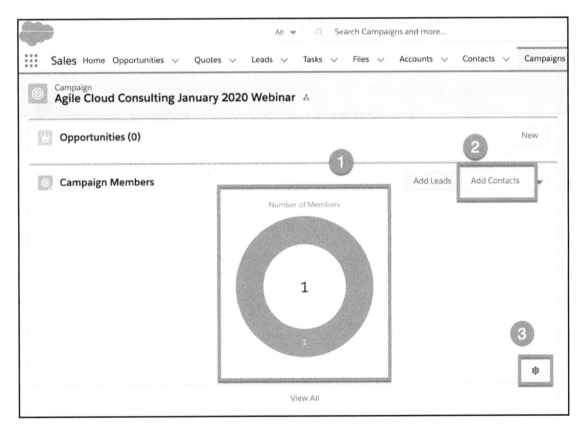

As you can see in the preceding screenshot, the lead now shows up under the **Number of Members** section (**1**). Let's click on **Add Contacts** (**2**) to add contacts as campaign members. (Note that the gear icon in the preceding screenshot (**3**) allows you to change the graph that shows here from a donut chart to a vertical or horizontal bar graph).

In the following screenshot, you can see the **Add Contacts to Campaign** page:

As you can see in the preceding screenshot, there are two actions to be taken:

- Choose the contacts you want to add (**1**). This is done by clicking on the checkbox next to the contact name.
- Click on Next (**2**) to move on to the final step of adding a campaign member.

In the following screenshot, you can see the final screen for adding the contact as a campaign member:

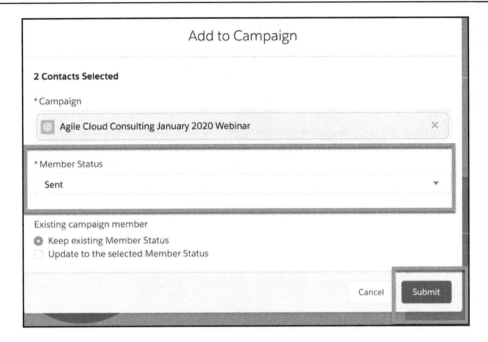

As you can see in the preceding screenshot, the default status is **Sent**. If the contact signs up for the webinar, this is updated to **Responded**. Clicking on **Submit** creates the campaign member record.

Next, let's take a look at how to view the campaign history of leads and contacts.

Viewing the campaign history of leads and contacts

The campaign history is a record of all the campaigns that a lead or contact has previously interacted with. Let's take a look at how to view the campaign history of leads and contacts.

In the following screenshot, you can see that you first need to navigate to the lead that was added as a campaign member:

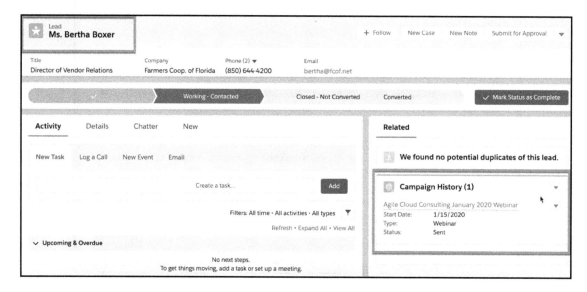

As you can see, the webinar campaign shows up under the **Campaign History** section of the lead. In the following screenshot, you can see that you can then navigate to the contact that was added as a campaign member:

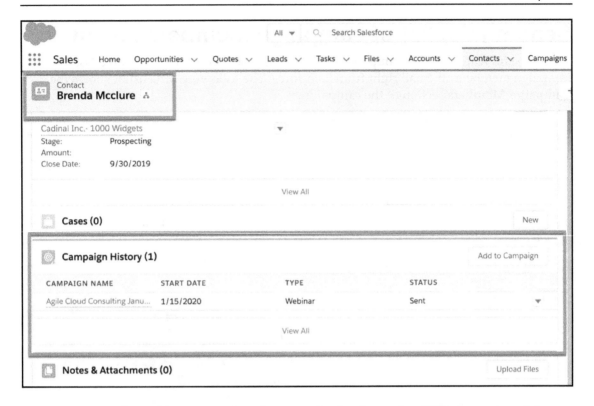

As you can see, the webinar campaign shows up in the **Campaign History** section of the contact. Let's take a look at one final feature of the **Campaign Members** section.

Sending the list of campaign members an email

A very useful feature in the **Campaign Members** section is the ability to send all of the campaign members an email right from Salesforce. The following screenshot shows the **Campaign Members** section of the campaign:

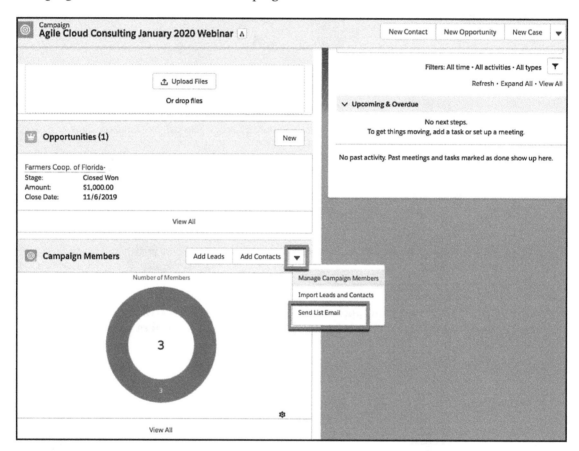

As you can see in the preceding screenshot, if you click on the drop-down arrow, there is the **Send List Email** option. This takes you to an email composition page, where you can write and send your email.

Now, we have seen how to create a campaign and how to add campaign members to a campaign. Next, let's look at what campaign hierarchies are and how to use them.

Using campaign hierarchies

Campaign hierarchies allow you to group campaigns under a top-level campaign. This can help in showing you the overall performance of a type of campaign over a year. For our webinar example, we want all the webinar campaigns that took place in 2020 to reside under a parent campaign called `2020 Webinar Campaigns`. Let's see how to do this.

In the following screenshot, you can see that the parent campaign for our January 2020 webinar is **2020 Webinar Campaigns**:

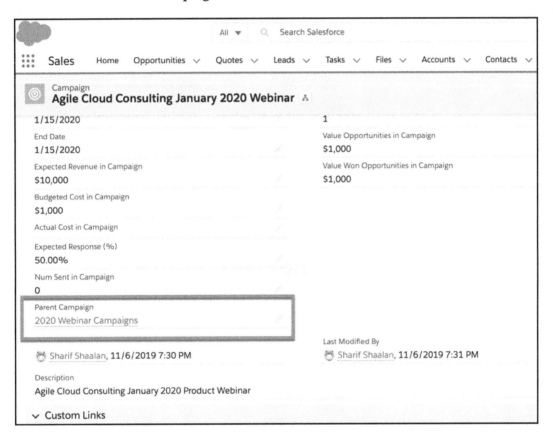

This means any numbers for this January campaign automatically come under this parent campaign.

In the following screenshot, we can see how the campaign hierarchy numbers show up under the parent campaign:

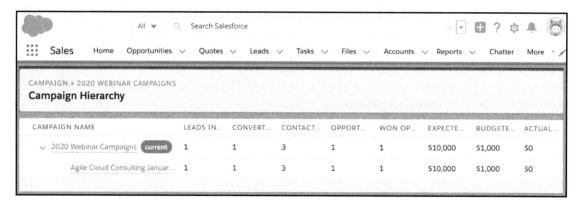

This shows the number of leads and contacts in the child campaigns, any opportunities that result from these campaigns, and any sales that result from these opportunities, which gives us a full picture of the performance of all the webinars in 2020.

Now that we have seen how to create and use campaigns, how to add campaign members, and how the campaign hierarchy shows us the performance of our campaigns across the year, let's look at how third-party apps contribute to automating campaigns.

Using third-party apps with campaigns

So far, we have seen how campaigns work. In our example, the marketing rep chooses leads and contacts and adds them to the webinar campaign. These campaign members default to a status of **Sent** and when they sign up for a webinar, the status updates to **Responded**. How does this status change happen? Without a third-party app, it would need to be updated manually.

In the following screenshot, we can see the campaign members that we added:

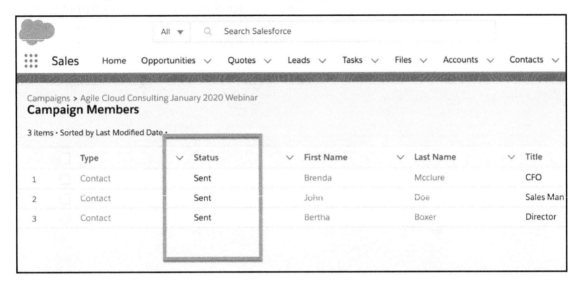

Notice that the status is set to **Sent** by default. There are many third-party apps available for campaigns such as webinars, events, conferences, or any other campaign use cases. Without using a third-party app, in our example, whenever a lead or contact signs up for the webinar, you would need to go into the system and update the status manually. This can be very time-consuming.

To find an appropriate third-party app, you can go to `https://appexchange.salesforce.com/`. AppExchange is the Salesforce store for third-party apps. You can go to AppExchange to search for and find relevant apps. Most apps allow you to test drive the app in a sandbox (test environment) for free before committing to the purchase. In the following screenshot, you can see the main AppExchange page:

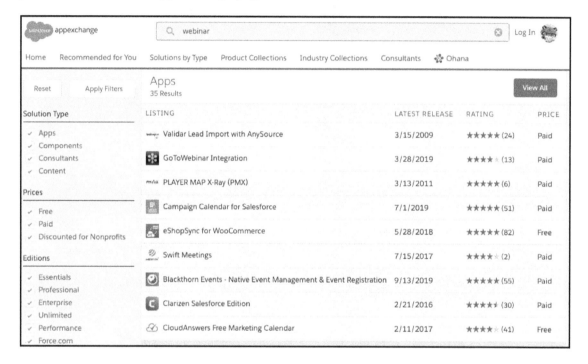

As you can see in the preceding screenshot, I entered `webinar` into the search box and all of the apps related to webinars that integrate with Salesforce were returned.

Assume that we have connected to a third-party webinar app that integrates with Salesforce:

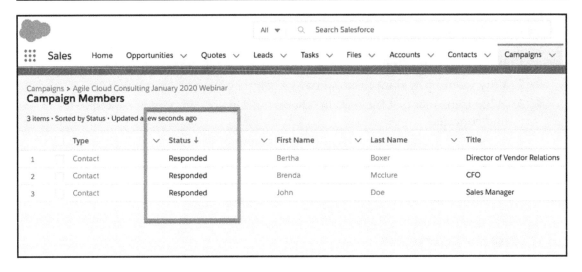

Notice that when someone signs up for the webinar through the third-party app, the app integration automatically updates the status to **Responded**.

This is how we use third-party apps with campaigns to know whether and when a member has signed up.

Summary

In this chapter, we learned how to create campaigns and what the important input fields are on campaign records to increase our visibility of the market. We learned that both leads and contacts can be added to campaigns, as well as how to add a lead and contact to a campaign.

We learned how to view the campaign history of both leads and contacts and we now know what a campaign hierarchy is and how to add a campaign to a hierarchy.

Finally, we learned how third-party apps can be used to automate campaign responses, cutting out manual work that could be inefficient and unreliable due to human error. We also now know where to find third-party apps on AppExchange to automatically find out when a member signs up.

Now that we have covered sales and marketing, we will look at how Salesforce handles customer service through cases in the next chapter!

Questions

1. What are the two types of campaign members that can be added to a Campaign?
2. Why would you want to add a parent campaign to your campaign?
3. What is the name of the section where you can see campaigns related to leads and contacts?
4. What field lets us know if a campaign is **Active**?
5. Why would you want to use a third-party app with campaigns?
6. What are three examples of types of campaigns?

Further reading

- Salesforce campaigns: `https://help.salesforce.com/articleView?id=campaigns_def.htmtype=5`
- Salesforce campaign members: `https://help.salesforce.com/articleView?id=campaigns_members_working_with_parent.htmtype=5`
- Campaign hierarchies: `https://help.salesforce.com/articleView?id=campaigns_hierarchy_setup.htmtype=5`

7
Enhancing Customer Service Using Cases

Cases are the foundation of the customer service experience in Salesforce. A customer can open a case to report an issue or ask a question. Cases are connected to a contact and the account related to that contact to show the person and the business that originated the Case. Sales Cloud includes the basic functionality for Cases, such as creating a Case, escalation rules, **Web-to-Case**, and **Email-to-Case**. This basic functionality supports sales operations that want to track the customer service experience but do not have a dedicated customer service department. Service Cloud includes add-ons and extended functionality that does not come with Sales Cloud. Service Cloud includes modules such as entitlements, a knowledge base, and a service console. These modules are meant for full customer service teams.

In this chapter, we will cover the basic case functionality that is the foundation for Service Cloud. The following topics will be covered in detail in this chapter:

- Using Cases and how to create them to enhance customer service
    - Case status and how this field drives the case life cycle
- Using escalation rules and how they are created
- Using **Web-to-Case** and how to generate the HTML code used for **Web-to-Case**
- Using **Email-to-Case** and how **Email-to-Case** is set up in the system

With the help of these topics, you will be able to gain the skills needed to create a case and see what the case record contains. You will learn what the case status field is, and how it is used to drive the case life cycle. You will learn the skills needed to set up and use escalation rules, and how to set up and use both **Web-to-Case** and **Email-to-Case** to enhance the customer experience.

Technical requirements

For this chapter, make sure to log in to your development org and follow along.

Using Cases to enhance customer service

Cases are issues that are raised by customers. The reason Cases are so important is that they are a primary means of resolving customer issues and keeping clients satisfied. These issues can range from basic questions to technical issues with a product.

Business use case

You are a customer service rep at XYZ Widgets. You get a call about a mechanical issue from one of your customers. You will need to create a case to log the issue. We will look at how to deal with this use case, and then explore how to create escalation rules and how customers submit cases through the web, as well as through email, that may end up in your queue.

Creating a Case

Let's take a look at how to create a case in Salesforce and go through the fields included when creating a Case.

In the following screenshot, I clicked on the **Cases** tab (1) to start the process:

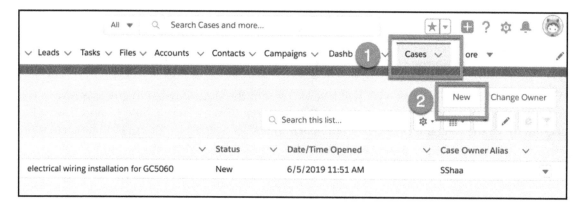

As you can see in the preceding screenshot, once I was on the **Cases** tab, I clicked on **New** (2).

In the following screenshot, you can see the beginning of the Case creation screen:

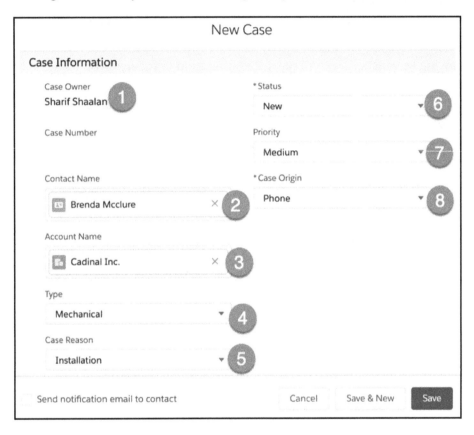

As you can see in the preceding screenshot, there are several fields here, as follows:

- **Case Owner** (1): This is the person that created the case and thus owns it in Salesforce.
- **Contact Name** (2): This is the person that raised the case.
- **Account Name** (3): This is the company associated with the person that raised the case.
- **Type** (4): This field defines the type of Case. This field is customizable for the business use case.
- **Case Reason** (5): This field defines the reason for the Case. This field is customizable for the business use case.

- **Status** (6): This field lets us know where in the life cycle the case is. When creating a case, it will default to **New**.
- **Priority** (7): This field lets us know how urgent the case is. It can be **High**, **Medium**, or **Low** priority.
- **Case Origin** (8): This field lets us know the source of the case. It can be **Phone**, **Web**, **Email**, or any custom origin you want to add.

In the following screenshot, we will see the continuation of the fields on the Case creation screen:

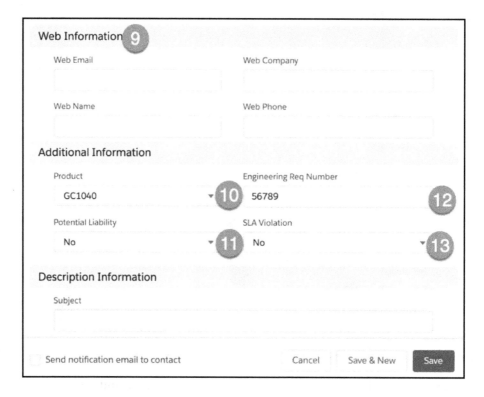

As you can see in the preceding screenshot, there are several more fields here, as follows:

- **Web Information** (9): This section is only utilized when a web form is submitted, so it is not relevant for this use case.
- **Product** (10): This field defines the product for the Case. This field is customizable for the business use case.
- **Potential Liability** (11): This field defines the potential liability for the Case. This field is customizable for the business use case, and may or may not be used.

- **Engineering Req Number** (12): This field defines the engineering request number for the Case. This field is customizable for the business use case, and may or may not be used.
- **SLA Violation** (13): This field lets us know if the **service-level agreement (SLA)** has been violated. The SLA defines how much time your business committed to responding to the issue.

In the following screenshot, we will see the continuation of the fields on the Case creation screen:

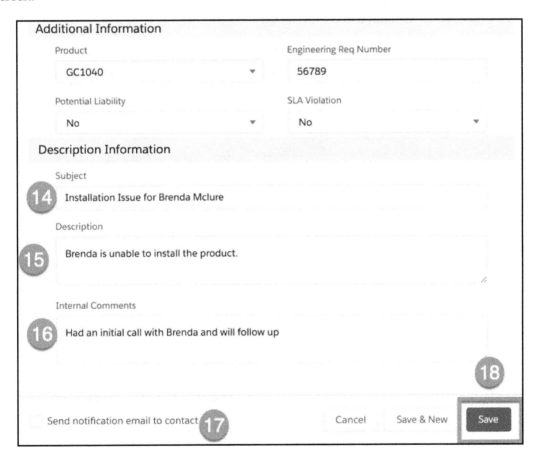

As you can see in the preceding screenshot, there are several more fields to finish off the case creation, as follows:

- **Subject** (14): This is where you enter the subject of the Case.
- **Description** (15): This is where you enter the details of the issue.
- **Internal Comments** (16): This is where you enter comments about the case that are not visible to the customer.
- **Send notification email to contact** (17): You can choose this option to notify the contact via email that the case has been created.
- **Save** (18): Click **Save** to create the Case.

The following screenshot shows the created case:

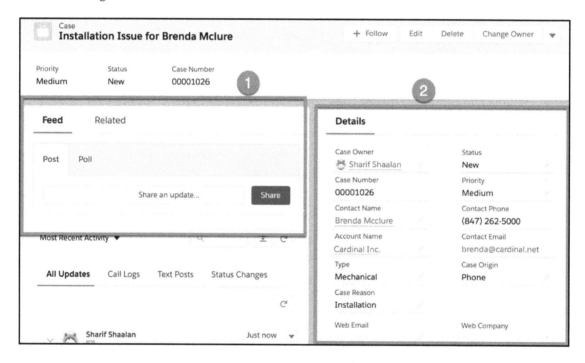

As you can see in the preceding screenshot, the case is now created. There are two important sections to note here, as follows:

- **Feed** (1): This is the chatter feed for the case.
- **Details** (2): All of the details you entered on case creation will show up here.

The following screenshot shows another very important section on the created Case:

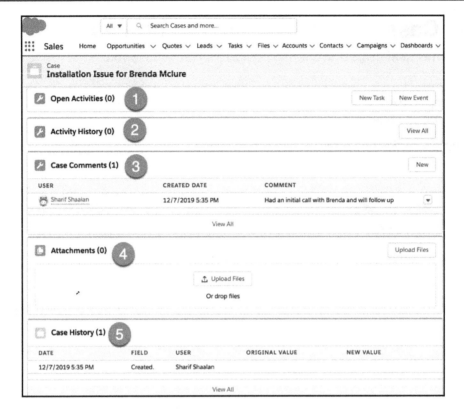

As you can see in the created case screenshot, there is one more very important section—the **Related** section. This section shows all records related to the Case, as follows:

- **Open Activities** (1): This section shows all open tasks and events related to the Case.
- **Activity History** (2): This section shows all tasks and events that have been completed.
- **Case Comments** (3): This section shows all comments, both internal and external, that have been added to the Case.
- **Attachments** (4): This section shows all attachments related to this Case.
- **Case History** (5): This section shows an audit of all actions on the Case.

Now that we have created the Case, let's see how the Case **Status** drives the case life cycle.

Using Case Status to drive the process

The case **Status** field drives the case life cycle. This field allows you to see where the case is at a point in time.

The following screenshot shows the options for Case **Status**. These values can be customized for the business use case, as needed:

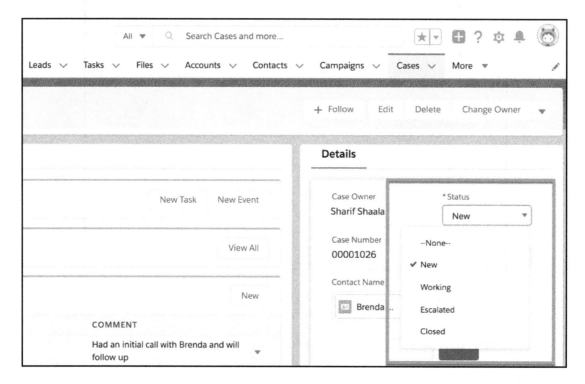

As you can see in the preceding screenshot, there are four Case **Status** values, as follows:

- **New**: This is the default status when a case is created.
- **Working**: This status lets us know that the case is being actively worked on.
- **Escalated**: This status lets us know that the case has been escalated to another department or a manager due to an issue.
- **Closed**: This status lets us know that the case has been resolved.

Now that we have created the case and seen how Case **Status** works, let's dig a little deeper into case escalation in the following section.

Using escalation rules for quicker case resolution

Escalation rules allow you to automatically reassign a case and/or notify a manager that there is an issue with a Case. An example would be a technical issue that needs to be escalated to a more skilled technician. Another example may be if a customer asks for a case to be escalated to a manager. Escalation rules allow you to automatically escalate cases based on criteria and set who the case is escalated to, as well as who to notify of the escalation. Let's take a look at how to build escalation rules.

In the following screenshot, I clicked on the gear icon (1) to start the process:

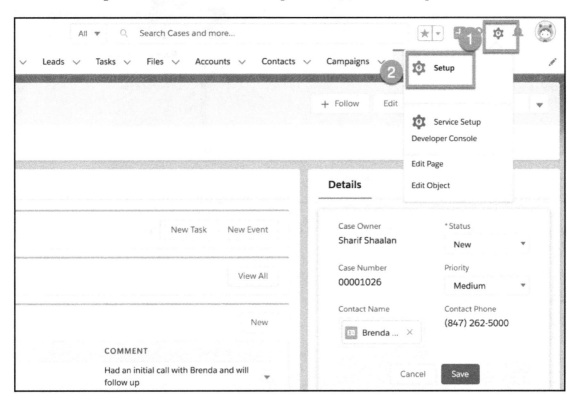

As you can see in the preceding screenshot, after clicking on the gear icon I clicked on **Setup** (2) to take me into the configuration section of Salesforce.

In the following screenshot, I started typing `esca` into the search bar (1). This brings up any items in **SETUP** that have these letters:

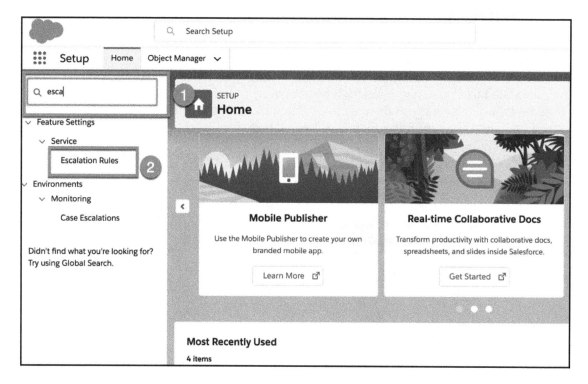

As you can see in the preceding screenshot, clicking on **Escalation Rules** (2) takes me into the section where I can set these rules up.

In the following screenshot, all of my escalation rules come up:

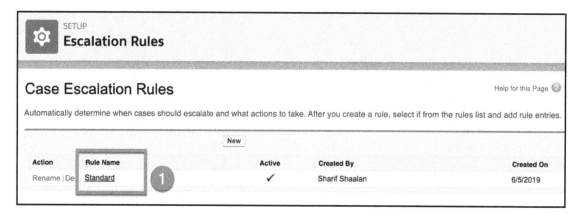

As you can see in the preceding screenshot, there is a standard escalation rule already set up. Let's click on the **Rule Name** (1).

In the following screenshot, all of the rule entries on the **Standard** escalation rule come up:

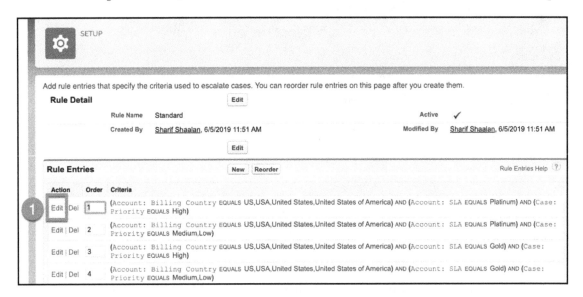

As you can see in the preceding screenshot, the rules are set with criteria for each rule. There is also an order of how the rules are executed, giving you the ability to check for multiple combinations of criteria within a single escalation rule. Let's click on **Edit** to look at the first entry (1).

In the following screenshot, you can see all of the configuration options for a single entry within an escalation rule:

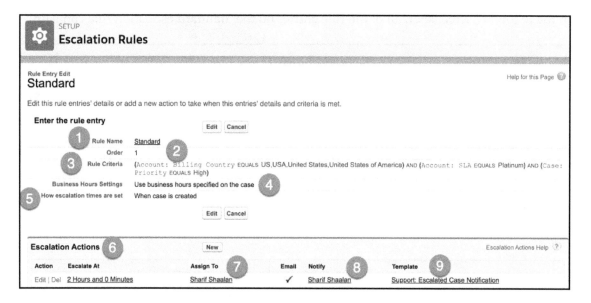

As you can see in the preceding screenshot, there are several options here, as follows:

- **Rule Name** (1): This is the name of the rule that this entry belongs to.
- **Order** (2): This is the order in which the entry executes within the rule.
- **Rule Criteria** (3): This is the criteria that, if true, will execute the action(s).
- **Business Hours Settings** (4): This allows the calculation of the hours. For example, if you only want business hours to count toward resolution time, this can be set here to exclude other times from the calculation.
- **How escalation times are set** (5): This allows you to set when the clock starts ticking on escalations. In this example, it is as soon as the case is created.
- **Escalation Actions** (6): These are actions you can set to execute if the criteria are met.
- **Assign To** (7): In this action, the case will be reassigned to whoever is set in the **Assign To** field if the criteria are met.
- **Notify** (8): In this action, a notification will be sent to whoever is set in the **Notify** field if the criteria are met.
- **Template** (9): This is the email template that will be used for the notification.

Now that we have seen how to create and use Cases, as well as how to create automatic escalation rules to reassign Cases and notify management of issues, let's take a look at another feature that will help automate Cases. In the next section, we will look at **Web-to-Case**.

Using Web-to-Case to create cases

Very similar to Web-to-Lead, which we covered in `Chapter 3`, *Creating and Managing Leads*, **Web-to-Case** is an easy way to generate HTML code that you can drop into your website to create a case capture form. A case capture form lives outside of Salesforce but creates a case directly in Salesforce when the form is saved. This can be a page on your website or any other form where you would want the case to be automatically added to Salesforce. Let's see how this is done.

In the following screenshot, I started typing `web` into the search bar (1). This brings up any items in **SETUP** that have these letters:

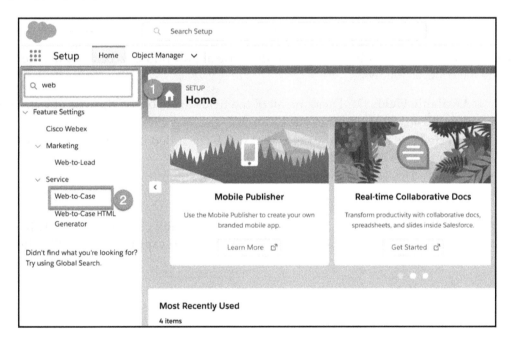

As you can see in the preceding screenshot, after clicking on **Web-to-Case** (2), it takes you into the section where you can set this up.

In the following screenshot, all of my options for setting up **Web-to-Case** come up:

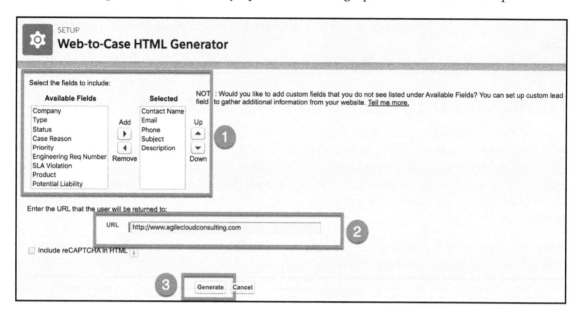

As you can see in the preceding screenshot, there are a few options to be filled in before you generate the code, as follows:

- **Available Fields** (1): These are all of the fields available on the case object. You can pull any of them into your form.
- **Selected** (1): These are the fields that will be included in the form once you generate the HTML code.
- **URL** (2): This is where the user will land after submitting the form.
- **Generate** (3): After this, click on **Generate**.

In the following screenshot, you can see the HTML code. Now, you have your HTML code! You can copy and paste this right into your website and start capturing Cases, like this:

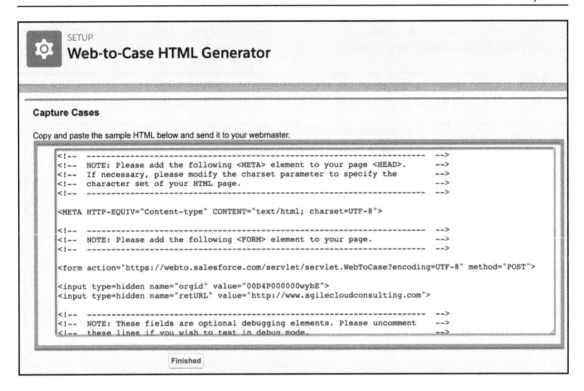

The preceding screenshot shows the final output.

You now have learned how to navigate to the **Web-to-Case** setup section and how to generate the HTML code needed to add a **Web-to-Case** form on an external website. Next, we will take a look at another powerful feature, **Email-to-Case**.

Using Email-to-Case to create Cases

Whereas **Web-to-Case** allows you to capture a case submission through your website, **Email-to-Case** allows you to set up a specific email address that converts any email sent to that email address to a Case. The business use case for this is a support email. You may want to set up an email address such as support@yourcompany.com, to which your clients can send an email with an issue. Salesforce will take that email and create a case for the issue. All subsequent correspondence will be captured on that case until the case is resolved. Let's take a look at how to set up **Email-to-Case**.

In the following screenshot, I started typing `case` into the search bar (1). This brings up any items in **SETUP** that have these letters:

As you can see in the preceding screenshot, I clicked on **Email-to-Case** (2) to take me into the section where we can set this up.

In the following screenshot, all of my options for setting up **Email-to-Case** come up:

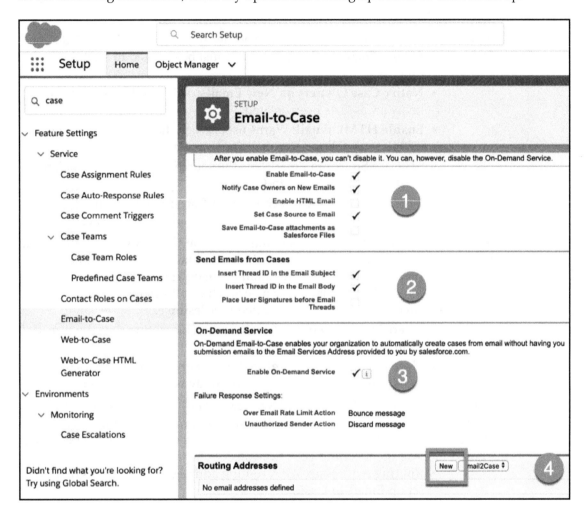

As you can see in the preceding screenshot, there are a few options to be filled in before you generate the code, as follows:

- **Initial Settings** (1): These are some initial settings to get you started, listed here:
  - **Enable Email-to-Case**: This box must be checked to start the process.
  - **Notify Case Owners on New Emails**: This is to let the case owner know a Case has been created.
  - **Enable HTML Email**: Warns users when the incoming email is HTML to avoid opening malicious emails.
  - **Set Case Source to Email**: Sets the source field to email for Cases created through **Email-to-Case**.
  - **Save Email-to-Case attachments as Salesforce Files**: If the incoming email has an attachment, it carries over to Salesforce.
- **Send Emails from Cases** (2): These settings allow you to set how responses work when corresponding with a Case created through **Email-to-Case**, as follows:
  - **Insert Thread ID in the Email Subject**: This setting makes sure the thread ID is in the email subject, which allows the replies to all emails in a thread to be created in Salesforce.
  - **Insert Thread ID in the Email Body**: This setting puts the thread ID in the email body as well.
  - **Place User Signatures before Email Threads**: This allows the user signature to show up in the email body before the thread.
- **On-Demand Service** (3): **On-Demand Service** makes it a bit easier to configure as it allows you to verify your email and set up forwarding to a unique Salesforce email address to set up **Email-to-Case**. The alternative is to download and install the **Email-to-Case** agent behind your firewall.
  - **Routing Addresses** (4): A routing address must be configured to set up **Email-to-Case**.

In the following screenshot, let's take a look at how to set up a routing address:

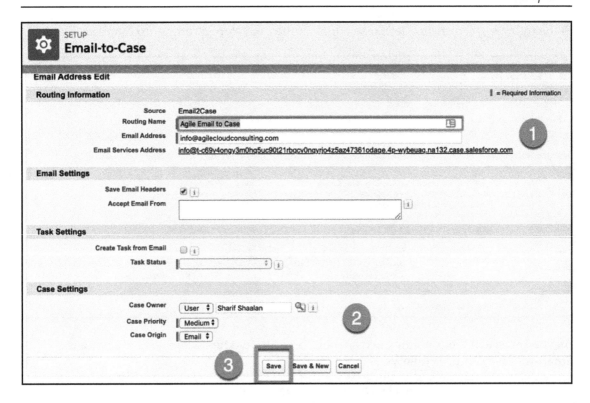

As you can see in the preceding screenshot, there are a few options when setting up your routing address, as follows:

- **Routing Information** (1): This is where you enter the routing name and email address.
- **Case Settings** (2): Here, you can set up the **Case Owner**, **Case Priority**, and **Case Origin** settings or cases created from this email address.
- **Save** (3): Click **Save** to start the verification process.

In the following screenshot, let's take a look at the final step in setting up **Email-to-Case**:

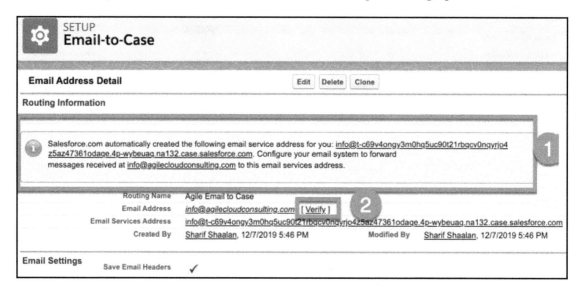

As you can see in the preceding screenshot, there are two final steps to completing the **Email-to-Case** setup, as follows:

- **Email Forwarding** (1): Once you set up a routing address, Salesforce will generate a unique email address for you. You must take this unique address and set it as the forwarding address for your **Email-to-Case** email address. As an example, if your email is support@yourcompany.com, all email sent to support@yourcompany.com will be automatically forwarded to your unique routing address. This is how a case is created in Salesforce.

- **Email Verification** (2): When you create a routing address, Salesforce will send you a verification email with a link to click on to make sure you have access to the email address. Clicking on this link is the final step. You have now set up **Email-to-Case**!

You have now learned how to navigate to the **Email-to-Case** setup section and how to configure Salesforce to support **Email-to-Case**. Let's summarize what we have learned in this chapter.

Summary

From this chapter, we have learned what a case is and how it is used to keep customers satisfied by being the building block of customer service. We understood what the case **Status** field is used for and how the values drive the process. We also learned how to create a case and update the Case **Status** field. We learned what escalation rules are, and gained the skills to configure escalation rules for our Cases. We gained an understanding of the use cases for **Web-to-Case** and **Email-to-Case**, as well as the steps needed to set these two features up in Salesforce.

In the next chapter, we will look at reports and dashboards, and how having visibility into **KPIs (Key Performance Indicators)** helps drive the business!

Questions

1. What is the main use case for Salesforce Cases?
2. Why is case status so important?
3. What is an example of when a case may be escalated?
4. Why is there an order field on case Escalation rule entries?
5. Why do you need to generate HTML code for **Web-to-Case**?
6. What is a use case for using **Email-to-Case**?
7. What happens if you don't set up **On-Demand Service**?
8. Why is it important to verify your email address when setting up **Email-to-Case**?

Further reading

- **Trailhead Module—Create and Manage Cases:** `https://trailhead. salesforce.com/en/content/learn/modules/nonprofit-client-services-with-service-cloud/create-and-manage-cases`
- **Trailhead Module—Create an Escalation Rule:** `https://trailhead. salesforce.com/en/content/learn/projects/create-a-process-for-managing-support-cases/create-an-escalation-rule`
- **Set up Web-to-Case:** `https://help.salesforce.com/articleView?id=setting_up_web-to-case.htmtype=5`
- **Set up Email-to-Case:** `https://help.salesforce.com/articleView?id=customizesupport_email.htmtype=5`

8
Business Analysis Using Reports and Dashboards

So far, we have covered the basic *objects* that are used to conduct business in Salesforce. Now, we will look at reports and dashboards.

Salesforce is a great tool for capturing the data needed to drive various business processes, but what good is the data if it isn't actionable? This is where reports and dashboards come in. They allow you to understand and act on your data.

To understand the data, you will need to learn how to create reports and how to use them. This underlying data is a combined visual output called a dashboard.

To help us learn all this, we will cover the following topics in detail:

- Using reports and how to create a report:
  - Using grouping to create various report types
  - Adding a chart to a report
  - Saving and running a report
- Using dashboards and how to create a dashboard using dashboard components

With the help of these topics, you will be able to create reports of various types in order to analyze data. You will also be able to use them as the underlying source for the visual dashboard components that will be used by the business to make important decisions.

Technical requirements

For this chapter, make sure to log into your development organization and follow along.

Using reports to understand data

Reports help you analyze data and come up with **Key Performance Indicators** (**KPIs**) that help drive business decisions. Reports can be created and run on any of the *objects* that we've covered. Reports can also be created and run for custom objects (we will cover custom objects in Chapter 12, *Configuring Objects for Your Business*).

Business use case

You are a Salesforce Admin for XYZ Widgets. Your users have asked for a report that shows how many contacts are associated with each business account, as well as a dashboard to show this. This information will help users make sure there is at least a primary contact associated with each account. Let's see how we can go about this.

Creating a report

Let's take a look at how to create a report in Salesforce:

1. On the Salesforce home page, click on the **Reports** tab (**1**) to start the process and click on **New Report** (**2**):

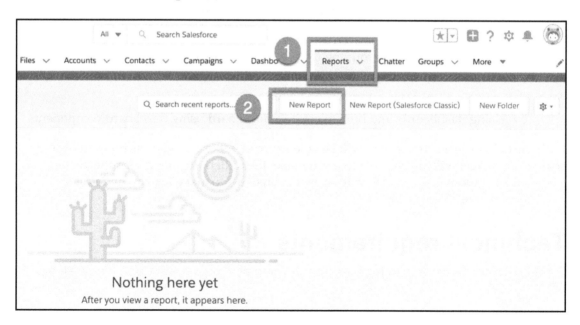

2. In the following screenshot, you can see a list of the objects you can choose to create a report for. For this example, I chose **Contacts & Accounts** (**1**) and then clicked on **Continue** (**2**) to move to the next step:

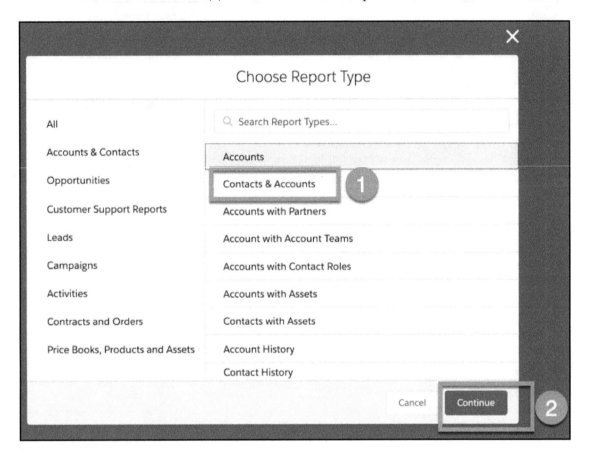

In the following screenshot, you can see we have landed on the report builder page, which defaulted to the **Outline** tab (**1**) within the report builder:

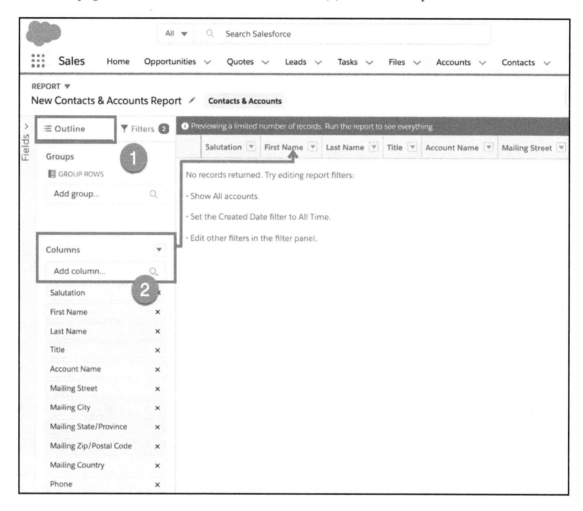

3. The **Columns** section (**2**) allows you to choose which fields show up as columns in the report you are creating. You can add and remove columns as needed.

4. Then, click on the **Filters** tab (**1**):

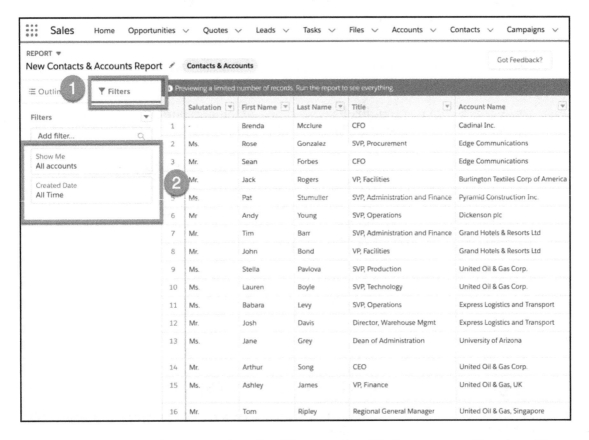

As shown in the preceding screenshot, the **Filters** section (**2**) allows us to add various filters so that we can gather the data needed for the report. An example is to look for all accounts created *this year*. In this case, you could set a filter where the **Created Date** field is set to **This Year**. When you run the report, it will return only the records that meet this criterion.

In the following sections, we will see how such grouping works in reports.

Using grouping to create report types

There are several report types that can be created using *grouping levels* within reports. A grouping level is a way to summarize data using one or more fields.

Let's use our previous example of a report that shows all accounts created this year. From this, we can infer the following:

- A report with no grouping levels is called a tabular report. If we ran the report in our example with no grouping, it would return a list of records. This is what is called a *tabular* report.
- If we added one grouping level – let's say, by calendar month – the report would return the set of records grouped by the creation month. This type of report is called a *summary* report since it is summarizing the data by a specific field; in this case, the created date field.
- Finally, we can group a report with two fields. Let's say we wanted to group our report by calendar month *and* billing state. This will give us a *Matrix* report since there are two levels of grouping.

We saw the tabular report in action in the *Creating a report* section, which shows a list of records. Now, let's take a look at how to create summary and Matrix reports using grouping.

Using grouping to create summary reports

In the previous section, we learned how to create a list of records in the report. Now, let's learn how to group them to create a summary.

On the Salesforce home page, click on the **Outline** tab and navigate to **GROUP ROWS (1)**:

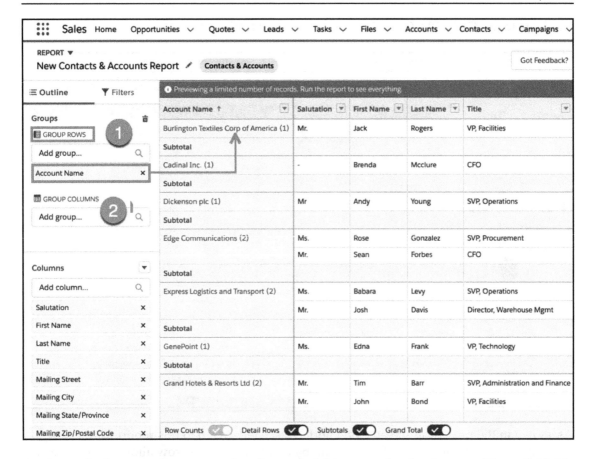

As shown in the preceding screenshot, I grouped this report by the **Account Name** field (**2**). Grouping by rows allows you to create a summary report. In this example, my report will be grouped by the name of the account.

Using grouping to create Matrix reports

Now that we've looked at the summary report, let's learn how Matrix reports work.

Navigate to the **GROUP COLUMNS** section under **Outline** (1):

As shown in the preceding screenshot, I added a second group to this report for the **Mailing State/Province Field** (2). Grouping by column as well as row allows you to create a Matrix report. In this example, my report will be grouped by the **Account Name** and **Mailing State/Province** fields.

Now that we have learned how to create a report and the various report types, let's add a chart to the report by clicking on **Add Chart** (3).

Adding a chart to a report

Adding a chart to a report helps provide our users with a better understanding of the reports as we can see the grouping being done in a visual manner.

In the following screenshot, you can see that the chart is automatically generated when you click on the **Add Chart** button (1):

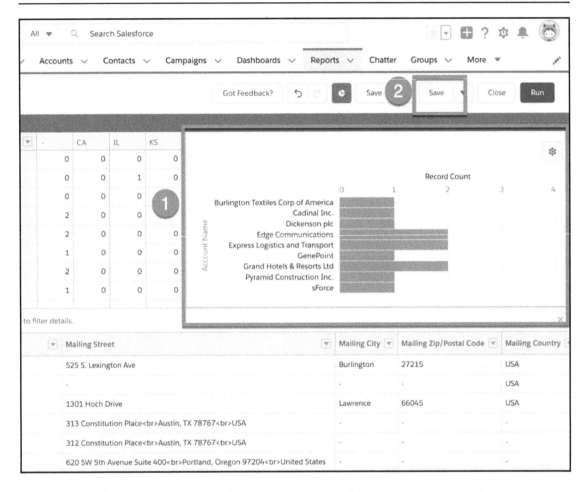

As shown in the preceding screenshot, we now have a Matrix report with a chart in preview mode. Click on the **Save** button (**2**) to save this report.

Saving and running a report

The final stage here, after creating a report and its data, is saving it and then running it to see how it appears. Let's learn how to do this.

In the following screenshot, you can see the page that comes up when you click on **Save**. Here, you can enter a name for your report (**1**):

I chose to save this report in the `Public Reports` folder (**2**) and then clicked **Save** (**3**) to save the report. There are three types of folders: private, public, and shared. Private folders are only visible to you, the logged-in user. Public folders are visible to everyone in the organization, while shared folders can be shared with particular users, roles, or public groups. For our example, I have made the report public.

After saving the report, we'll land back on the preview page:

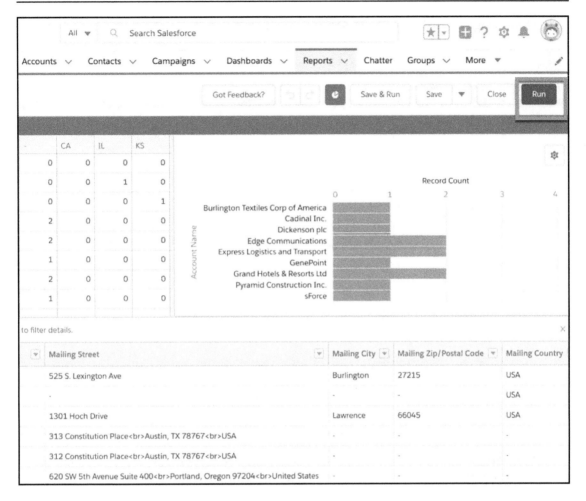

Now, click on **Run** to see how the actual report looks.

In the following screenshot, you can see how the final report looks:

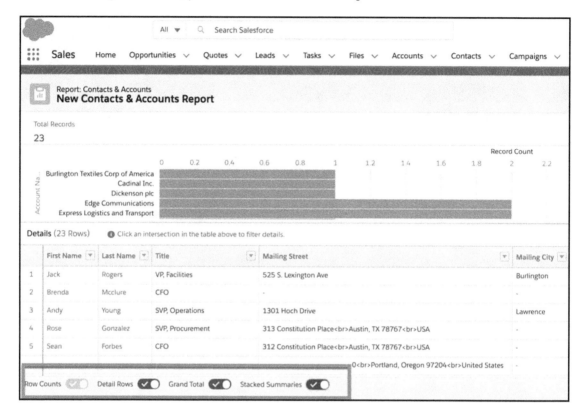

There are various options available showing **Row Counts**, **Detail Rows**, **Grand Total**, and **Stacked Summaries**. You can toggle these options on and off to adjust the report as needed.

In the following screenshot, you can see the additional chart properties that can be edited to the report:

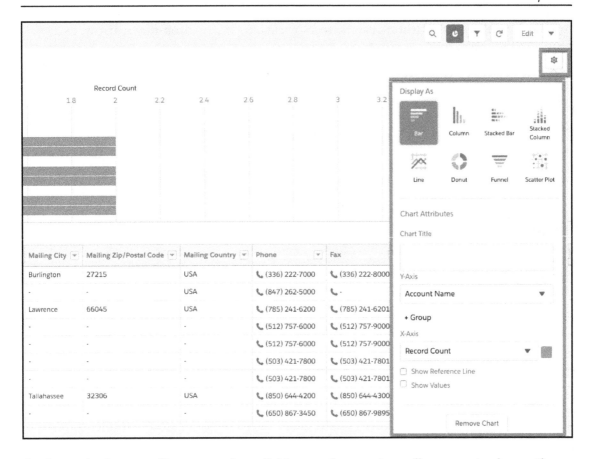

As shown in the preceding screenshot, clicking on the gear icon allows you to change the way the chart is displayed, add a chart title, control the fields displayed on the Y and X axes, and remove the chart if needed.

Another useful reporting feature can be seen by clicking on the drop-down arrow, as shown in the following screenshot:

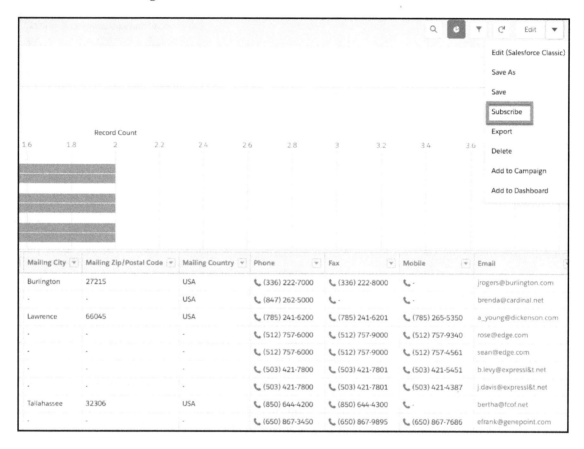

Now, click on **Subscribe**, which will bring you to the following screen:

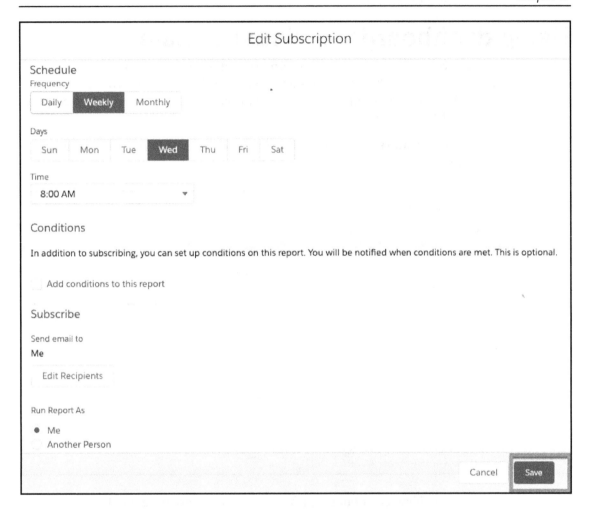

As shown in the preceding screenshot, we can subscribe to a report so that it's automatically sent to **Me** on a specific day and time.

Now that we have learned how to create a report, let's learn how to add this report to a dashboard as a dashboard component.

Using dashboards to visualize data

While reports allow you to gather and filter information, dashboards allow you to visualize various reports together through dashboard components. A dashboard is always built as an overlay to reports. We built an example report in the previous section, so now, let's add this report to a dashboard component:

1. Click on the **Dashboards** tab (**1**) to start the process, as shown in the following screenshot:

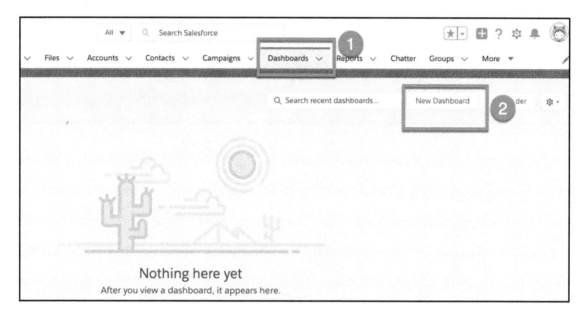

2. Then, click on **New Dashboard** (**2**). You can name it anything you like; I have named my dashboard `Account and Contact Dashboard` (**1**).

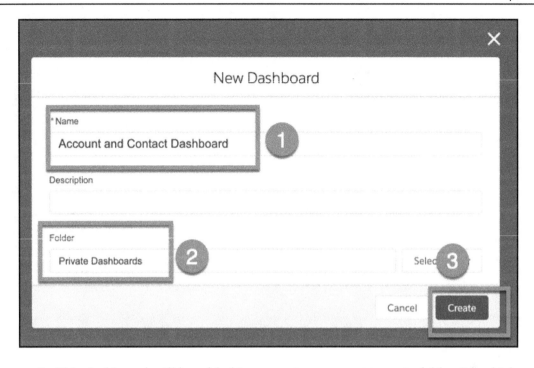

3. This dashboard will be added to my `Private Dashboards` folder (**2**), which means it will only be visible to me. Once I've finished building it, I can choose to move it to a public folder that can be widely shared. Click on **Create** (**3**).

4. After creating a private dashboard, we'll land on the dashboard builder page. Click on **+ Component** to add a new dashboard component to the dashboard:

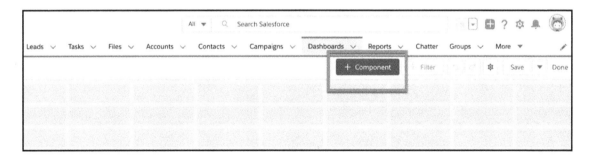

5. Then, click on the report that you would like to use as the underlying source for the dashboard component (**1**) and click **Save** (**2**):

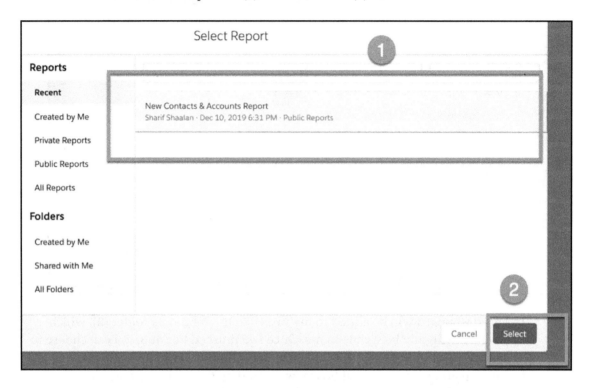

6. Next, choose the chart type you would like to use for the component and update the formatting settings (**1**), as shown in the following screenshot:

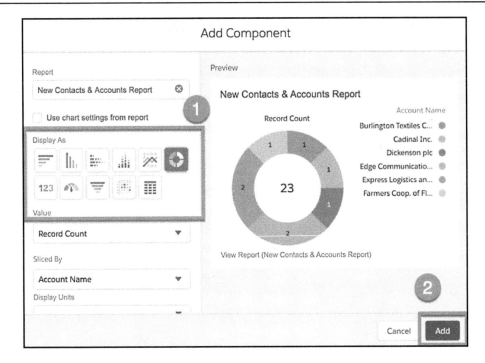

Once you're done, click on **Add** (2) to create the component.

In the following screenshot, you can see that the component we've created is still in preview mode. Click **Save** (2) to see the final result:

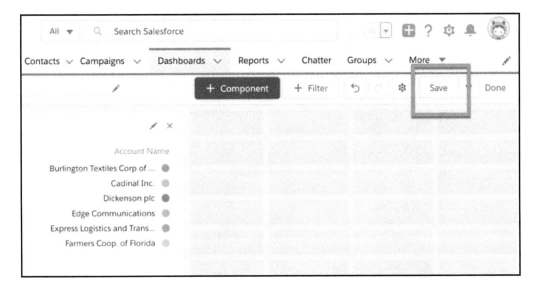

The following screenshot shows the completed dashboard:

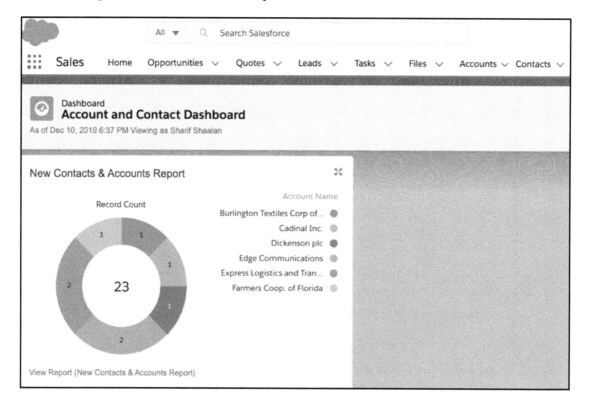

From the preceding screenshot, you can see that there is one component for our example. A dashboard can contain up to 20 dashboard components. Each of these components will have an underlying report.

Finally, another useful dashboard feature can be seen by clicking on the **Subscribe** button, which can be found on the upper-right of the page. This brings us to the following screen:

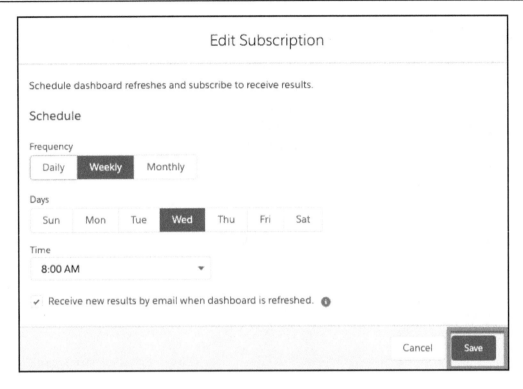

As shown in the preceding screenshot, we can subscribe to a dashboard to have it automatically sent to me on a specific day and time.

Now that we have learned how to create, view, and subscribe to a dashboard, let's go over what we have learned in this chapter.

Summary

In this chapter, we learned what a report is and how to create a report to help the business understand and take action on data. We learned how to add columns, filters, groupings, and charts to customize the report's output and make it more useful. We also learned how to take a report and make it the underlying data source for a dashboard component.

Reports allow us to gain an understanding of what dashboards are and how to create dashboards in order to help the business visualize and act on data.

In the next chapter, we will look at Salesforce Administration, starting with its setup and configuration!

Questions

1. What type of report has no grouping?
2. What type of report has only a row grouping?
3. What type of report has both a row and column grouping?
4. How do you add a chart to a report?
5. How does a report relate to a dashboard?
6. How many components can you add to a dashboard?
7. What does **KPI** stand for?

Further reading

- **Quick Start: Reports and Dashboards**: `https://trailhead.salesforce.com/en/content/learn/projects/quickstart-reports`
- **Explore Reports and Dashboards**: `https://trailhead.salesforce.com/en/content/learn/modules/lex_migration_whatsnew/lex_migration_whatsnew_analytics`

Section 2: Salesforce Administration

This section will cover the basics of Salesforce administration to get you started with using the software.

In the following chapters, we will cover the setup and configuration, sharing and visibility, sandboxes and change sets, configuring objects for your business use cases, and third-party applications:

- Chapter 9, *Setup and Configuration*
- Chapter 10, *An Overview of Sharing and Visibility*
- Chapter 11, *Using Sandboxes and Change Sets*
- Chapter 12, *Configuring Objects for Your Business*
- Chapter 13, *Third-Party Applications and Salesforce Mobile*

Setup and Configuration

9

Now that we have gone through the basic Salesforce objects and how they are used in the context of businesses, we will turn to Salesforce administration for this part of the book. Salesforce administration has endless possibilities and we would need a complete book in its own right to cover them all. For our purposes, we will focus on how to navigate the most crucial sections you will use overall and on a day-to-day basis as an admin. Some of these features will be covered in further detail in later chapters of this book. This chapter is best used as a reference for all the setup and configuration items. It will help you when going through future chapters in this book, as well as in future admin work within your organization.

In this chapter, we will cover the following topics:

- Navigating to the **Setup** page
- Delving into the **ADMINISTRATION** section under **Setup** and understanding what the items are used for
- Exploring the **PLATFORM TOOLS** section under **Setup** and what the items are used for
- Understanding what is included in the **SETTINGS** section under **Setup** and what the items are used for
- Understanding the **Object Manager** tab and what **Object Manager** is used for

With the help of these topics, you will be able to navigate to **Setup** and you will know where to find the settings to help you carry out your job as a system administrator.

Technical requirements

For this chapter, make sure you log in to your development org (which stands for organization) and follow along as we go through the different settings available to a system administrator. Your development org will be automatically set up with the system administrator profile, but do note that in other Salesforce orgs, you need to have the system administrator profile set up to access all of the areas we will cover in this chapter.

Navigating to the Setup page

Setup is the key to the administrator kingdom. Once you have access to this page, you can look under the hood of your system and make the changes needed to help drive business processes. Let's take a look at how to get to this page.

We start off on the home page of Salesforce, as shown:

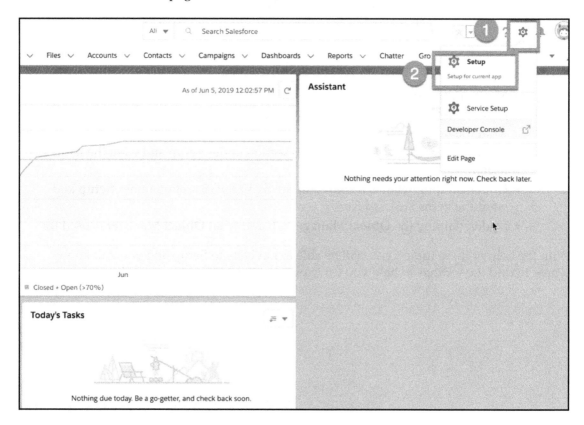

Click on the gear icon at the top of the page (**1**) and then click on **Setup** (**2**).

The following screenshot shows the landing page after clicking on **Setup**:

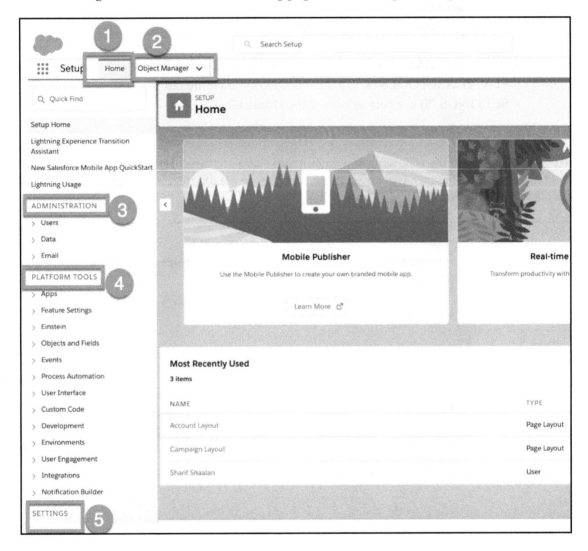

As you can see in the preceding screenshot, there are several items that are of interest:

- The **Home** tab (**1**) contains all of the settings related to administration outside of the **Object Manager** tab.
- The **Object Manager** tab (**2**) contains all of the administration options related to standard and custom objects.
- **ADMINISTRATION** (**3**) is a sub-section of the **Home** tab.
- **PLATFORM TOOLS** (**4**) is a sub-section of the **Home** tab.
- **SETTINGS** (**5**) is a sub-section of the **Home** tab.

All of these items will be covered in this chapter.

Then, you can see in the following screenshot that there are three items that fall outside of the **Home** sub-sections; we will cover these here before we dig deeper into the list of items directly under the **Home** sub-sections:

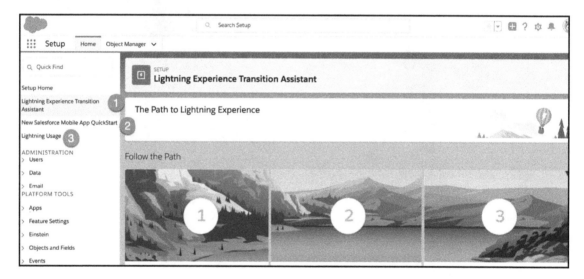

As you can see in the preceding screenshot, the following three items fall outside of the
ADMINISTRATION, PLATFORM TOOLS, and **SETTINGS** sub-sections:

- **Lightning Experience Transition Assistant** (**1**): This tool allows admins that use
  Salesforce Classic to analyze and transition their org to Salesforce Lightning.
- **New Salesforce Mobile App QuickStart** (**2**): This tool provides a step-by-step
  guide for admins to configure the Salesforce mobile app.
- **Lightning Usage** (**3**): This tool allows admins to track the usage and adoption of
  Salesforce Lightning for organizations that are in the middle of making the
  transition to Salesforce Lightning.

Now that we have seen how to navigate to **Setup** and looked at the components of the
page, let's look at the various sub-sections in more detail.

Using the **Quick Find** search bar in **Setup** takes you directly to the section
in **Setup** that you wish to navigate to as you carry out your day-to-day
admin work.

Using the ADMINISTRATION section

Of the three sub-sections, we will first begin by understanding what **ADMINISTRATION**
covers.

Under the **Home** tab, the first sub-section is the **ADMINISTRATION** section. This section allows you to make changes to three sub-sections within **ADMINISTRATION**—**Users**, **Data**, and **Email**. The following screenshot shows you this section:

Now, let's look at these sub-sections in more detail.

Users

The following screenshot shows you the **Users** section under the **Home** tab:

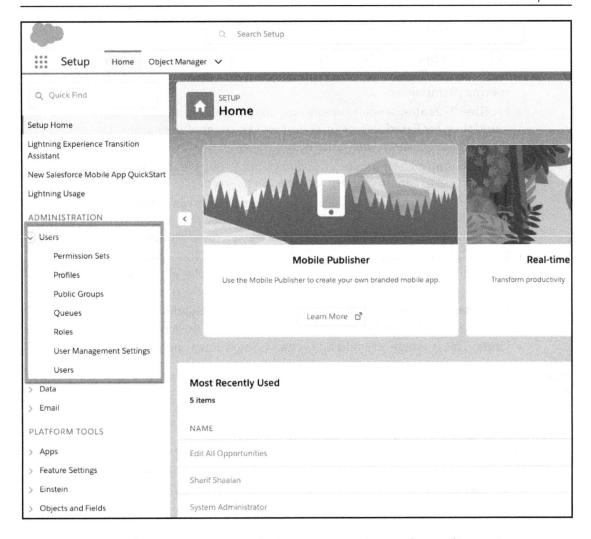

The **Users** section focuses on user permissions, user creation, and recording assignments. This is a section that is very heavily used by admins as this is where the initial set up of users and assigning their permissions happens. When a new user is created in Salesforce, a role and a profile are assigned to them. You can also assign one-off permissions using permission sets. A user can be assigned to a public group, which is used for sharing folders and views, among other items. A user can also be part of a lead or case assignment queue. All of these settings can be found under this **Users** section.

The following settings are included under the **Users** section:

- **Permission Sets**: Permission sets allow you to add a subset of permissions to a user's profile. This is for one-off permissions that do not apply to all users with specific permissions.
- **Profiles**: This allows you to create and adjust profiles for users. Profiles are a foundation for Salesforce security and will be covered in Chapter 10, *An Overview of Sharing and Visibility*.
- **Public Groups**: Users can be added to public groups and these groups can be given access to certain Salesforce items, such as report folders or views.
- **Queues**: Queues are used by leads and cases. A user can belong to a queue and they will be able to view records assigned to a specific queue and, in turn, take one of these records and reassign it from the queue to themselves.
- **Roles**: Roles are another security bedrock that will be covered in more detail in Chapter 10, *An Overview of Sharing and Visibility*. Roles allow the admin to set up a company hierarchy to help control the security options.
- **User Management Settings**: These are the settings that relate to specific users, such as scrambling personal information if the user does not want it to be visible.
- **Users**: This is where you add and remove Salesforce users.

Now that we have looked at the items under the **Users** section, let's take a look at the **Data** section.

When managing users, there is an option to freeze users. This option is useful when you need to deactivate a user, but the user is connected to a feature or functionality in some way and there needs to be some analysis before carrying out the actual deactivation. This feature makes sure the user cannot log into Salesforce while the analysis is conducted.

Data

The following screenshot shows the **Data** section:

The **Data** section contains the settings for all the data-related items. This is another section that is heavily used by admins. This section contains the tools needed for data transformation (that is, importing, exporting, updating, and deleting), as well as the tools for duplicate management that are needed to keep the database clean of duplicates. This section also contains the picklist settings that are often used as a basis for data integrity.

Let's take a look at all of the sub-sections under **Data**:

- **Big Objects**: Big objects are special custom objects to store large data-volume objects. This is where you would navigate to create big objects.
- **Data Export**: This setting allows you to export all of your organization's data as a backup.
- **Data Integration Metrics**: This section shows you the metrics related to data integration rules.

- **Data Integration Rules**: Data integration rules are tied to any activated data services, such as data cleansing services.
- **Duplicate Management**: This section allows you to create duplicate rules and matching rules for data that comes into Salesforce to help maintain the data quality.
- **ISV Hammer Opt Out**: This setting ensures testing for new Salesforce releases is carried out and helps **Independent Software Vendors** (**ISVs**) stay compliant with upgrades. It is recommended to opt into this setting.
- **Mass Delete Records**: This wizard allows you to mass delete records based on filters.
- **Mass Transfer Approval Requests**: This allows you to mass transfer record approvals to another user if, for instance, someone leaves the company or is on an extended vacation and they have specific approvals assigned to them.
- **Mass Transfer Records**: This setting allows you to mass transfer records to another user.
- **Mass Update Addresses**: This wizard allows you to mass update the address field on records.
- **Picklist Settings**: This setting allows you to disable editing the picklist values' API names.
- **Schema Settings**: This setting allows you to restrict certain access to schema, such as custom metadata.
- **Secure Agent Clusters**: Secure Agent clusters provide failover protection, ensuring that your users can always access on-premises external data sources from Salesforce.
- **Secure Agents**: Secure Agents let you safely connect Salesforce to external data stored on-premises.
- **State and Country/Territory Picklists**: This setting allows you to set up the state and country picklist values.
- **Storage Usage**: This setting shows you your data storage and how close you are to the limit.

Now that we have looked at the items under the **Data** section, let's take a look at the **Email** section.

 While this section includes wizards to import, export, update, and delete records, there is a limit. If you are going to work with more than 50,000 records, you will need to use the standalone data loader.

Email

The following screenshot shows you the **Email** section:

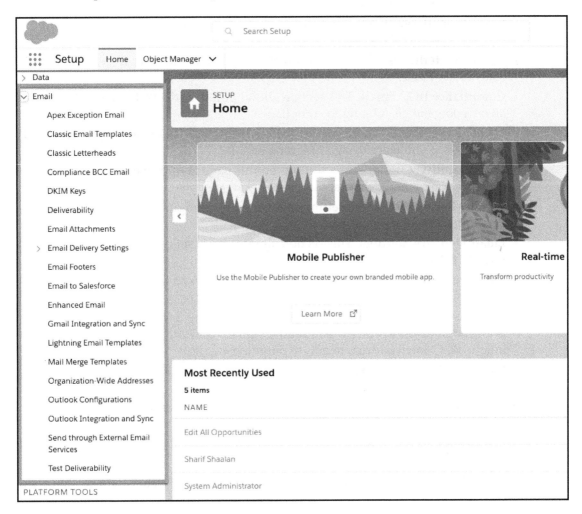

The **Email** section contains the settings for all email-related items. As an admin, you will find yourself doing a lot of work here as this section contains items related to third-party email integration tools, email templates, and organization-wide email addresses that may be used by your sales and support teams.

Let's take a look at all the sub-sections under **Email**:

- **Apex Exception Email**: Here, you can set the email addresses that receive alerts when there is an apex exception.
- **Classic Email Templates**: This section contains any email templates that were built in Salesforce Classic.
- **Classic Letterheads**: This section contains any letterheads that were created in Salesforce Classic.
- **Compliance BCC Email**: This section allows you to add a BCC email address for all outgoing emails relating to compliance.
- **DKIM Keys**: This is where you set the **DKIM** (which is **DomainKeys Identified Mail**) keys if you want to sign outgoing emails.
- **Deliverability**: Configure the settings on this page to improve your organization's email deliverability.
- **Email Attachments**: These settings allow you to configure settings such as the email-attachment size allowance.
- **Email Delivery Settings**: This section allows you to set up email relays and email domain filters.
- **Email Footers**: This setting allows you to add footers to emails sent from Salesforce.
- **Email to Salesforce**: This section allows you to set up a feature where an activity is logged in Salesforce when you send an email from a third party by providing a unique BCC email address to add to outgoing emails.
- **Enhanced Email**: This section allows you to set up emails in their own objects, rather than as a type of activity.
- **Gmail Integration and Sync**: This contains the settings to turn on Gmail integration.
- **Lightning Email Templates**: This section contains email templates created for Lightning.
- **Mail Merge Templates**: This section contains the mail merge templates you create.

- **Organization-Wide Addresses**: This setting is used to set up an organization-wide email address, such as `support@yourcompany.com`, and make it available for use by any user as they send out emails.
- **Outlook Configurations**: This section contains the rules used for Outlook integration.
- **Outlook Integration and Sync**: This section contains further settings related to Outlook integration.
- **Send through External Email Services**: This section allows you to send emails directly from Gmail or Office 365.
- **Test Deliverability**: Here, you can test the deliverability to specific email addresses to see whether emails are blocked for any reason.

Now that we have looked at an overview of all the settings under the **ADMINISTRATION** section, let's take a look at the **PLATFORM TOOLS** section.

 If you have issues with sending emails from production or from a sandbox, the first place to check is the **Email Delivery Settings**.

Using the PLATFORM TOOLS section

The **PLATFORM TOOLS** section deals with the configuration and development features of the Salesforce application. This section of the chapter teaches you where you need to go to create and manage metadata in Salesforce. You will also learn where to access workflow automation tools. The **PLATFORM TOOLS** section is heavily used when customizing your Salesforce instance.

The following screenshot shows you how to access this section on the **Setup** page:

Let's take a look at what the sections highlighted in the preceding screenshot contain.

Apps

Apps provide a set of functionality grouped together. Some of the use cases of this section for an admin include creating an app for a specific division in your company, finding a third-party application to install, and customizing and setting up Salesforce Mobile.

The following settings are available under the **Apps** section:

- **App Manager**: This section shows you all of your Classic and Lightning apps and allows you to edit them.
- **AppExchange Marketplace**: This section links you directly to AppExchange, where you can download pre-built apps (both free and paid).
- **Connected Apps**: This section allows you to create and view connected apps, such as OAuth apps.
- **Lightning Bolt**: Bolt solutions address the needs of specific industries and functions with tailored apps and business processes.
- **Mobile Apps**: This section allows you to customize your mobile apps.
- **Packaging**: This section allows you to view your installed packages and create your own packages.

Now that we have looked at items under the **Apps** section, let's take a look at the **Feature Settings** section.

The AppExchange marketplace is a great place to search before building custom functionality. There are both free and paid apps that you could find very helpful.

Feature settings

This section covers features for specific categories and business processes in Salesforce. As an admin, some of the use cases for this section include settings related to specific objects, such as opportunities as leads. It also includes the settings related to specific features, such as Quip or Salesforce files.

The following settings are available for the **Feature Settings** section:

- **Analytics**: This section contains all the settings related to reporting and dashboards.
- **Chatter**: This section contains all the settings related to Chatter. Chatter is an internal business social network for Salesforce.
- **Cisco Webex**: This section contains the settings for using Webex within Salesforce.
- **Communities**: This section contains all settings to create and manage a Salesforce community. Communities are customer- or partner-facing portals.

- **Data.com**: This section contains all settings related to setting up Data.com, a data quality add-on.
- **Home**: This section allows you to set up and manage different home page layouts.
- **Marketing**: This section contains the settings for marketing-related objects, such as leads and campaigns.
- **Office 365**: This section contains the settings for setting up Skype on Salesforce.
- **Quip**: This section contains settings for Quip, a shared document tool add-on for Salesforce.
- **Sales**: This section contains all the settings for sales-related objects, such as accounts, opportunities, products, and quotes.
- **Salesforce Files**: This section contains the settings for files. Files are documents that you upload to records or libraries in Salesforce.
- **Service**: This section contains the settings for all service-related objects, such as cases, Omni-Channel, and Field Service.
- **Survey**: This section contains the settings for Salesforce Surveys.
- **Topics**: This section contains the settings for Salesforce Topics.

Now that we have taken a look at items under the **Feature Settings** section, let's take a look at the Einstein section.

The **Sales** section is very heavily used by admins, especially the lead and opportunity settings.

Einstein

Einstein is the AI tool for Salesforce. Some of the use cases of this section include configuring the **Einstein** search and checking whether your organization is ready to work with **Einstein AI**. Let's take a look at the available settings:

- **Einstein Platform**: This section allows you to turn on the paid portion of **Einstein**.
- **Einstein Sales**: This section allows you to set up Einstein Activity Capture.
- **Einstein Search**: This section allows you to configure Einstein Search.
- **Readiness Assessor**: This wizard allows you to analyze your organization's data to see whether you are ready to use **Einstein**.

Now that we have looked at the items under the **Einstein** section, let's take a look at the **Objects and Fields** section.

Objects and Fields

This section covers the **Object and Field** settings. This is a section that you will use quite frequently as an admin since the **Object Manager** tab takes you to the settings for all of the objects and items related to objects such as custom fields, page layouts, and record types.

The following settings are available under the **Objects and Fields** section:

- **Object Manager**: This section redirects you to the **Object Manager** tab. We will cover this in more detail in the *Using the Object Manager settings* section of this chapter.
- **Picklist Value Sets**: This setting allows you to set global picklists, which allow you to use one picklist across lots of different objects and create values for those picklists.
- **Schema Builder**: This section allows you to view a dynamic **Entity Relationship Diagram** (**ERD**) for your organization.

Now that we have looked at the items under the **Objects and Fields** section, let's take a look at the **Events** section.

If someone requests an ERD, the schema builder is a good place to start as it shows you all of your Salesforce objects and how they connect to each other.

Events

Event monitoring helps you audit your Salesforce instance for all types of activities. This is an add-on service. It can be used from the **Event Manager** page, which allows you to view all events.

Next, let's take a look at the **Process Automation** section.

Process Automation

This section contains the settings to create all things related to automation. As an admin, you will use this section quite often as it contains process builders, workflows, approval processes, and flows.

The following settings are available under the **Process Automation** section:

- **Approval Processes**: This section allows you to create and edit approval processes.
- **Automation Home (Beta)**: This section provides a dashboard to monitor and manage automation.
- **Flows**: This section allows you to create and edit flows.
- **Next Best Action**: This section allows you to create strategies for the **Einstein** tool's next best action.
- **Paused Flow Interviews**: This section allows you to monitor and troubleshoot flows that didn't run.
- **Post Templates**: Approval post templates allow you to customize the content of approval request posts.
- **Process Automation Settings**: This section is a one-stop-shop for the high-level settings related to the different automation options.
- **Process Builder**: This section allows you to create and edit process builders.
- **Workflow Actions**: This section shows you all the workflow actions that have been created.
- **Workflow Rules**: This section allows you to create and edit workflow rules.

Now that we have looked at the items under the **Process Automation** section, let's take a look at the **User Interface** section.

 Automation Home is a great place to bring all the things related to automation together. This is a new feature that will undoubtedly only get better going forward.

User Interface

This section contains all the settings related to the UI. This is another section that you will heavily use as an admin. Some of the use cases for this section include creating Lightning record pages and creating global actions.

The following settings are available under the **User Interface** section:

- **Action Link Templates**: An action link is a button on a feed element that targets an API, a web page, or a file. This section allows you to create action links.
- **Actions & Recommendations**: This section allows you to create actions and recommendations to guide users in specific processes.
- **App Menu**: This section allows you to customize what shows up in the App Launcher.
- **Custom Labels**: This section allows you to create custom labels. These can be accessed and used in code.
- **Density Settings**: This setting allows you to change aspects of the UI.
- **Global Actions**: This section allows you to create and edit global actions.
- **Lightning App Builder**: This section allows you to create Lightning pages.
- **Lightning Extension**: This section allows you to configure the Lightning Extension settings. Lightning Extension is a browser extension that's designed to complement the user experience with continuous productivity feature releases.
- **Path Settings**: This section allows you to create different paths to help guide users on specific records and next steps.
- **Quick Text Settings**: This section allows you to configure the settings related to Quick Text, which helps users be more productive.
- **Record Page Settings**: This section allows you to choose different layouts for Lightning pages.
- **Rename Tabs and Labels**: This section allows you to rename tabs and objects. For example, you may want to rename accounts to organizations or rename specific standard fields.
- **Sites and Domains**: This section allows you to manage domains, sites, and custom URLs.
- **Tabs**: This section allows you to create and manage tabs.
- **Themes and Branding**: This section gives you the theme and branding options for your organization.
- **Translation Workbench**: This section provides you with the various Salesforce translation options.
- **User Interface**: This section provides you with the various high-level user interface settings.

Now that we have looked at the items under the **User Interface** section, let's take a look at the **Custom Code** section.

Remember that the Lightning App Builder allows you to create and edit Lightning pages. The page layout section of an object allows you to edit the **Details** and **Related Lists** sections of your Lightning pages.

Custom Code

This section contains all the code-related settings. Depending on how complex your organization is, you may spend a significant amount of time here, especially if you are working with a developer. Some of the use cases for this section include creating Apex triggers and the Apex classes used for custom automation and custom UIs.

The following settings are available under the **Custom Code** section:

- **Apex Classes**: This section shows all the Apex classes that exist in the org.
- **Apex Settings**: This section has a few Apex-related settings options.
- **Apex Test Execution**: This section allows you to run test classes as needed.
- **Apex Test History**: This section shows you all the tests that have run and which tests passed and failed.
- **Apex Triggers**: This section contains all the Apex triggers that exist in the org.
- **Canvas App Previewer**: Canvas apps are another type of app that can be utilized. This section allows you to preview your canvas apps.
- **Custom Metadata Types**: Custom metadata types enable you to create your own setup objects whose records are metadata rather than data. This section allows you to create custom metadata types.
- **Custom Permissions**: This section allows you to create custom permissions accessed by code.
- **Custom Settings**: This section allows you to create custom settings related to code.
- **Email Services**: This section allows you to create email services. Email services are automated processes that use Apex classes to process the contents, headers, and attachments of inbound emails.
- **Lightning Components**: This section contains all of your custom Lightning components.
- **Platform Cache**: Platform cache partitions let you segment the org's available cache space. This section allows you to create partitions.
- **Remote Access**: Remote access is no longer used; it has been moved to connected apps.

- **Static Resources**: This section allows you to create static resources that can be referenced in code.
- **Tools**: This section provides links to various development tools.
- **Visualforce Components**: This section contains all of your orgs, Visualforce components.
- **Visualforce Pages**: This section contains all of your org's Visualforce pages.

Now that we have looked at the items under the **Custom Code** section, let's take a look at the **Development** section.

 Knowing where the **Custom Settings** section is is useful since many third-party apps use this functionality to store settings related to their apps.

Development

This section allows you to access the **Dev Hub** page. The **Dev Hub** page allows you to create and manage scratch orgs. Scratch orgs are disposable Salesforce orgs that are used to support development and testing. They are fully configurable, allowing developers to emulate different Salesforce editions with different features and preferences.

Now that we have looked at the item under the **Development** section, let's take a look at the **Environments** section.

Environments

The **Environments** section contains the settings related to moving code and metadata between environments. As an admin, you will spend a significant amount of time here since you should always build features in a sandbox for testing and then move them to production. Some of the use cases for this section include creating change sets to deploy code between environments, creating custom jobs, and monitoring these jobs.

The following settings are available under the **Environments** section:

- **Deploy**: This section contains the settings related to deploying code.
- **Jobs**: This section contains the settings to view and set up various Apex jobs.
- **Logs**: This section contains debug logs and email file logs. Debug logs are very important to admins as they allow you to monitor the actions of a specific user and view detailed system logs of the actions they take. An example use case here is a user that gets an error when carrying out an action. You add a user under **User Trace Flags** (**1**), as you can see in the following screenshot:

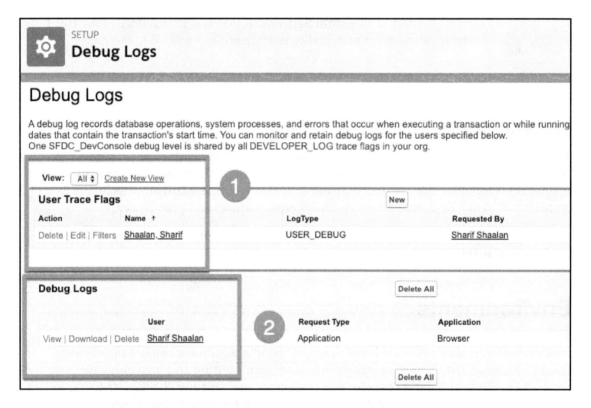

The next step is to ask the user to replicate the action that produced the error. Once the action is replicated, you can download the **Debug Logs** (**2**), as you can see in the preceding screenshot, to get details on the error. The user is traced for 24 hours.

- **Monitoring**: This section allows you to monitor various types of jobs and automation.

- **System Overview**: This section shows a complete overview of the system and where your org is with certain limits.

Now that we have looked at the items under the **Environments** section, let's take a look at the **User Engagement** section.

> **System Overview** is a great place to monitor your Salesforce limits to make sure you are not close to exceeding any of them.

User Engagement

This section focuses on driving user engagement. Let's take a look at these settings:

- **Adoption Assistance**: This section contains settings specific to switching to Lightning and driving user adoption.
- **Help Menu**: This section allows you to customize the **Help** menu.
- **In-App Guidance**: This section allows you to set up in-app guidance to help drive user adoption.

Now that we have looked at the items under the **User Engagement** section, let's take a look at the **Integrations** section.

Integrations

This section focuses on the integration settings. Some of the use cases for this section include building integrations with external systems, importing data, and working with external objects. Let's take a look at what these settings are:

- **API**: This section contains links to help you build integration with various APIs.
- **Change Data Capture**: This sends notifications for created, updated, deleted, and undeleted records. All custom objects and a subset of standard objects are supported.
- **Data Import Wizard**: This allows you access to the data import wizard to import data.
- **Data Loader**: This allows you to access the data loader, which offers more features than the data import wizard.

- **Dataloader.io**: This links to `dataloader.io`, which is a web-based data loader and has paid options.
- **External Data Sources**: This allows you to manage external data sources connected to Salesforce.
- **External Objects**: These are custom objects that connect to external data sources.
- **External Services**: This section allows you to add and configure external services.
- **Platform Events**: Platform events are used to define the data that is delivered in custom notifications.

Now that we have looked at the items under the **Integrations** section, let's take a look at the **Notification Builder** section.

> **Dataloader.io** is free to use to load data up to a certain amount of records. It is worth looking into as it has several usability features that are not included in the regular data loader.

Notification Builder

This section contains the settings for the notification builder:

- **Custom Notifications**: This section allows you to create custom notifications.
- **Notification Delivery Settings**: This allows you to choose where notifications show up, such as on mobile, desktop, and so on.

That was a lot of information! As you use Salesforce as an admin, you will come across many of these settings. Let's take a look at the last main section under the **Setup** home tab—**SETTINGS**.

The SETTINGS section

The last of the three main sections under the **Setup** home tab is **SETTINGS**. This section contains various settings that were not captured in the **ADMINISTRATION** and **Platform Tools** sections. The following screenshot shows you where you can find the **SETTINGS** section:

Let's take a look at what settings are included here.

Company Settings

The **Company Settings** section includes settings related to the organization. Some of the use cases for this section include finding your org ID for a Salesforce case, setting up your fiscal year, and setting up company holidays. Let's look at all of these settings:

- **Business Hours**: This setting allows you to set your organization's business hours.
- **Calendar Settings**: This section allows you to add public calendars and resources for your company.
- **Company Information**: This contains all of your basic company settings, including licenses and your org ID.
- **Critical Updates**: This section allows you to view and activate critical updates.
- **Data Protection and Privacy**: This setting allows you to give access to data protection and privacy details in lead, contact, and person accounts.
- **Fiscal Year**: This setting allows you to set the fiscal year for your organization.
- **Holidays**: This section allows you to add the holidays your company observes.
- **Language Settings**: This section allows you to add the languages you want to be available to your users.
- **My Domain**: This is where you set up My Domain to get a custom domain for your org.

Now that we have looked at the items under the **Company Settings** section, let's take a look at the **Data Classification** section.

It is a good idea to set up **My Domain** as it lets you customize your login page with your company branding, as well as set up **single sign-on** (**SSO**), among other benefits.

Data Classification

The **Data Classification** settings are related to data marked as sensitive in Salesforce:

- **Data Classification Download**: This allows you to download your data classification information to a `.csv` file.
- **Data Classification Settings**: This section allows you to set up data sensitivity picklist values.

- **Data Classification Upload**: This section allows you to upload data classification information through a `.csv` file.

Now that we have looked at the items under the **Data Classification** section, let's take a look at the **Identity** section.

Identity

This section contains all the identity-related settings. A use case for this section includes using Salesforce as an identity or service provider for SSO. Let's look at all of the settings in this section:

- **Auth. Providers**: This section allows you to add and manage authentication providers.
- **Identity Connect**: This section contains the Identity Connect settings. Identity Connect provides **Active Directory** (**AD**) integration, so users can log in with AD credentials and connect to Salesforce using SSO.
- **Identity Provider**: This section allows you to set up and manage Salesforce as an identity provider.
- **Identity Verification**: This section contains various identity verification settings.
- **Identity Verification History**: This section shows all verification attempts.
- **Login Flows**: This section allows you to set up login flows that introduce business processes during login.
- **Login History**: This section shows all the login history.
- **OAuth Custom Scopes**: This section allows you to create custom OAuth scopes.
- **Single Sign-On Settings**: This section allows you to set up and manage SSO.

Now that we have looked at the items under the **Identity** section, let's take a look at the **Security** section.

Login History is a good place to start if you need to monitor the login activity of a user for dates or times as needed. This is sometimes requested by HR departments within an organization.

Security

This section contains all the security-related settings. As an admin, you will spend a lot of time here, initially setting up security and updating settings as needed. Some of the use cases for this section include running the security heath check and controlling network access.

The following settings are available under the **Security** section:

- **Activations**: This section shows the login IP address of the browser or application that the user used to log in.
- **CORS**: This page lists the origins that are whitelisted for **Cross-Origin Resource Sharing** (**CORS**).
- **CSP Trusted Sites**: This page has a list of web addresses (URLs) that your organization can use to access resources for Lightning components, either within your organization's Lightning Experience or through CSP-secured Lightning communities.
- **Certificate and Key Management**: This section allows you to manage your certificates to authenticate single sign-on with an external website, use your org as an identity provider, or verify requests to external sites from Salesforce orgs.
- **Delegated Administration**: This allows you to delegate user administration, custom object administration, or both to the delegated administrators of a group.
- **Event Monitoring**: This allows you to access the event monitoring settings and set transaction security policies.
- **Expire All Passwords**: This setting allows you to expire all passwords for users in your organization for cases where you need to deny access to all users for a business reason.
- **Field Accessibility**: This section allows you to set field-level security for all fields.
- **File Upload and Download Security**: This section allows you to control how various file types are handled during the upload and download processes.
- **Health Check**: This page allows you to run a security health check on your instance.
- **Login Access Policies**: This section allows you to grant login access to Salesforce and third-party applications.
- **Named Credentials**: This setting allows you to set a callout endpoint and its required authentication parameters.
- **Network Access**: This page allows you to set trusted IP ranges to access your org.

- **Password Policies**: This section allows you to set various login policies for your org.
- **Platform Encryption**: This section allows you to access the platform encryption settings and key management.
- **Remote Site Settings**: This section allows you to set the web addresses that your organization can invoke from Salesforce.
- **Security Alerts**: This section gives you instructions on the steps you need to take to roll out various security settings on Salesforce.
- **Session Management**: This page allows you to view information about active user settings.
- **Session Settings**: This page allows you to set the session security and session expiration timeout for your organization.
- **Sharing Settings**: This page allows you to set up organization-wide security defaults for objects, as well as sharing rules.
- **View Setup Audit Trail**: This section allows you to see the last 20 entries for actions carried out in Salesforce. You can also download the last 6 months of entries to a CSV file.

Now that we have looked at the items under the **Security** section, let's take a look at the **Optimizer** section.

 The **Field Accessibility** section is a very important section. Many admin troubleshooting items end up being field-level security issues.

Optimizer

The **Optimizer** page allows you to simplify customizations and drive feature adoption. It is recommended that you run the optimizer once a month, before installing a new app, and before each Salesforce release.

Now that we have gone through all of the items under the **Home** tab, let's take a look at the last section in this chapter—the **Object Manager** tab.

Using the Object Manager settings

The **Object Manager** section allows you to manage settings related to standard and custom objects. You can see all of the listed objects in the following screenshot:

As you can see in the preceding screenshot, both standard and custom objects are included.

In the following screenshot, you can see the options available when clicking on one of these objects:

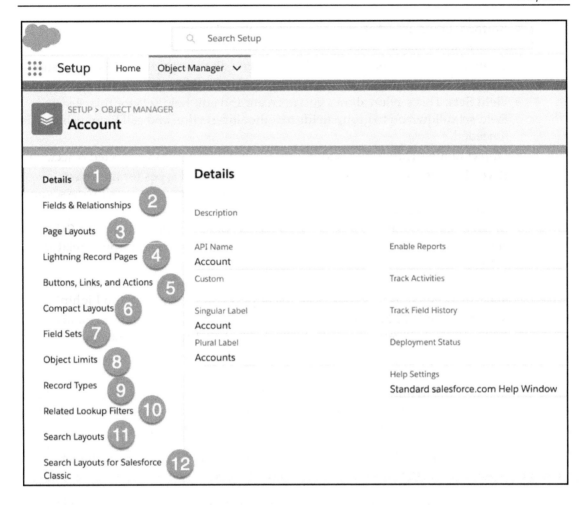

There are 12 sections that relate to our example, the standard **Account** object. Let's take a look at the options here:

- **Details**: This section shows you the details of the selected object, such as its name, the API name, and the labels.
- **Fields & Relationships**: This section allows you to create new fields, including relationship fields to other objects.
- **Page Layouts**: This section allows you to edit the core page layouts available for this object. This layout shows up in the **Details** section of the Lightning layout and is the main classic layout.
- **Lightning Record Pages**: This section allows you to edit the Lightning page layouts related to the object.

- **Buttons, Links, and Actions**: This section allows you to create new buttons, links, and actions, as well as edit existing ones for the object.
- **Compact Layouts**: This section allows you to edit the compact layouts that show up in various places both on the desktop and on mobile.
- **Field Sets**: This section allows you to create and edit field sets for this object. Field sets allow you to group fields together in a section and call them using code if needed.
- **Object Limits**: This section shows you all object limits for the selected object.
- **Record Types**: This section allows you to create record types for the object. Record types allow you to use the same object for various business processes and assign different page layouts for the record types.
- **Related Lookup Filters**: This section allows you to add filters to lookup fields to allow only specific records to be connected to the chosen object from a related object.
- **Search Layouts**: This section allows you to customize what columns are returned in various search pages throughout the application for this object in Lightning.
- **Search Layouts for Salesforce Classic**: This section allows you to customize what columns are returned in various search pages throughout the application for this object in Classic.

These settings are used to fully configure an object in Salesforce. Once you create an object, you navigate to this section to create all of the fields for the object, the relationships to other objects, the page layouts, the record types, and any search-related settings.

That was a lot of information! In this section, we learned about the features of **Object Manager**. We will now summarize what we covered in this chapter.

 Field Sets is a great feature, especially when working with custom code. For custom pages, you can reference a field set instead of individual fields. This gives the admin the ability to swap fields in and out of the changeset without needing the developer to update code.

Summary

Setup is where much of the admin work happens. We took a look at the high-level functions of the sections on this page, some of which will be covered in more detail in later chapters. In this chapter, we learned that there are two tabs on the **Setup** page—**Home** and **Object Manager**. Under the **Home** tab, we learned that there are three main sections—**ADMINISTRATION, PLATFORM TOOLS**, and **SETTINGS**. We looked at the settings under these three sections and learned, to a high level, what each one does. We also learned that under the **Object Manager** section, we can access various settings that help admins configure metadata and customize the application to meet the business needs.

In the next chapter, we will take a deep dive into sharing and visibility!

Questions

1. Which tab is used for non-object settings?
2. Which tab is used for managing object settings?
3. Under the **ADMINISTRATION** section, which sub-section allows you to mass delete records?
4. Under the **ADMINISTRATION** section, which sub-section allows you to create users?
5. Under the **PLATFORM TOOLS** section, which sub-section allows you to access Process Builder?
6. Under the **SETTINGS** section, which sub-section allows you to see your org ID?
7. Under the **Object Manager** tab, which setting allows you to edit the Lightning page layout?

Further reading

- Explore the Salesforce Setup Menu: `https://help.salesforce.com/articleView?id=basics_nav_setup.htmtype=5`
- Navigate the Setup page: `https://trailhead.salesforce.com/en/content/learn/modules/starting_force_com/starting_tour`

An Overview of Sharing and Visibility

10

Sharing and visibility are the cornerstones of data security in Salesforce. In the context of a business, the first decision that an organization makes is whether to have an open policy, which means all the users can see all the records. Depending on the nature of the business, this is not always possible and some records and/or fields need to be secure and only visible to certain people. If this is the case, the system needs to be set to completely private from the start; then, access is granted using several layers of administration features.

In this chapter, we will cover the following sharing and visibility security features in detail:

- Using organization-wide defaults
- Understanding the role hierarchy and its use
- What sharing rules are and how they are used
- What team access is and how it is used
- What profiles are and how they are used
- What permission sets are and how they are used
- Additional sharing and visibility features

With the help of these topics, you will be able to set up sharing and visibility for your org and learn about the different options available to grant and restrict access to data.

Technical requirements

For this chapter, make sure you log in to your development org and follow along as we work through the different sharing and visibility settings available to a system administrator.

Using organization-wide defaults

The first decision that needs to be made, as mentioned in the introduction, is whether you want to have an open organization, where all data is visible and editable by everyone, or whether any data needs to be restricted from being viewed or edited by certain people. Let's see how this works with a use case.

A business use case

You are the Salesforce admin for XYZ Widgets. You need to limit the visibility of accounts to account owners and their managers only. The first step is to make sure the **organization-wide** (**org-wide**) default settings for the account objects are set to private.

Setting up org-wide defaults

Org-wide defaults allow you to adjust these settings on an object-by-object basis. The following org-wide defaults are available for standard and custom objects:

- **Private**: This means the records in the object are only visible to and can only be edited by the record owner and anyone above the record owner in the role hierarchy (we will cover the role hierarchy later in this chapter).
- **Public read-only**: This means the records in the object are visible to all users but can only be edited by the record owner and anyone above the record owner in the role hierarchy.
- **Public read/write**: This means the records in the object are visible to and can be edited by all users.
- **Public read/write/transfer**: This is the setting in certain objects, such as leads and cases. It means the records in these objects are visible to and can be edited by all users and the records can also be transferred to new owners by anyone.
- **Controlled by parent**: This is the setting in objects that are a detail/child in a master/detail relationship. It means the child object inherits the org-wide default of the parent object.

These settings are the core of the security model. If any restrictions are required on an object, they must first be set to `private`, then access is granted using one of the many security features that we will cover in this chapter.

Let's take a look at how we access these settings. As the following screenshot shows, we can access this setting from the **Setup** page, as discussed in `Chapter 9`, *Setup and Configuration*:

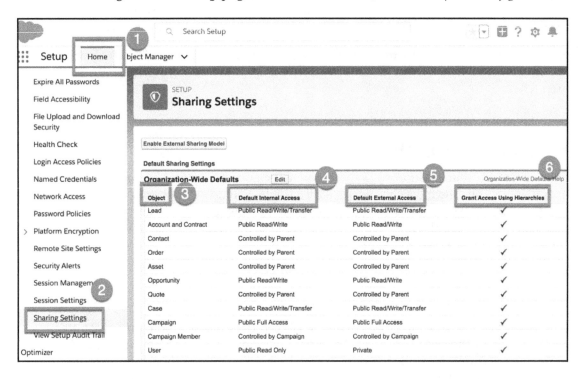

As you can see in the preceding screenshot, there are several items to review:

1. You can access the **Sharing Settings** page by clicking on the **Home** tab on the **Setup** page.
2. Once you have opened the **Home** tab, click on **Sharing Settings**. This brings up the following columns:
    - **Object (3)**: This is the object that you set the org-wide default for.
    - **Default Internal Access(4)**: This is the org-wide default setting for internal use, such as your regular internal Salesforce users.
    - **Default External Access (5)**: This is the org-wide default setting for external use, such as communities. This access setting defaults to the same as the internal access setting and can be adjusted accordingly.
    - **Grant Access Using Hierarchies (6)**: This setting lets you allow users higher up in the role hierarchy to inherit the access of users below them in the hierarchy.

As the admin, you can set the account object to **Private** to achieve the first part of the requirement, allowing only the account owner to see the accounts they own. Note that whenever you make changes to the org-wide defaults, the sharing privileges are reevaluated and recalculated so that access is added or removed accordingly.

Now that we have seen how to set the foundation for data security, let's see how we can open up access once an object is set to **Private**. The first feature we will look at is the role hierarchy.

Role hierarchy

Every user record in Salesforce has the option to be added to a role. That role is part of an overall hierarchy. The most common use case is when someone higher in the role hierarchy inherits the permissions to objects of users that are below them. For example, the sales manager role inherits the permissions of someone in the sales rep role as the manager comes above the sales rep in the hierarchy.

A business use case

As the Salesforce admin for XYZ Widgets, you need to limit the visibility of accounts to account owners and their managers. The previous step of setting up the org-wide default settings for accounts to private assures you that only the account owners can see the accounts they own. Setting up a role hierarchy will take care of the second part of the requirement, allowing managers to also be able to view the accounts owned by the reps they manage.

Let's take a look at how we can access this setting.

Using the role hierarchy

As the following screenshot shows, we can access this setting from the **Setup** menu, as discussed in Chapter 9, *Setup and Configuration*:

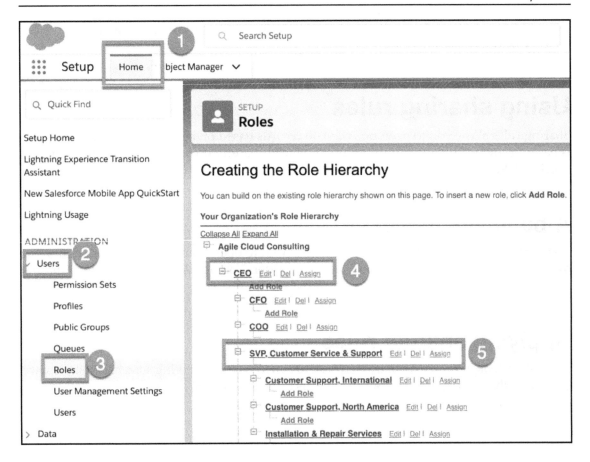

As you can see in the preceding screenshot, there are several items to review:

1. You can access the **Role Hierarchy** page by navigating to the **Home** tab on the **Setup** page.
2. Under the **Home** tab, go to the **Users** section.
3. Under the **Users** section, click on the **Roles** link.
4. In this example, the CEO inherits all the settings for users below **CEO** in the hierarchy (as long as the **Grant access using hierarchies** checkbox is checked on the org-wide default settings).
5. The **SVP, Customer Service & Support** role inherits the access of all of the users below **SVP, Customer Service & Support**. Note that since **SVP, Customer Service & Support**, **COO**, and **CFO** are on the same hierarchy level, **COO** and **CFO** do not inherit the access of the users directly under **SVP, Customer Service & Support**.

Now that we have seen how to open up access using roles, let's take a look at another security feature—sharing rules.

Using sharing rules

Sharing rules allow you to open up access to records based on record ownership (which is based on ownership) or specific criteria (which is based on criteria) on a record such as a specific field value.

A business use case

As the Salesforce admin for XYZ Widgets, you need to open up view access to accounts owned by a specific user with a specified team leader. You decide to use an account-sharing rule.

Applying sharing rules

Let's take a look at how we can access these settings. As the following screenshot shows, we can access this setting from the **Setup** page, as discussed in Chapter 9, *Setup and Configuration*:

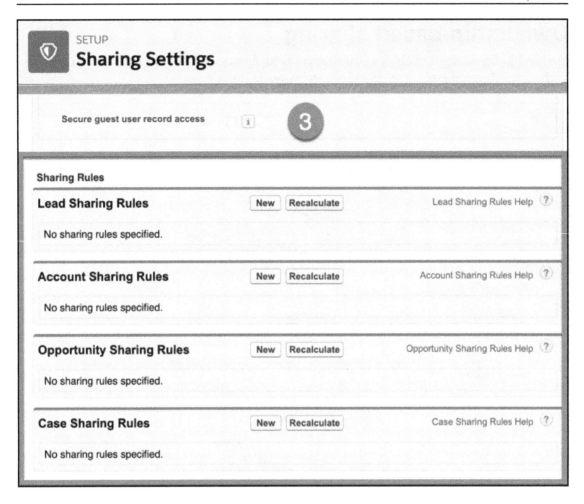

In the preceding screenshot, we can see that there are several items to review:

1. You can access the **Sharing Settings** page by navigating to the **Home** tab on the **Setup** page.
2. Once you have opened the **Home** tab, click on **Sharing Settings**.
3. Here, when you scroll down, you will see the option to add sharing rules for each object.

Let's take a look at the two kinds of sharing rules.

Ownership-based sharing

Ownership-based sharing allows you to share records based on ownership. As you can see in the following screenshot, there are several ways to do this:

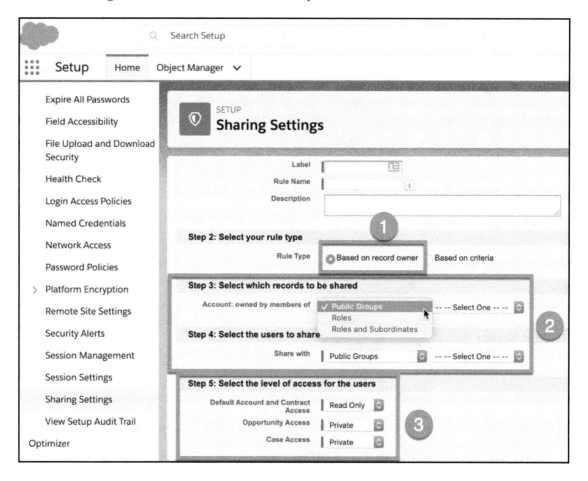

As you can see in the preceding screenshot, there are several items to review:

1. The **Based on record owner** radio button allows you to set this rule up as an ownership-based rule.
2. The records to be shared could be owned by a specific group (a group of owners), owners within a specific role, or owners within a specific role and all subordinates of the role. The same options are available for sharing these records with specific groups, roles, or roles and subordinates.

3. Finally, if the object to be shared is a parent in a master-detail relationship, you can control the access to the child records. This option is available for standard objects, such as accounts.

To cover this business use case, you would create an ownership-based account-sharing rule.

Next, let's take a look at criteria-based sharing rules.

Criteria-based sharing rules

Criteria-based sharing allows you to share records based on specific criteria on a record. As you can see in the following screenshot, there are several ways to do this:

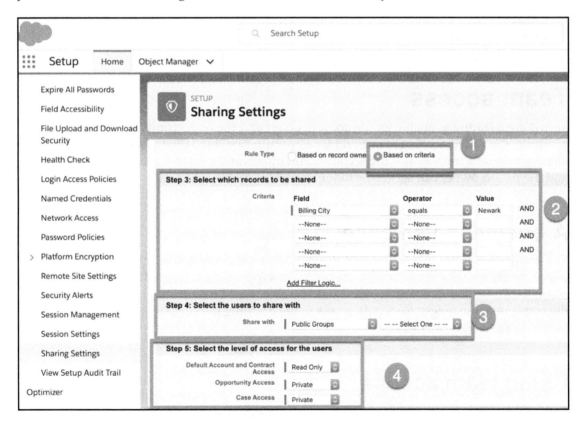

From the preceding screenshot, we can see the following:

1. The **Based on criteria** radio button allows you to set this rule up as a criteria-based rule.
2. The criteria can be set based on any field on the record. In this example, we set `Billing City` to `Newark`. This means that any record with this billing city is shared according to the rule.
3. The records can be shared with a specific group (a group of owners), owners within a specific role, or owners within a specific role and all subordinates of the role.
4. Finally, if the object that is shared is a parent in a master-detail relationship, you can control the access to the child records. This option exists for standard objects, such as accounts.

Now that we have seen how to open up access using sharing rules, let's take a look at another security feature—team access.

Team access

Teams are a feature available on the account object and the opportunity object. For accounts, it is called account teams and for opportunities, it is called sales teams. Teams allow you to add users to specific accounts and opportunities. They consist of specific users and the record owner can set access to the record for each specific user.

A business use case

You are the Salesforce admin for XYZ Widgets. The sales manager wants an account team, which consists of an engagement manager and a support specialist, to have access to certain accounts. The account record owner should be able to add two users to the team and grant the engagement manager read-only access while granting the support specialist read/write access. Let's see how this works.

Using team access

Team-related lists are available on the account and opportunity objects when the teams feature is enabled. Let's take a look at what this looks like when adding team members to the account team in the following screenshot:

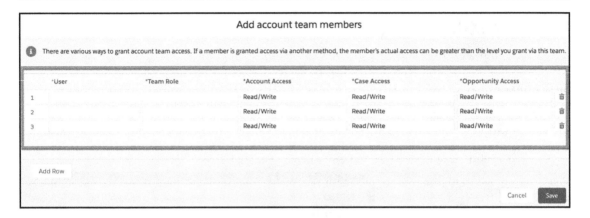

As you can see in the preceding screenshot, you can select a specific user and the role on the team, as well as set the access to the account and related objects for the user.

Now that we have seen how to open up access using teams, let's take a look at another security feature—profiles.

Profiles

Profiles are a very important and powerful security feature. The same way each user in Salesforce can have a role, each user must have a profile. Profiles allow you to set access to objects that are more powerful and overwrite other security settings. While profiles cover a multitude of settings, we will only focus on the object settings in the context of sharing and visibility here.

A business use case

You are the Salesforce admin for XYZ Widgets. The sales manager has requested that a group of users, all of which have the **Service Manager** profile, should have **View All** access to the accounts object. You will do this by updating the **Service Manager** profile.

Using profiles

Let's take a look at how we access the profile settings. As the following screenshot shows, we can access this setting from the **Setup** page, as discussed in Chapter 9, *Setup and Configuration*:

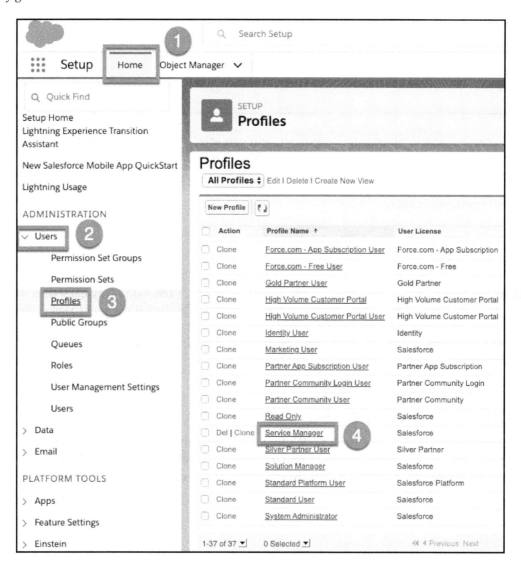

In the preceding screenshot, we can see the following:

1. You can access the **Sharing Settings** page by navigating to the **Home** tab on the **Setup** page.
2. Once on the **Home** tab, expand the **Users** section.
3. Under the **Users** section, click on **Profiles.**
4. There are many standard and custom profiles. Click on the **Service Manager** profile.

In the following screenshot, you can see the landing page that shows up when you click on **Service Manager**:

As you can see in the preceding screenshot, there are many settings available on the **Profiles** page. Let's take a look at the **Object Settings** section as it relates to sharing and visibility.

In the following screenshot, you can see the options available for the **Accounts** object:

In the preceding screenshot, you can see **Object Permissions**. Let's look at what these permissions do:

- **Read**: This allows read-only access to the object. This is applied if you want users to be able to see a record but not be able to make any changes to it.
- **Create**: This allows create access to the object. This is applied if you want users to be able to create a record on a specific object.
- **Edit**: This allows edit access to the object. This is applied if you want users to be able to read as well as make changes to a record on an object.
- **Delete**: This allows delete access to the object. This is applied if you want users to be able to delete a record on the object from Salesforce.
- **View All**: This is very important as it overrides the org-wide defaults. For example, you may have the org-wide default set to private, but if someone has a profile with **View All** on the object, they will be able to view all records for the object, regardless of the org-wide setting.
- **Modify All**: This is, again, very important as it overrides the org-wide defaults. For example, you may have the org-wide default set to private, but if someone has a profile with **Modify All** on the object, they can modify all records for the object, regardless of the org-wide setting.

Choose the **View All** option and save to complete the setup for this requirement. Now that we have seen how to open up access using profiles, let's take a look at our last security feature—permission sets.

Permission sets

Permission sets are the last feature we will look at to open up access. You use permission sets if you have a group of users that all have the same profile but there is one person that needs extra access for a business reason. It would not make sense to create a whole other profile for just one permission. Permission sets allow you to add a single permission to the user's record, letting you bypass creating a whole new profile for one additional setting.

A business use case

You are the Salesforce admin for XYZ Widgets. The sales manager has requested for a certain sales team lead to be able to modify all accesses to **Opportunities** in order to edit all the opportunities for their team. You do not want to create a separate profile for this user, so using a permission set would be perfect! Let's see how to go about this.

Using permission sets

Let's take a look at how we can access the permission sets settings. As the following screenshot shows, we can access this setting from the **Setup** page, as discussed in `Chapter 9`, *Setup and Configuration*:

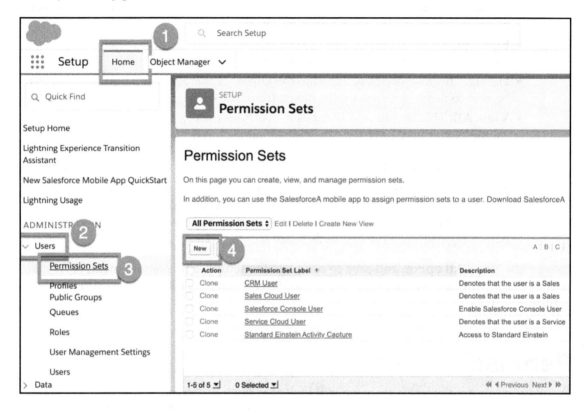

As you can see in the preceding screenshot, there are several items available:

1. You can access the **Permission Sets** page by navigating to the **Home** tab on the **Setup** page.
2. Once on the **Home** tab, expand the **Users** section.
3. Under the **Users** section, click on **Permission Sets**.
4. Click on **New** to create a permission set.

In the following screenshot, you can see the **Permission Sets** creation page:

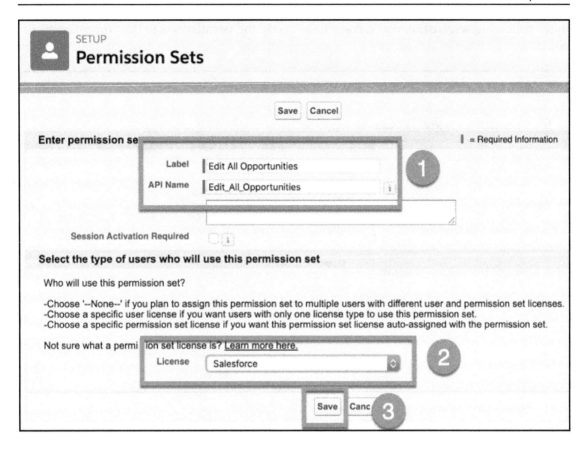

From the preceding screenshot, we can observe the following:

1. Here, you can set the name of the permission set and edit all the opportunities.
2. Here, you can set the Salesforce license for the permission set.
3. Click **Save** to save this permission setting.

In the following screenshot, you can see how to add the permissions to the **Opportunities** object:

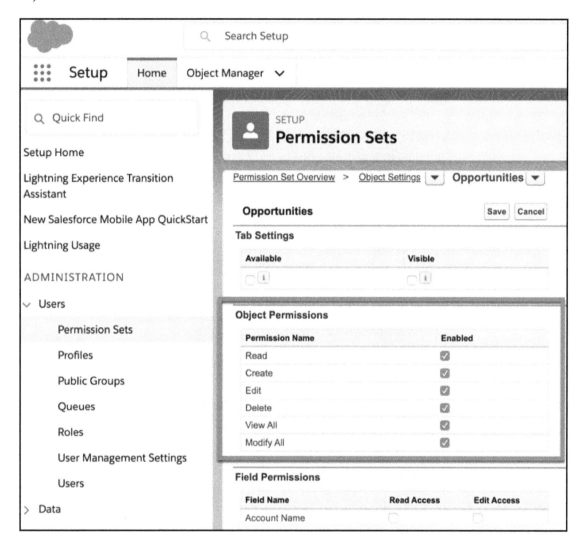

By selecting the appropriate options, the required permissions are set. From the preceding screenshot, you can see that I have added all the object permissions, including **Modify All**.

In the following screenshot, you can see how to add this permission to the user record:

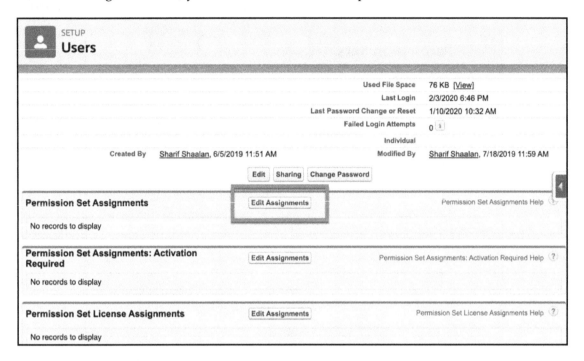

Navigate to the user record, scroll down to the **Permission Set Assignments** list, then click on **Edit Assignments**.

In the following screenshot, you can see the final step to add the permission set:

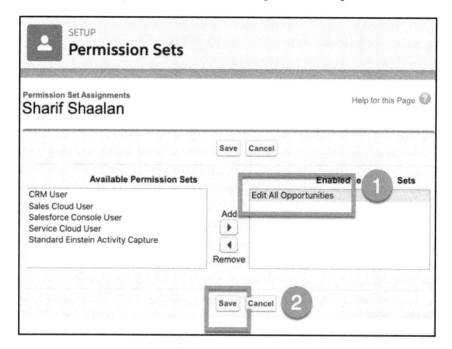

The preceding screenshot shows all of the available permission sets on the left:

1. I added the **Edit All Opportunities** permission set.
2. Then, click on **Save** to save this.

The team lead can now edit all the opportunities, even though they share the same profile as the other sales reps. Next, let's take a look at some additional sharing and visibility features.

Additional sharing and visibility features

There are a few more sharing and visibility features that should be reviewed. In this section, we will touch on system and user permissions, implicit sharing, and apex sharing.

System and user permissions

System permissions are permissions that apply to all apps, such as `view all data` or `modify all data`. User permissions are permissions that are tied to user management and access. Both of these sections can be found on profiles and permission sets under the **System Permission** link, as you can see in the following screenshot:

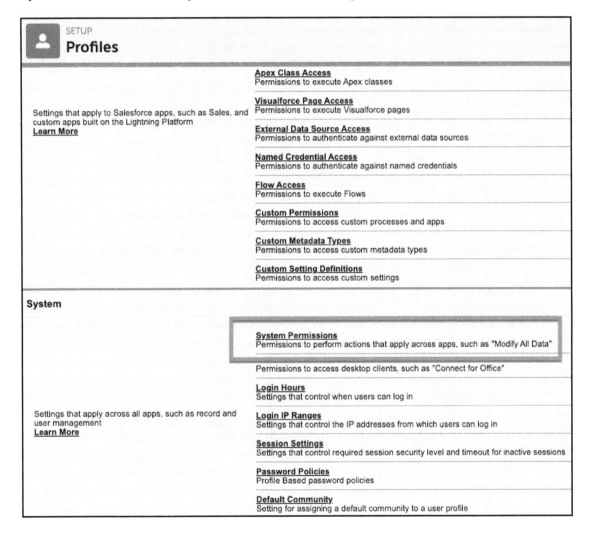

This takes us to the next page, which shows us a list of the permissions:

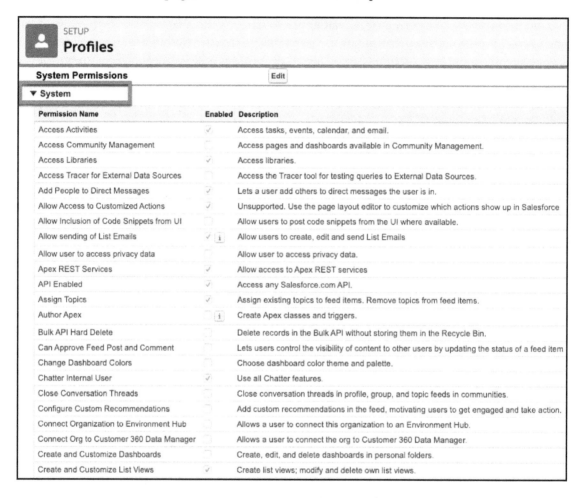

As you can see in the preceding screenshot, all of the available system permissions appear under **System**. Scrolling down on this page takes you to the following section:

▼ Users		
Permission Name	**Enabled**	**Description**
Assign Permission Sets		Assign permission sets to users.
Manage Internal Users		Create and edit internal users.
Manage IP Addresses		Create, edit, and delete trusted IP ranges.
Manage Login Access Policies		Specify the login access policies that apply to administrators and support organizations.
Manage Password Policies		Set password restrictions and login lockout policies for all users.
Manage Profiles and Permission Sets		Create, edit, and delete profiles and permission sets.
Manage Roles		Create, edit, and delete roles.
Manage Sharing		Create, edit, and recalculate sharing rules, edit organization-wide defaults, and enable the external sharing model.
Manage Users	*i*	Create, edit, and deactivate users, and manage security settings, including profiles and roles.
Reset User Passwords and Unlock Users	*i*	Unlock users whose accounts are locked, and reset user passwords.
View All Users		View all users, regardless of sharing settings.

As you can see in the preceding screenshot, the **Users** section contains the available user permissions, such as **Manage Roles** and **Manage Profiles and Permission Sets**. Next, let's look at what implicit sharing is.

Implicit sharing

Implicit sharing is built-in sharing, which occurs in the following use cases:

- If you have access to a child record of an account, you implicitly have read-only access to the account.
- If you have access to an account, you implicitly have access to the associated child records. The account owner's role determines the child record access you have.
- Account portal users have implicit read-only access to the account and to all of the contacts on an account.
- If a portal user is a contact on a case, that portal user has implicit read and write access to the case.

Finally, let's look at apex sharing.

Apex sharing

Apex sharing is a way of sharing a record programmatically. Each object has a share object that can be accessed programmatically to grant sharing access via code. An example is an account object that has an **AccountShare** object associated with it. A developer can access this object via apex code to fulfill the sharing requirements.

Next, let's summarize what we have learned in this chapter.

Summary

In this chapter, we learned that the foundation of sharing and visibility is the org-wide setting. If anything needs to be restricted, you need to first remove all access by making the object private, then open up access as needed using various security features.

We learned what roles are and how they are used to grant access to records. We learned how to add ownership-based and criteria-based sharing rules to grant access to records. We saw what the account and sales teams are and how to add them to accounts and opportunities. We learned how to further grant record access using profiles and permission sets.

In the following chapter, we will cover sandboxes and change sets for project management.

Questions

1. What is the first decision that should be made when looking at org-wide settings?
2. What does the **Grant Access Using Hierarchies** checkbox do?
3. What are the two types of sharing rules?
4. Who can add team members to the account and sales teams?
5. Does the **Modify All** data setting on a profile work if the org-wide setting for an object is private?
6. When would you use permission sets?
7. Where is a permission set added after it is created?

Further reading

- An overview of data security can be found at https://trailhead.salesforce.com/en/content/learn/modules/data_security/data_security_overview.
- More information on apex sharing can be found at https://developer.salesforce.com/docs/atlas.en-us.apexcode.meta/apexcode/apex_bulk_sharing_creating_with_apex.htm.

Using Sandboxes and Change Sets

11

One of the key things when it comes to managing effective projects on the Salesforce platform is understanding sandboxes. It also helps to understand how the right environment management strategy can help you ensure your code and configuration have been built and tested with quality before it's deployed to your production environment.

Consequently, we will cover the following topics in this chapter:

- Creating and using sandboxes
- Using different types of sandboxes
- Creating change sets
- Deploying change sets

With the help of these topics, you will be able to understand how to create sandboxes, as well as knowing which type of sandbox to create. You will also learn how to build and deploy change sets so that you can move your changes from a sandbox to another or move them to your production environment.

Technical requirements

For this chapter, all you need to do is follow along with the screenshots provided—development environments *do not* contain sandboxes.

Creating and using sandboxes

When working day to day as an admin it is important that you do not make changes that can disrupt your active users. For this reason we create and test new features in Sandboxes. Sandboxes are environments that are isolated from your production Salesforce environment. This means you can make and test changes and they will have no impact whatsoever on your live users. In this section we will introduce a business use case and learn how to create a sandbox.

Business use case

You are the Salesforce admin at XYZ Widgets. You have some configuration and automation ideas that you would like to build and test, but you don't want to cause any interruptions in the live production organization. You decide to spin off a sandbox to complete and test your work. Once the work has been completed and tested, you will push it to production using change sets. Let's see how all of this works.

Creating a sandbox

When you create a sandbox, all of your *metadata* is copied to the sandbox. Metadata is the actual object and field configuration, as well as your setup items. This is the opposite of regular *data*, which is what is entered into those objects. There is one type of sandbox that copies both metadata and data; we will discuss this in the next section. Follow these steps to create a sandbox:

1. Let's take a look at how to create a sandbox. First, navigate to **Setup** and then the **Home** tab (1), as shown in the following screenshot:

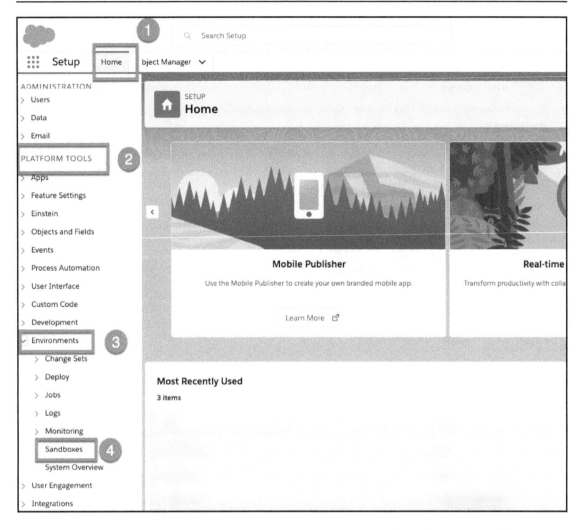

2. From the **Home** tab, go to **PLATFORM TOOLS (2)** | **Environments (3)**|
   Sandboxes (4).

3. The following screenshot shows the sandbox management and creation screen:

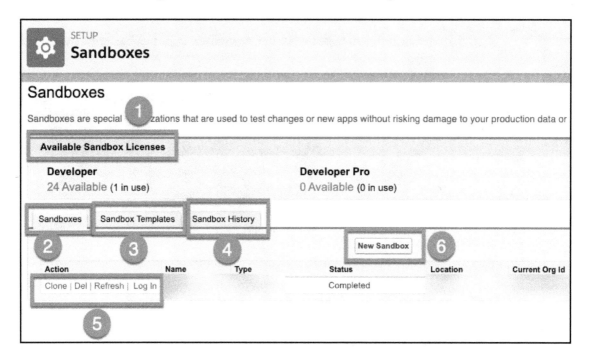

Let's check out the sections that are numbered in the preceding screenshot:

1. **Available Sandbox Licenses**: This section shows you how many sandboxes of each type you have available. We will discuss the different types of sandboxes in the next section.
2. **Sandboxes**: This tab shows you all of your created sandboxes and the status of each.
3. **Sandbox Templates**: This section allows you to build templates so that you can pull specific testing data into your sandbox if you are using a partial copy or a full copy sandbox. For example, you can use a template to copy a sample dataset from the Account, Contact, and Opportunity objects in production so that they're displayed within the sandbox when it is created.
4. **Sandbox History**: This tab shows the history of when the sandbox was created, who it was created by, and the last time it was refreshed.
5. **Sandbox Actions**: These are the actions you can perform on an existing sandbox. They include the following:
   - **Clone**: Allows you to copy a sandbox to a new sandbox.
   - **Del** (Delete): Allows you to delete a sandbox.
   - **Refresh**: Allows you to refresh a sandbox, which means recreating the sandbox with the latest production metadata.
   - **Log In**: Allows you to log into the sandbox.
6. **New Sandbox**: Allows you to create a new sandbox.

In the following screenshot, you can see the sandbox creation screen that appears when **New Sandbox** is clicked:

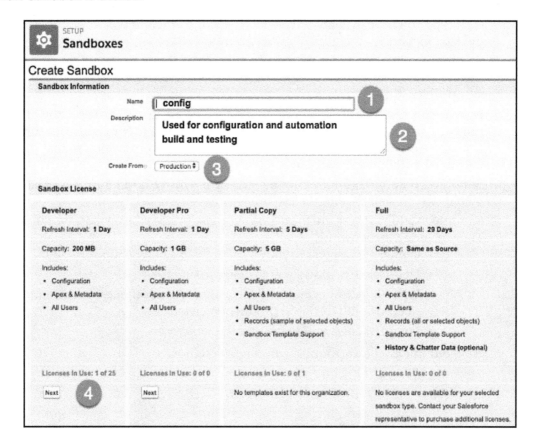

As numbered in the preceding screenshot, there are several important items here:

1. **Name**: This is where you name the sandbox. Your sandbox name will be added to your production username when you log into the production environment. For example, if your production username is `john.doe@xyz.com` and you name your sandbox `testing`, your username for the testing sandbox will be `john.doe@xyz.com.testing` and your password will be the same as your production password. It is also a good time to mention that when you log into production, you log in at `login.salesforce.com`, but when you log into a sandbox, you log in at `test.salesforce.com`.

2. **Description**: This is where you can add the purpose of the sandbox. I have added `Used for configuration and automation build and testing.`

3. **Create From**: This gives you the option to create the sandbox from production, meaning it will copy the data and metadata from your live production organization or from another sandbox that already exists.

4. **Next**: Click **Next** to create the type of sandbox type you wish to create.

Once the sandbox starts being processed, it may take from a few minutes to 24 hours or longer to complete, depending on your position in the request queue and how big your sandbox is, capacity-wise. Once it is complete, you will receive an email and then you can log in. Now that we have learned how to create a sandbox, let's look at the different types of sandboxes and their uses.

Using different types of sandboxes

There are four types of sandboxes:

- Developer
- Developer Pro
- Partial Copy
- Full Copy

Each type of sandbox has different features and possible uses within the business. Their main differences have to do with refresh interval, capacity, and sandbox features. Let's take a look at these types and the differences between them in the following sections...

Developer sandboxes

Developer sandboxes are the most common types of sandboxes. There is no extra fee for this sandbox and it can be refreshed daily. This sandbox has a capacity of 200 MB and includes all **Configuration**, **Apex & Metadata**, and **All Users** from the production organization. The most common use case for this sandbox is for coding since you have to build code in a sandbox in order to push it to production. It can also be used to make configuration changes, as well as to test those changes before you make them live in your production environment.

Developer Pro sandboxes

Developer Pro sandboxes are exactly the same as Developer sandboxes except for two things: there is usually an extra fee for the Developer Pro sandbox and the capacity is 1 GB instead of 200 MB. The use case for this sandbox is the need to test with a bit more data than what's allowed in the Developer sandbox.

Partial Copy sandboxes

Partial Copy sandboxes contain everything a Developer Pro sandbox contains, but with the following exceptions:

- It will cost more than a Developer Pro sandbox
- The refresh interval is 5 days
- The capacity is 5 GB
- It includes a sample of data from select objects
- It has sandbox template support

The use case for this sandbox is testing with data samples and training it for organizations where a full sandbox is cost-prohibitive.

As shown in the following screenshot, when you create a partial sandbox, you have the option to choose a data template. This is where you define the objects that the data sample is created from:

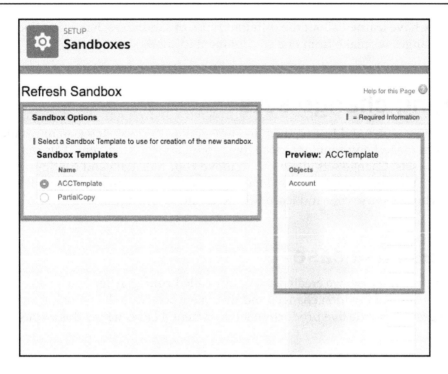

As you can see in the preceding screenshot, we have defined a template and can see a preview of the objects included in that template. Next, let's look at Full Copy sandboxes.

Full Copy sandboxes

Full Copy sandboxes contain everything a Partial Copy sandbox contains, but with the following exceptions:

- It will cost more than a Partial Copy sandbox
- The refresh interval is 29 days
- The storage capacity is the same as production
- It includes *all* data from the source
- It has sandbox template support
- It allows you to copy chatter and history data

The use case for this sandbox is **user acceptance training** (**UAT**) as it is an exact data and metadata replica of production. It can also be used for data migration and integration testing.

Now that we have learned about the different types of sandboxes, let's take a look at how to move the changes we make from one environment to another.

Creating change sets

After creating features and testing them in our sandbox the next step is to move these features from the test environment to the live production environment. This can be done using change sets. Change sets allow you to move your metadata and configuration changes from the source environment to a target environment. In this section we will introduce a business use case and learn how to create a a change set.

Business use case

In the preceding use case, we created a sandbox called **config**. After you've made your configuration and automation changes and they have been tested, you will want to move those changes over to the live production environment. Let's see how this works with change sets.

Creating change sets

Let's take a look at how to create change sets. We need to perform the following steps:

1. First, click on the **Home** tab (**1**) from **Setup**, as shown in the following screenshot:

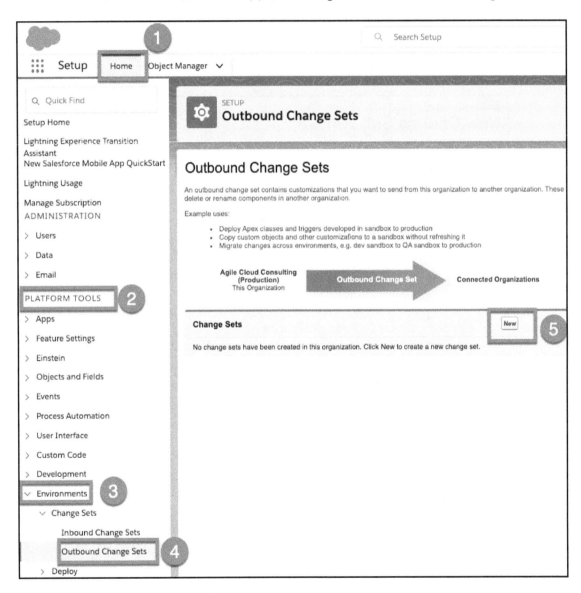

2. From the preceding screenshot, we can see the following:
    1. Go to **PLATFORM TOOLS (2)** | **Environments (3)** | **Outbound Change Sets (4)**. **Outbound Change Sets** means I am building the change set in the source organization (sandbox) so that I can send it outbound to the target organization (production).
    2. Click on **New (5)** to create the change set.

3. The following screenshot shows the first screen you'll see when you start creating your change set:

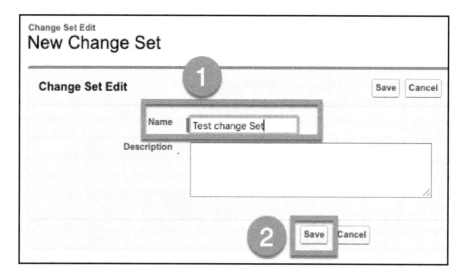

4. Here, enter the change set **Name (1)** and click on **Save (2)**. You can also add a description if you wish.

5. The following is the second screen you'll see when creating the change set:

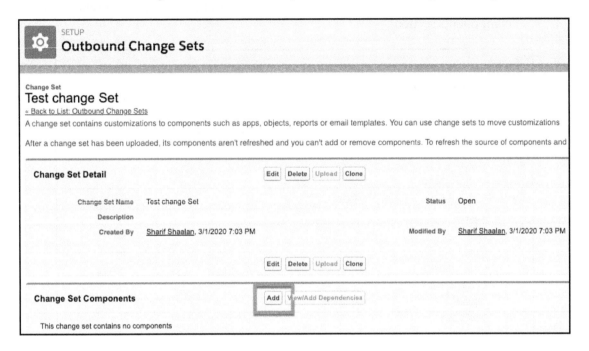

As shown in the preceding screenshot, the first step is to add the change set's components. Let's see what it looks like when we click on **Add** in the change set components section:

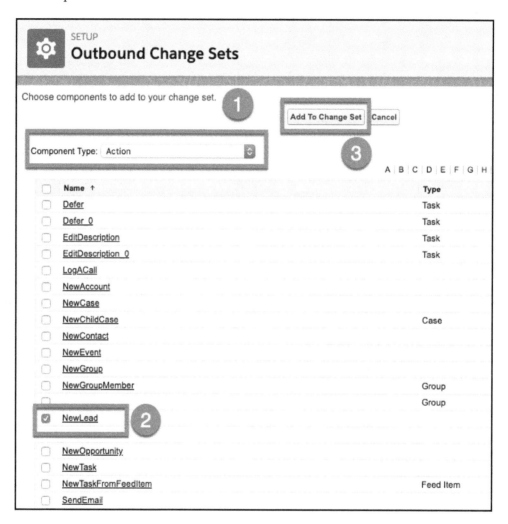

6. As you can see, you can add all of the components you wish to push to production. This can include any metadata or configuration changes you have made. You can choose from a list of component types (**1**), choose one or many components of that type (**2**), and then add them to the change set (**3**). Let's take a look at the remaining steps we need to follow in order to upload the change set:

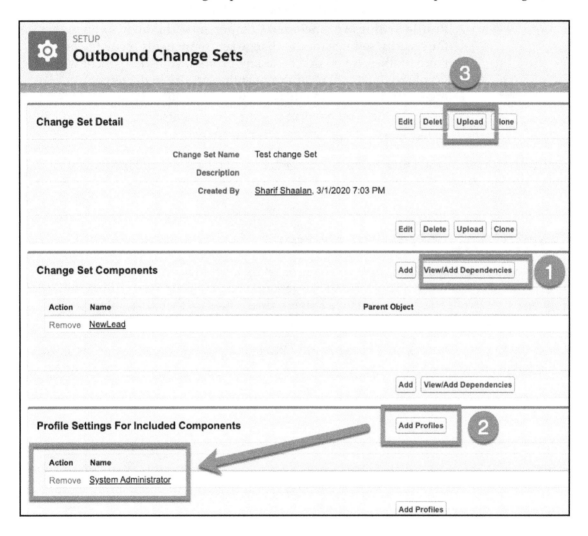

7. As you can see, there are several steps we need to complete to finish creating the change set:

   1. **View/Add Dependencies**: This allows you to see any dependent components and add them to the change set. This helps make sure you don't forget sections of the code that are needed for your functionality to work, such as custom fields, page layouts, and so on.

   2. **Profile Settings For Included Components**: This allows you to add the security settings for the change set components related to one or more profiles. If you don't add any profiles, your component won't be visible and you will need to adjust the security in the target organization, so adding this here will save a lot of time.

   3. **Upload**: Once you have all of your components, you can upload the changes to the target organization (production).

Now that we have learned how to create change sets, let's take a look at how to deploy them to production.

Deploying change sets

Before you can deploy a change set, you have to set up a deployment connection between the source organization (sandbox) and the target organization (production), or a connection from one sandbox to another if you have that use case. You can do this by going to the deployment connections in the target organization and allowing inbound change sets.

Under the **Deploy** tab, click on **Deployment Settings** in the target organization, as shown in the following screenshot:

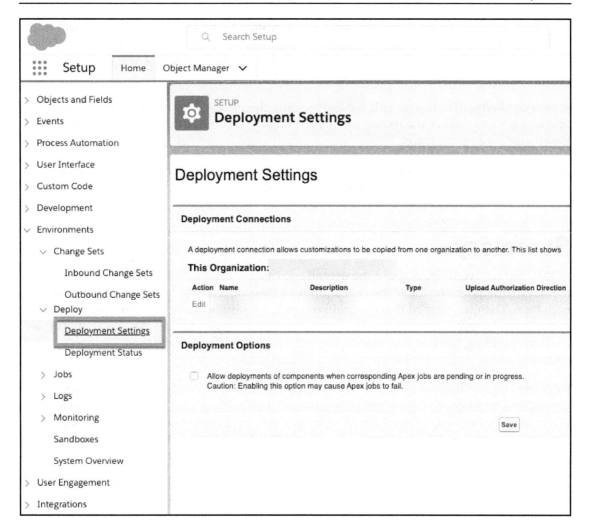

As you can see, some production data has been masked. Let's take a closer look at this screen:

- On this screen, under **Upload Authorization Direction**, you can set up the organization so that it receives inbound change sets from the target organization. Once you've set this connection up, you'll be ready to deploy a change set to production.
- After clicking upload on the outbound change set in the source organization, it will take up to 30 minutes for the change set to show up in the production (target) organization.

- In the production organization, go to **Inbound Change Sets**. Here, you will find the uploaded change set. On the change set, you will see a **Deploy** button. This will deploy the change set to production. Once the deployment is complete, you will get a status showed failed or succeeded.

If your deployment fails, you will see a log stating the reason why it failed. At this point, you will have to resolve the issues, rebuild the change set from the sandbox, and redeploy the change set to production.

Now that we have learned how to connect to organizations and deploy a change set to production, let's go over what we have learned in this chapter.

Summary

In this chapter, we learned about the overall use cases for sandboxes and how to create them. We discussed the four types of sandboxes, their differences, and the use cases for each type. Then we learned that the main use case for sandboxes is building and configuring features without disrupting the production environment. We saw that once we are done building these features in a sandbox, we can use change sets to move their features.

By doing this, we learned how to create change sets, how to upload the change sets to production, and how to deploy the change sets. These skills will help you build and test your configuration and automation features in a safe environment where you cannot disrupt users and push those features to users with the confidence that they will work in production.

In the next chapter, we will learn about some of the most common configuration changes we need to make when configuring objects for our businesses.

Questions

1. What are the four types of sandboxes?
2. Which type of sandbox is commonly used for development?
3. Which type of sandbox is commonly used for data migration testing?
4. Why would you add a profile to a change set?
5. Before you upload a change set, what step must you take?
6. Should the outbound change set be set up in the source or the target organization?
7. What is the refresh interval for a Full Copy sandbox?

Further reading

- **Sandbox Types and Templates**: `https://help.salesforce.com/articleView?id=create_test_instance.htmtype=5`
- **Sandboxes: Staging Environments for Customizing and Testing**: `https://help.salesforce.com/articleView?id=deploy_sandboxes_intro.htmtype=5`

12
Configuring Objects for Your Business

One of the core features of using Salesforce is *declarative development*, also known as *clicks, not code*. This feature allows admins to build on the platform without actually having to write code. Admins have the ability to build custom objects to hold the necessary data and configure these custom objects for the business use case. By adding fields and different layouts to the objects, admins give end users the ability to easily interact with the objects as required for their day-to-day work.

In this chapter, we will cover the following topics in detail:

- Creating custom objects
- Creating custom fields
- Creating and using page layouts
- Creating and using record types
- Adding a certification to a contact

With the help of these topics, you will be able to understand the use case for creating a custom object, as well as how to configure custom objects using custom fields, page layouts, and record type so that they can be used by end users.

Technical requirements

For this chapter, log into your development organization and simply follow along as we create and customize a custom object.

Creating custom objects

As we discussed in the first section of this book, there are several *standard objects*, such as **Accounts**, **Contacts**, **Opportunities**, **Leads**, and **Cases**, all of which are part of the foundations for customer relationship management and sales.

Outside these core objects, there may be other use cases where you'll need to create new *custom* objects to handle a business use case. Objects, also known as **database tables**, allow you to build the infrastructure needed to store this information. Objects are similar to spreadsheets, where the *object* is the *tab*, the *columns* are the *fields*, and the *rows* are the *actual data* that's created and inserted into these objects. Let's take a look at a business use case where you may need to create a custom object.

Business use case

You are the Salesforce admin at XYZ Widgets. A business use case has come up where your manager has asked you to track the Salesforce certifications held by the customers that are currently doing business with XYZ Widgets. Knowing which Admin and Developer certifications a customer has can help the sales representatives at XYZ Widgets present the right products to these customers when on a call. Let's gather the requirements and start building!

Creating a custom object

Looking at the requirements, the first step is to create a Certifications custom object.

Perform the following steps to do this:

1. Navigate to the **Setup** | **Object Manager** tab **(1)**, as shown in the following screenshot:

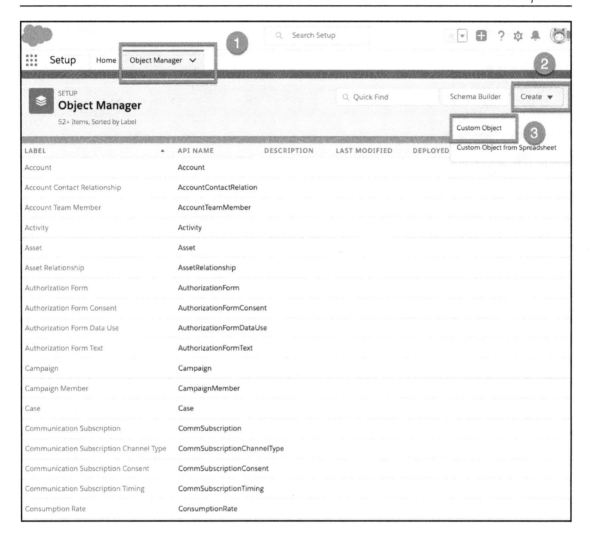

2. Next, click on **Create (2)** and then **Custom Object (3)** in order to start creating the custom `Certifications` object.

In the following screenshot, you can see the **New Custom Object** creation screen:

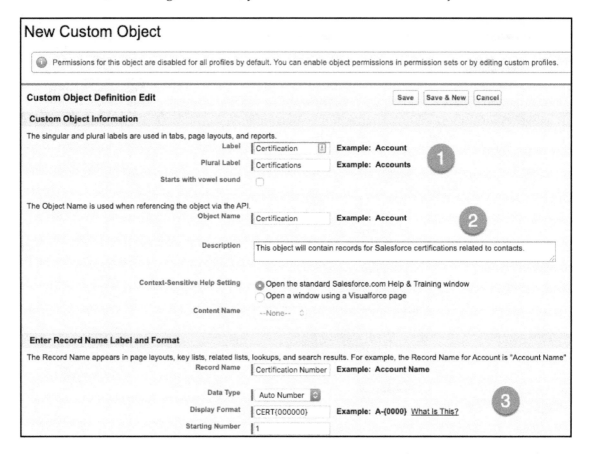

From the preceding screenshot, we can see that there are several important sections when creating a new object (the following points have been labeled in the preceding screenshot):

1. In this section, I entered the object's **Label** and **Plural Label** (`Certification` and `Certifications`, respectively).

2. Next, I entered the **Object name** of the API (the name used for programmatic purposes) and a **Description**. Additionally, a personal choice is to opt for the standard help and training, as opposed to customizing them.

3. In the third section, I opted for the records in the object to be auto-numbered, as opposed to them having text names. So, I set the **Data Type** to **Auto Number**, added a **Display Format**, and added a **Starting Number**.

In the following screenshot, you can see some more features that can be added when creating a custom object:

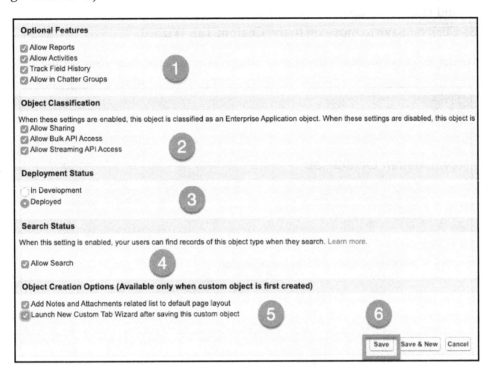

As shown in the preceding screenshot, there are several more items that can be configured when creating the custom object (the following points have been labeled in the preceding screenshot):

1. **Optional Features** provides the following options:
    - **Allow Reports**: Allows you to report on records that will be created in this object.
    - **Allow Activities**: Allows you to create tasks and events on this object.
    - **Track Field History**: Allows you to track field change history on up to 20 fields of this object.
    - **Allow in Chatter Groups**: Allows this object to be accessible in Chatter Groups.
2. **Object Classification**: Check these boxes to classify the object as an Enterprise custom object without API limitations.
3. **Deployment Status**: Set to **Deployed** when you are ready for this object to show up.

4. **Search Status**: Allows you to search for records for this object.
5. **Object Creation Options**: Here, you can add a **Notes and Attachments** section and launch the **Custom Tab Wizard**.
6. Click on **Save** to move on to the **Custom Tab Wizard**.

The following screenshot shows the screen you land on after saving your settings:

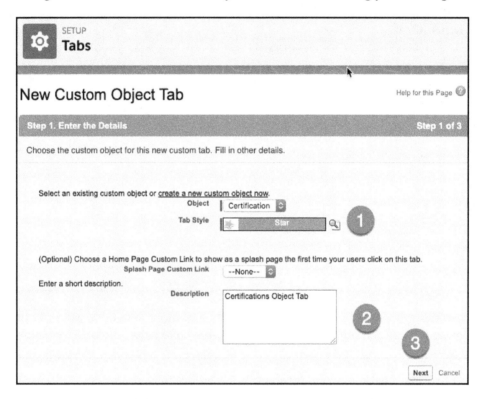

From the preceding screenshot, you can see that I added an object name, selected a tab icon, added a description, and clicked on **Next** on the custom tab screen.

The following is the next page you will see:

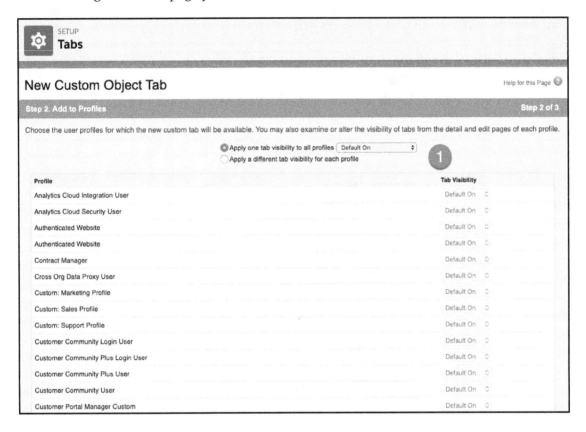

Here, you have the option to apply tab visibility to all or some of the profiles. Tab visibility determines whether the application contains a tab for this new object. For example, you may want the certification tab to show up in the **Sales** app:

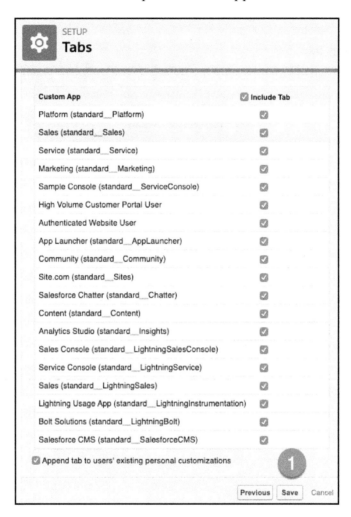

In the preceding screenshot, you can see that you have the option to add the tab to one or more custom apps. This will make it easier to access this object when a user is using any of the apps the tab is added to. Click **Save** to finish creating the object.

The following screenshot shows the page you'll land on when you've finished creating the custom object:

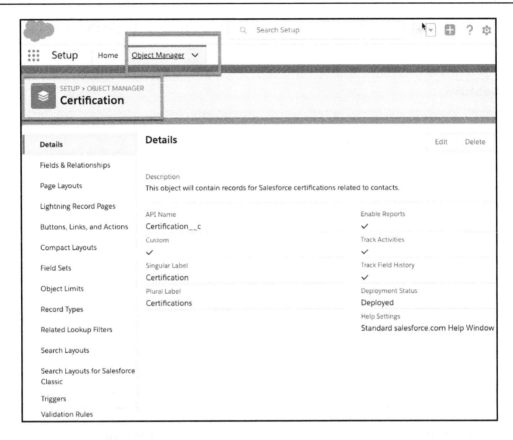

In the preceding screenshot, you can see we have landed back on the object manager and that there is now a new **Certification** object.

With that, our first requirement is complete – we have created the **Certification** object. The next step is to create some fields for the information you would like to capture on the **Certification** object.

Creating custom fields

Now that we have created our custom **Certification** object, the next step is to create the fields that will capture information on these objects. The first and most important field to create will be the relationship field so that we can connect **Certifications** to **Contacts**.

By going to the **Setup > Object Manager** tab, you can see how we begin the process of creating this field:

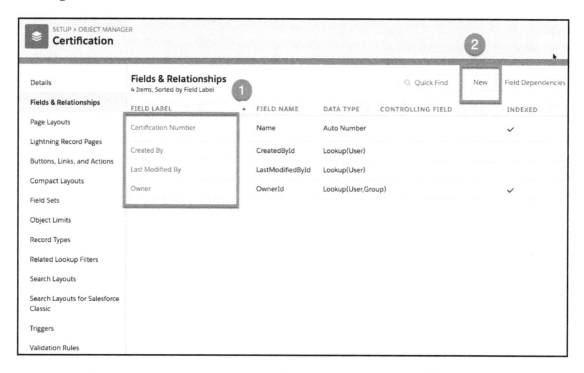

As shown in the preceding screenshot, there are four fields that were automatically created when the object was created **(1)**. These are **Certification Number**, **Created By**, **Last Modified By**, and **Owner**. To create a new field, click on **New (2)**.

The following screenshot shows the **New Custom Field** page. Notice the description of each field type as you create the necessary fields:

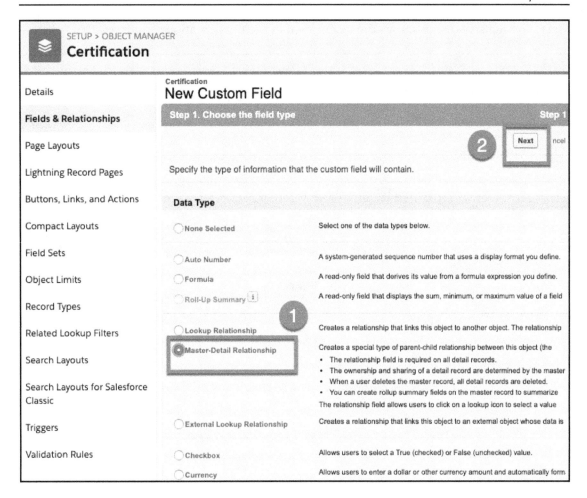

As shown in the preceding screenshot, there are two types of internal relationships (1):

- You can choose a **Lookup Relationship**, which allows you to look up any object and connect the certification object.
- I chose to make this a **Master-Detail Relationship**, which means that the certification has to have a contact before it can be created. This makes sense because if the contact were to be deleted, the certification would have no use for the certification records related to that contact in Salesforce.

After selecting an internal relationship, click **Next (2)**.

The following screenshot shows the next screen in the field creation sequence:

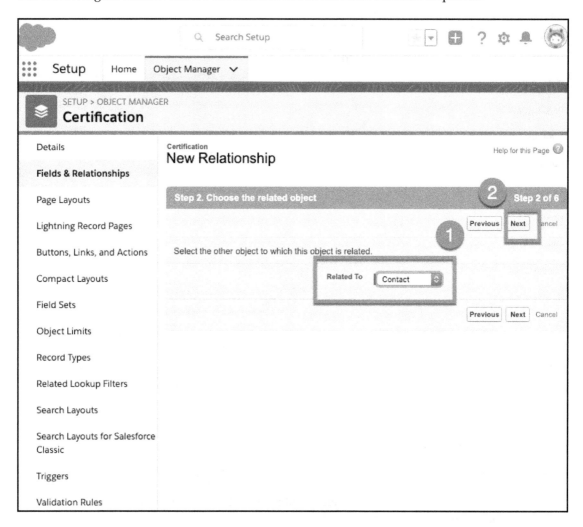

Next, we choose the related object – in this case, **Contact (1)** – and click **Next (2)**.

The following screenshot allows us to add some details about this field:

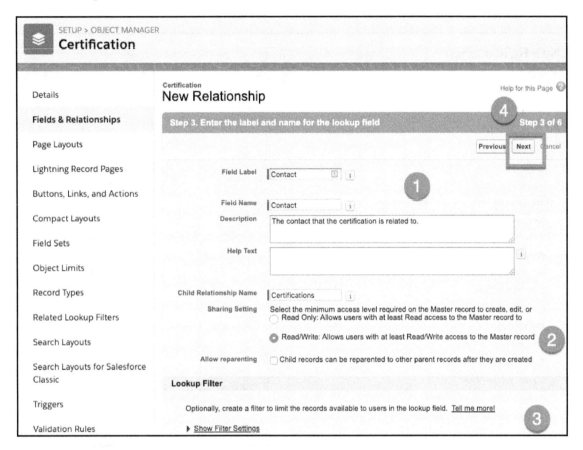

As shown in the preceding screenshot, we have added a few things (the following points have been labeled in the preceding screenshot):

1. Here, we added the **Field Label** and API name, as well as a **Description** and optional **Help Text**.
2. In this section, we have several sharing options. We chose **Read/Write** as the minimum sharing access on the contact record so that we can create a certification record.
3. Optionally, you can add a **Lookup Filter** to allow a certification record to be created for certain types of contacts. We won't create one for this example.
4. Click **Next** to proceed to the next step.

The next step is to set the field-level security for the new field, as shown in the following screenshot:

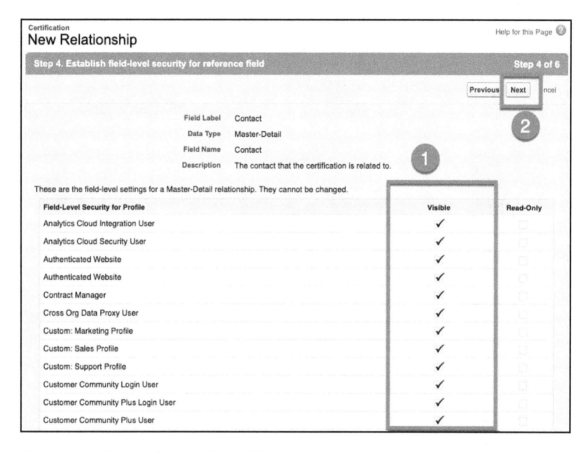

Here, we can choose which profiles will be able to see the new field **(1)**. Click on **Next (2)**.

On the next page, you can add the field to specific layouts:

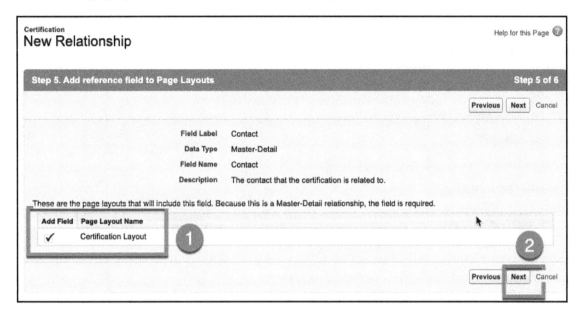

As shown in the preceding screenshot, I added the field to the existing certification **Page Layout (1)** and clicked **Next (2)** to proceed to the next step.

The following screenshot shows the final steps in creating a custom field:

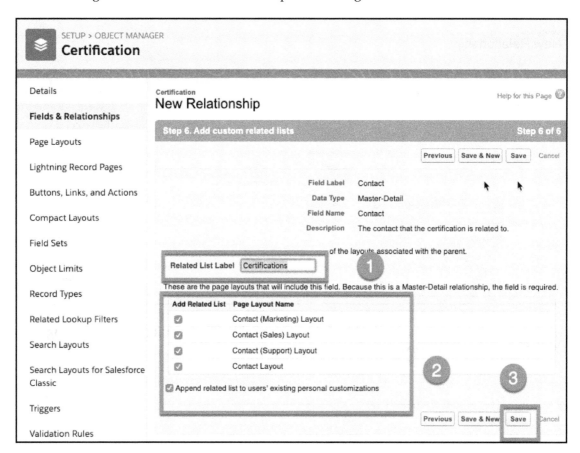

As shown in the preceding screenshot, I have set a few final options for the field (the following points have been labeled in the preceding screenshot:

1. The **Related List Label** of **Certifications** that will show up on the contact record.
2. The contact page layouts to add this related list to.
3. Save to finish creating the field.

Now that we have created this field, we can create a few more in our developer organization that we can then use in our example:

- Create a **Date** field called **Certification Start Date**.
- Create a **Checkbox** field called `Active`.
- Create a **Picklist** field called `Certification` with the following options:
  - `Admin`
  - `Advanced Admin`
  - `Platform Developer I`
  - `Platform Developer II`

With that, we have created our fields! The relationship field is very important because it ties two objects together. Next, let's take a look at custom page layouts for the new object and its related fields.

Creating and using page layouts

Page layouts are the user interfaces where we interact with the object and fields that we created. When looking at page layouts, there are two types to consider. The first is the Lightning page layout, which is used for configuring the layout for a record in the Lightning experience and includes many usability options. We will add some resources for the Lightning page layout at the end of this chapter. The second is the page layout related to the actual object. This is the page layout we will look at in this section. It maps directly to the **Details** section of a Lightning page's layout.

Page layouts are used to display the fields related to objects and allow you to enter data into those fields. This gives admins the flexibility to show different page layouts to different users based on profiles and/or record types. We will cover record types in the next section. Now, let's take a look at how to create page layouts using our previous **Certification** object example. Although a page layout is automatically created when you create an object, we will create a new page layout for the purpose of this exercise.

In the following screenshot, you can see that we've navigated to the certification object we created in the previous section:

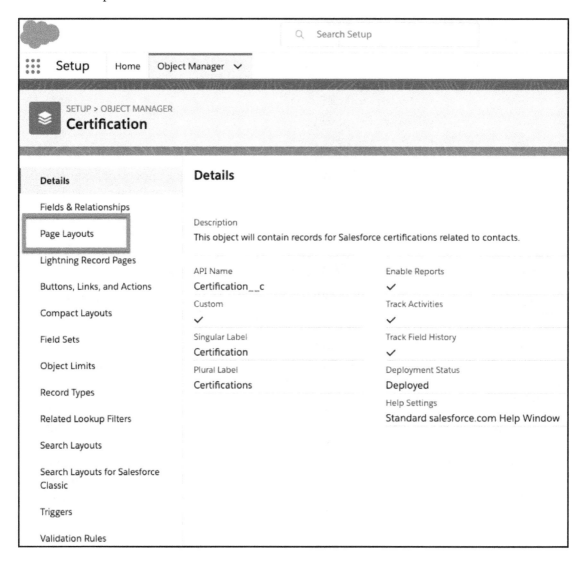

Then, click on the **Page Layouts** section under **Details**.

In the following screenshot, you can see that I clicked on **New** and was brought to the **Create New Page Layout** page:

Add the new **Page Layout Name (1)** and **save (2)**. Note that you have the option to clone an existing page layout.

In the following screenshot, you can see the **Page Layouts** edit screen:

From the preceding screenshot, we can see that we clicked on the **Fields** section (1). Now, we can create a section and drag fields onto the layout (2).

In the following screenshot, you can see the section and fields we added:

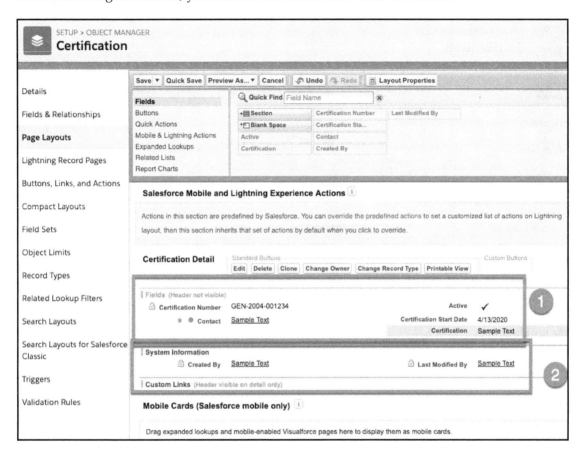

I added the new custom fields to the top section **(1)** and added the **Created By** and **Last Modified By** fields under a new **System Information** section.

In the following screenshot, you can see the final step when it comes to editing the layout:

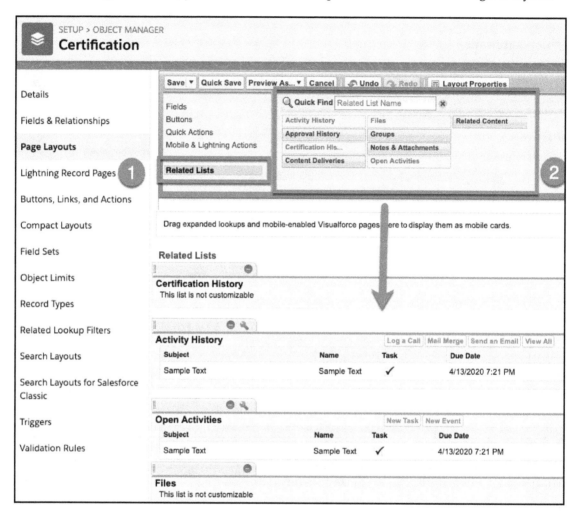

Finally, navigate to the **Related Lists** section **(1)** and add the related lists **(2)** to the bottom section of the page layout.

Using the certification object, we have successfully created a page layout. Now, let's take a look at record types.

Creating and using record types

Record types are the last piece of the puzzle. It is important to note that record types are not always needed; this depends on your business process. Record types are used when you need to show different page layouts, apply different processes, and/or need to show different picklist values based on a business use case. In this example, we will create two record types for the **Certification** object in order to show the correct picklist values in the **Certification** custom field. The record types will be **Admin** and **Developer**, and the goal is to show the Admin Certifications for **Admin** and the Developer Certifications for **Developer**. Let's learn how to create these two record types and update the available picklist values.

First, navigate back to the Certification custom object, as shown in the following screenshot:

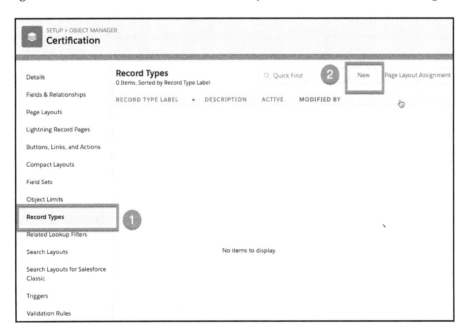

Click on **Record Types (1)** | **New (2)**.

The following screenshot shows the **Record Type** creation screen:

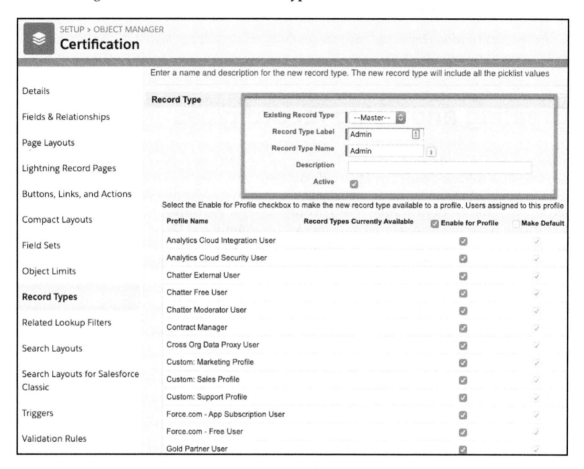

I added **Admin** as the **Record Type Label** and **Record Type Name** and also enabled this record type for all profiles before clicking on **Next**.

The following screenshot shows the next step in this process:

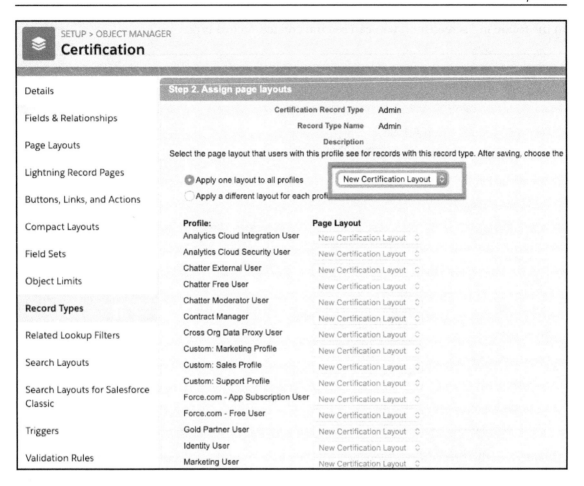

Apply the **Certification** page layout we created in the previous section to all profiles and click **Next**.

In the following screenshot, you can see the created record type:

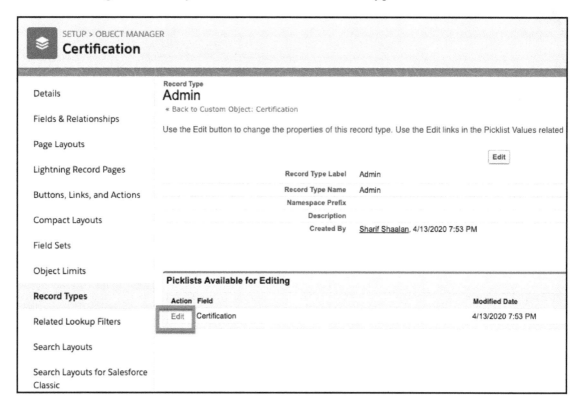

As shown in the preceding screenshot, all the picklists of the objects are available for editing.

In the following screenshot, you can see the option to **Add** and **Remove** values to/from the picklist for this specific record type:

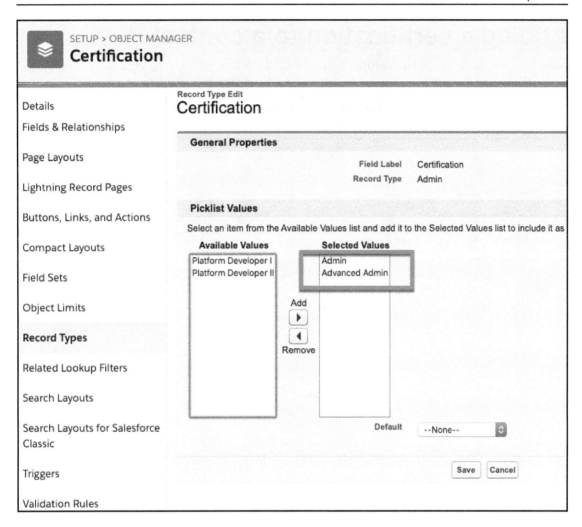

From the preceding screenshot, you can see that I have added the Admin certifications for the **Admin Record Type**. Replicate this exercise for the **Developer Record Type**.

Record types allow us to have flexibility when working with an object. We can show different page layouts and different picklist field values based on which record type is chosen. This makes it easier for Admins to use an object for multiple purposes within a similar business case.

Adding a certification to a contact

Now that we have created a custom object, created custom fields, created a page layout, and created record types, let's learn how to add a **Certification** to a **Contact**:

1. Navigate to the **Contacts** tab **(1)**, as shown in the following screenshot:

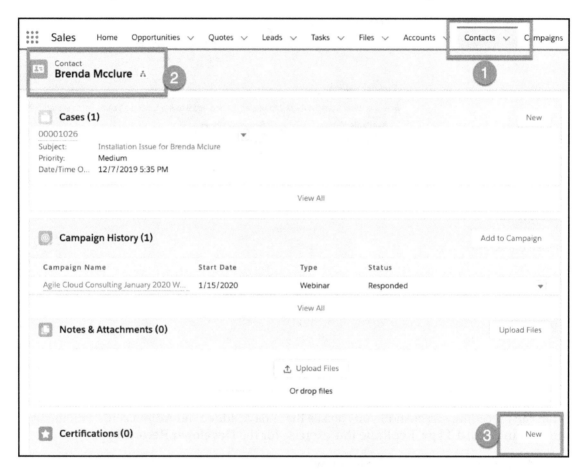

In the preceding screenshot, you can see that I navigated to the **Brenda Mcclure** contact **(2)** and scrolled down to the **Certifications** section. Click on **New (3)** to add a new certification.

2. In the following screenshot, you can see the record type selection screen:

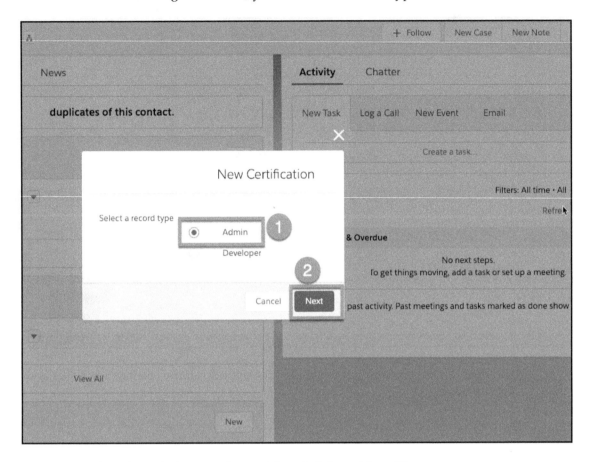

3. Select the **Admin** record type **(1)** and click on **Next (2)**.

In the following screenshot, you can see the **Certification** edit page:

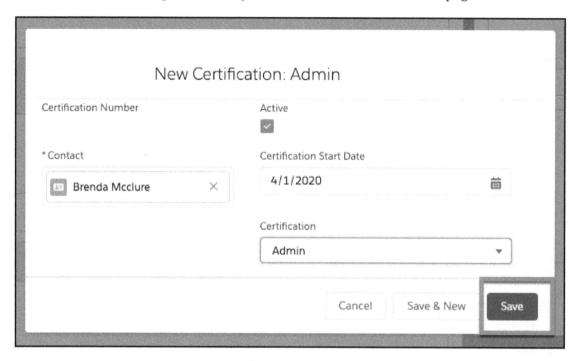

As shown in the preceding screenshot, I have filled out the certification fields and clicked **Save**.

In the following screenshot, you can see the newly created certification:

As shown in the preceding screenshot, the **Admin** certification has been created. Let's go over what we have learned in this chapter.

Summary

In this chapter, we learned how to create a custom object. We learned how to add elements to a custom object, such as relationship fields that allow you to tie objects together. We also learned how to create page layouts and record types so that we can control how picklist values are displayed. With the skills you've learned in this chapter, you can extend Salesforce using *clicks, not code* to handle multiple use cases outside of standard objects.

In the next chapter, we will learn about third-party applications and setting up Salesforce Mobile.

Questions

1. Why would you create a master-detail relationship as opposed to a lookup relationship?
2. What are some of the optional features when creating a custom object?
3. What are the two types of internal relationship fields you can create on an object?
4. What part of the page layout shows related items on a record?
5. What is a possible use case for using record types?

Further reading

- **Creating custom objects**: https://help.salesforce.com/articleView?id=dev_objectcreate_task_parent.htmtype=5
- **Creating custom fields**: https://help.salesforce.com/articleView?id=adding_fields.htmtype=5
- **Page layouts**: https://help.salesforce.com/articleView?id=customize_layout.htmtype=5
- **Lightning page layouts**: https://help.salesforce.com/articleView?id=layouts_in_lex.htmtype=5
- **Creating record types**: https://trailhead.salesforce.com/en/content/learn/projects/customize-a-salesforce-object/create-record-types

13
Third-Party Applications and Salesforce Mobile

One of the core tenets of requirements gathering for a business is not re-inventing the wheel. This means that if someone has already built the functionality you are looking to implement, why not use it? In the Salesforce ecosystem, third-party applications serve this purpose. Third-party applications are created and published for installation on Salesforce AppExchange, and they can be free or paid for. Another hot topic for business requirements gathering is accessing Salesforce through your mobile phone or tablet.

In this chapter, we will cover the following topics in detail:

- Using third-party applications
    - What are managed and unmanaged package applications?
    - Using Salesforce AppExchange
    - Installing third-party applications
    - Uninstalling third-party applications
- Configuring Salesforce Mobile using the Mobile App Quickstart

With the help of these topics, you will be able to understand business use cases for third-party applications. You will also find out how to find, install, and uninstall a package. Finally, you will learn how to easily configure the Salesforce Mobile App experience. These skills will help the Salesforce admin to become more efficient in finding possible pre-built solutions as well as help the admin to set up Salesforce Mobile quicker through clicks, not code, when a functionality is requested by users.

Technical requirements

For this chapter, log in to your development org and follow along as we find, install, and uninstall a third-party application as well as configure Salesforce Mobile.

Using third-party applications

Third-party applications are a way to find and use business-specific functionality that may be needed as an add-on to the Salesforce platform. Think of Salesforce as similar to your iPhone or Android phone. While the platform is robust and delivers a lot of functionality out of the box, some things are not there and must be custom-built or installed as an add-on.

The job of an admin or business analyst is to perform a cost-benefit analysis to determine whether an organization should custom build functionality or decide to go with a third-party application. There are two types of third-party applications, managed and unmanaged. We will study them in the following sections.

Managed and unmanaged package applications

Managed package applications are applications that are built by a publisher and the code is *managed*, meaning it is not open source and available for all to see. The intellectual property of the code is protected with a managed package, which has other benefits, as follows:

- The package can be published and listed on Salesforce AppExchange for free or as a paid option.

- The package is *upgradeable,* meaning the publisher can push an update or allow admins to install an update.

Unmanaged package applications are applications that are usually built in a dev org similar to the one you are using for this book. These packages are open source, meaning all of the code is visible, and are typically not for sale. The unmanaged packages are not upgradeable once installed. These applications are usually used to move functionality from one Salesforce environment to the other. This would be one production Salesforce environment to another production Salesforce environment since change sets would not work in that use case. When discussing third-party applications within the context of Salesforce AppExchange, the applications are always managed. Let's see how this works.

Business use case

You are the Salesforce admin for XYZ Widgets. Your executive team wants to make sure Salesforce has maximum adoption and asks you to build a dashboard to track user adoption progress using some key metrics. This will be a big project for you and needs to be prioritized. If only there was a way to make this easier—"*Other organizations have to be doing this!*", you think to yourself. After doing some research, you find out that Salesforce Labs, a publisher that provides free applications on Salesforce AppExcahnge, has built this exact dashboard and made it available for free! Let's find it and install it!

Using Salesforce AppExchange

Salesforce AppExchange is a marketplace for apps that you can find and install on the Salesforce platform. There are both free and paid apps. Let's take a look at how to find an app on AppExchange:

1. Navigate to `https://AppExchange.salesforce.com/`, which takes us to the landing page with a few categories of available solutions, as shown in the following screenshot:

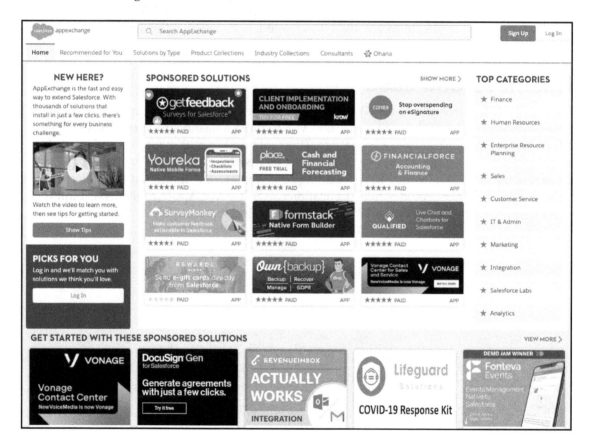

2. In the search bar, look for a keyword based on our business use case. Here, I have searched for **Adoption** (1). This brought up some options that include the word *adoption* such as **Salesforce Adoption Dashboards** (2), which is exactly what you need! Refer to the following screenshot for this:

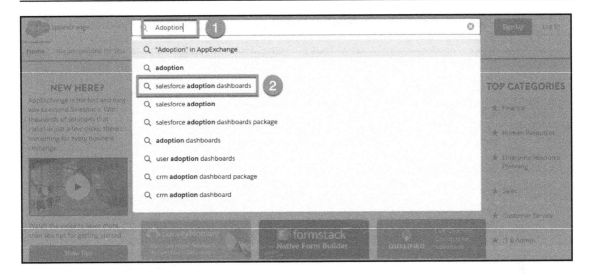

By selecting **Salesforce Adoption Dashboards**, you land on the following screen:

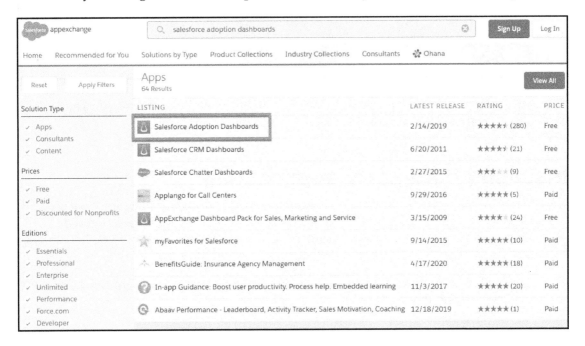

3. Clicking on **Salesforce Adoption Dashboards** brings us to the following page:

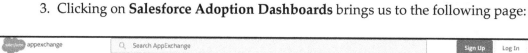

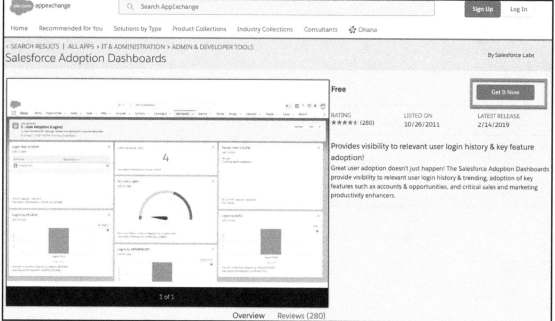

This is the Salesforce Labs app you were looking for! After reading some reviews and checking the great ratings, you decide to install this app.

Installing third-party applications

Now that we have found the app we're looking for, we decide to install it. Since we are working in a dev org, we will install it in production, since a dev org is considered a production org. You would normally install an app in a sandbox to test it if you had a paid Salesforce production org. Let's take a look at how to install the app:

1. In the following screenshot, you can see the page you are brought to when you click on **Get it Now**:

Here, you have the option to log in using Salesforce credentials or continue as a guest. We will choose to log in using Salesforce credentials.

2. Then, once logged in with your Salesforce credentials, you have the option to install in production or a sandbox. We chose to install this app in production since we are using a dev org, as shown in the following screenshot:

Once we choose to install in production, we are brought to the following screen:

3. After agreeing to the terms and conditions (1), click on **Confirm and Install** (2).

This brings us to the following screen, where we can choose whom to install the application for. I chose **Install for All Users** (1) and clicked **Install** (2):

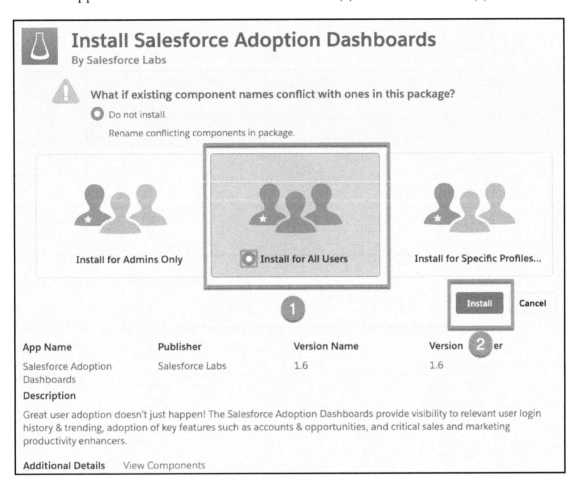

Installing it will bring up the following screen, which will last a few minutes at most:

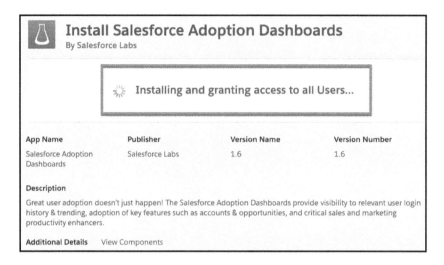

Sometimes it will time out and give you a message that you will be emailed when the installation is complete if it is a big package.

4. Once the installation is complete, you will see the following screen:

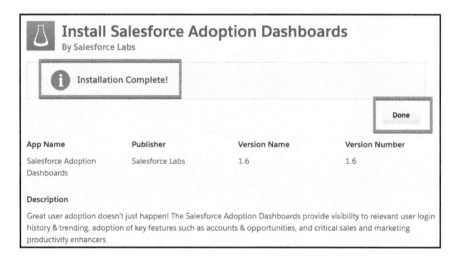

Now that the package is installed, clicking on **Done** will bring you to the following screen:

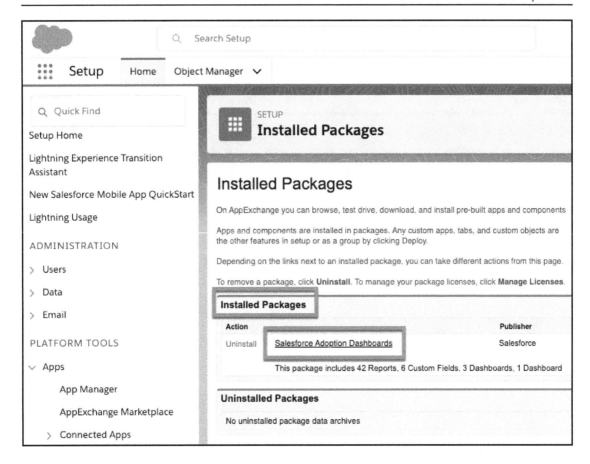

The preceding screenshot shows you that the package has been installed under the **Installed Packages** section. Clicking on the package name will allow you to see the package components such as any **Tabs**, **Custom Fields**, **Custom Page Layouts**, **Apex Classes**, or any other components that are included in the installed package.

Now, let's take a look at the installed dashboard in the following screenshot:

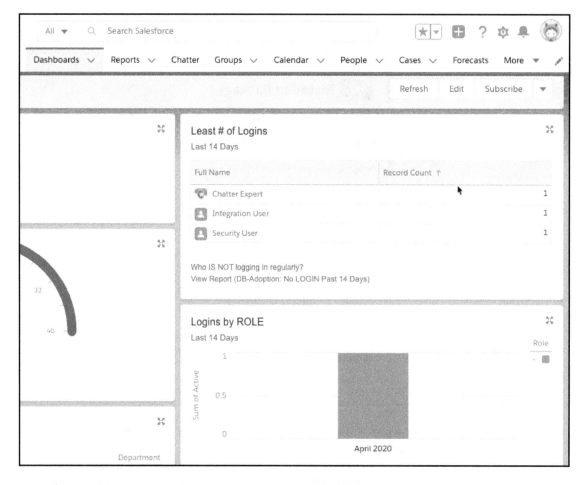

As you can see in the preceding screenshot, the user adoption dashboard now shows up for all users. Now, let's take a look at how to uninstall the package if you ever need to do so.

Uninstalling third-party applications

To uninstall an application, navigate to the **Setup** section. In the following screenshot, you can see I typed `Installed` in the **Setup** search bar to bring up the **Installed Packages** section:

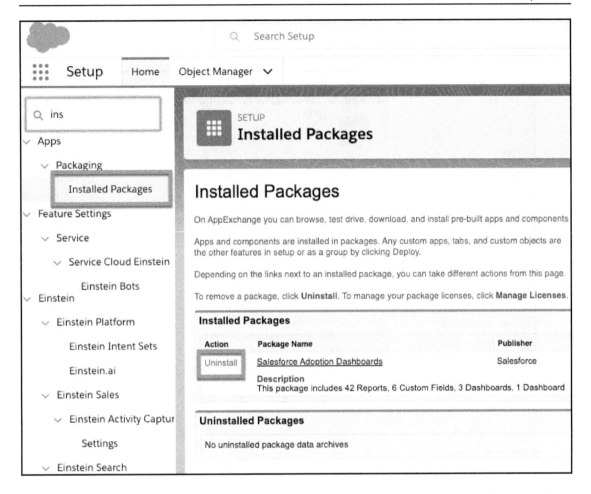

Once you are on the **Installed Packages** page, click on **Uninstall** as shown in the preceding screenshot.

This will bring you to the following screen where all of the components that are to be uninstalled will appear:

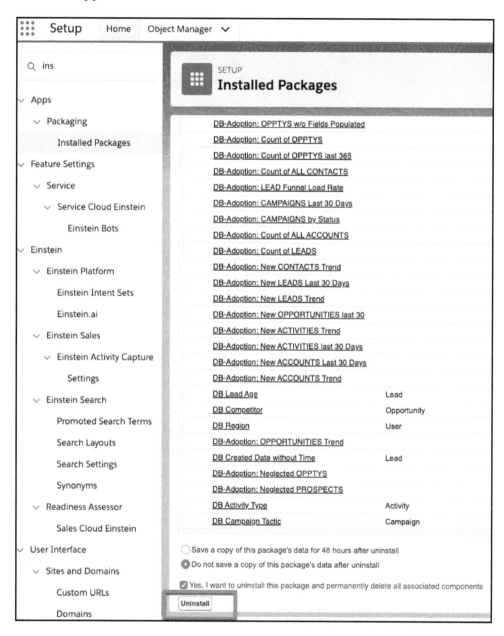

I chose not to save a copy of the package and clicked on **Uninstall**, which brings us to the following screen:

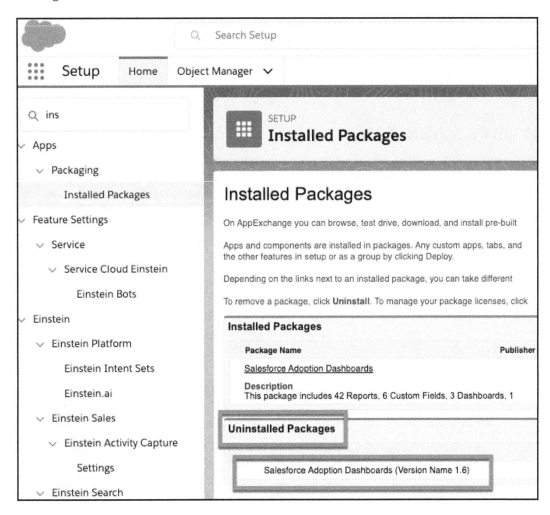

As you can see in the preceding screenshot, the package is now uninstalled and shows up under the **Uninstalled Packages** section.

Now that you have learned how to find, install, and uninstall a package, let's look at how you would set up Salesforce Mobile for your organization.

Configuring Salesforce Mobile using the Mobile App Quickstart

Salesforce provides a quickstart to help you to set up the mobile experience for your users. The quickstart includes a few intuitive configuration sections. So, let's take a look at how to navigate to these sections.

Business use case

As the admin for XYZ Widgets, your users have requested the ability to use Salesforce on their mobile devices. You need to get this up and running quickly for a quick win. This should be very straightforward since Salesforce provides a mobile app out of the box. You go to the Mobile App Quickstart to set this up.

So, first, we navigate to the **Setup** section of Salesforce, as shown in the following screenshot:

Once in the **Setup** section, click on **New Salesforce Mobile App Quickstart**, as you can see in the preceding screenshot.

The following screenshot shows the first three options available in the Mobile App Quickstart:

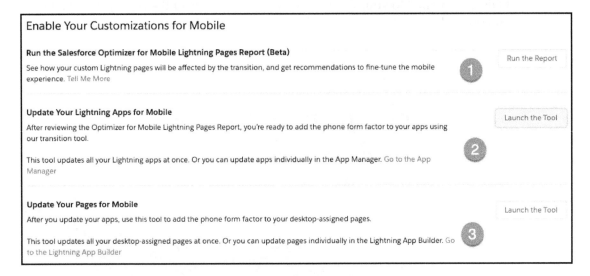

Enable Your Customizations for Mobile

Run the Salesforce Optimizer for Mobile Lightning Pages Report (Beta)

See how your custom Lightning pages will be affected by the transition, and get recommendations to fine-tune the mobile experience. Tell Me More

Run the Report

1

Update Your Lightning Apps for Mobile

After reviewing the Optimizer for Mobile Lightning Pages Report, you're ready to add the phone form factor to your apps using our transition tool.

This tool updates all your Lightning apps at once. Or you can update apps individually in the App Manager. Go to the App Manager

Launch the Tool

2

Update Your Pages for Mobile

After you update your apps, use this tool to add the phone form factor to your desktop-assigned pages.

This tool updates all your desktop-assigned pages at once. Or you can update pages individually in the Lightning App Builder. Go to the Lightning App Builder

Launch the Tool

3

The options are explained as follows:

- **Run the Salesforce Optimizer for Mobile Lightning Pages Report (1)**: This report will show you how your custom Lightning pages will be affected in the mobile experience. When you click **Run the Report**, the report is generated as a PDF and emailed to you. The following is an example of the page you see when you open the report:

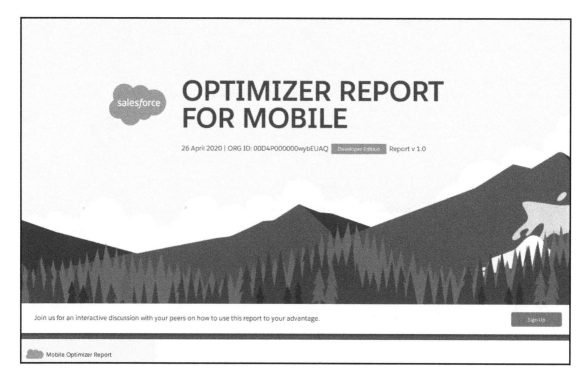

This report contains all of the recommendations for setting up a mobile in the context of your current setup. Let's look at the next available option on the quickstart.

- **Update Your Lightning Apps for Mobile (2):** This section will automatically update all of your apps and make them ready for the mobile experience. When you click on **Launch the Tool,** you will get a popup with all of the apps available to update, as shown in the following screenshot:

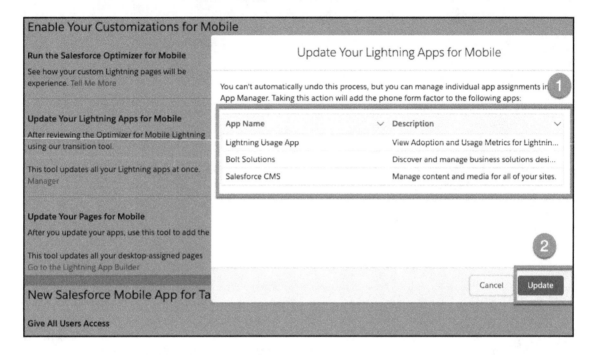

Once you click on **Update**, your lightning apps will be updated. Let's look at the next available option on the quickstart.

- **Update Your Pages for Mobile (3)**: This tool allows you to make your desktop-assigned pages ready for mobile. This will also come up as a popup when you click on **Launch the Tool**, as shown here:

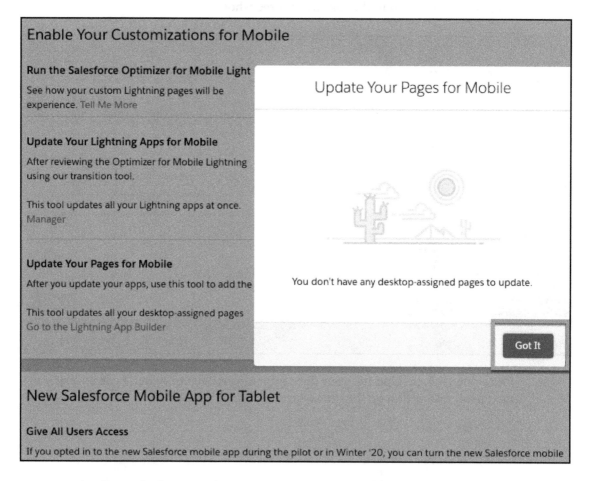

As shown in the preceding screenshot, in my org I didn't have any desktop assigned pages; if you do, they will show up here and you can update. Let's look at the next set of options on the quickstart.

The following screenshot shows the final four options available in the Mobile App quickstart:

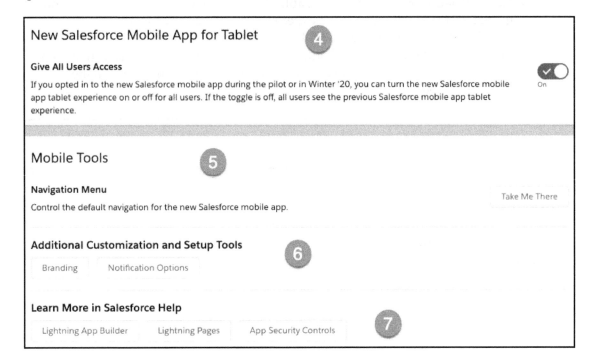

The options are explained as follows:

- **New Salesforce Mobile App for Tablet (4)**: This section allows you to turn on the Salesforce Mobile App tablet experience for all users using a toggle switch. Let's look at the next available option on the quickstart.
- **Mobile tools (5)**: This section allows you to control the default navigation menu for the mobile app. When you click on **Take Me There**, you will be on the following screen:

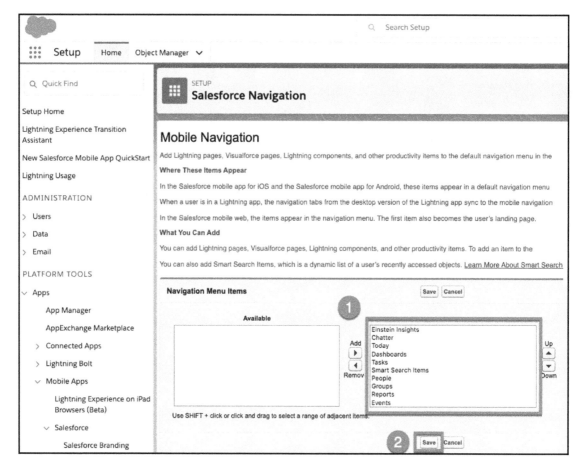

As you can see, you can add all of the navigation tabs you wish to show up on the mobile experience (1) and click **Save** (2). Let's look at the next available option on the quickstart.

- **Additional Customization and Setup Tools (6)**: This section allows you to set up branding and notification options for your mobile app. The following screenshot shows the branding page:

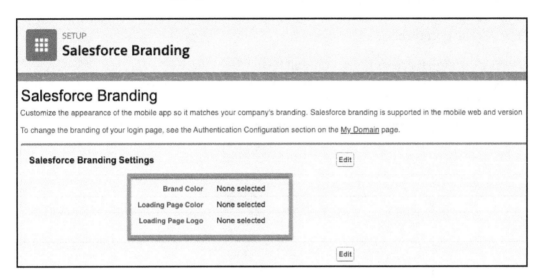

You now have the option to add a brand color, loading page color, and loading page logo to your mobile app. In the following screenshot, you can see the notification options page:

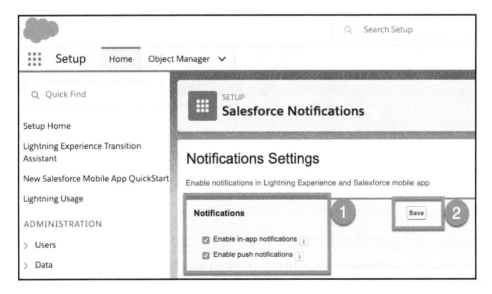

Here we have enabled in-app and/or push notifications **(1)** and saved our settings **(2)**. Let's look at the final available option on the Quickstart.

- **Salesforce Help** (7): This section gives you further resources related to configuration options for a Lightning App Builder, Lightning pages, and app security controls.

After going through these sections, you will have what you need to launch Salesforce Mobile for your users! Let's take a look at what the mobile app looks like. The following screenshot shows the mobile login screen:

As you can see, I added my username and password and clicked on **Log In**. This will take me to the following screen:

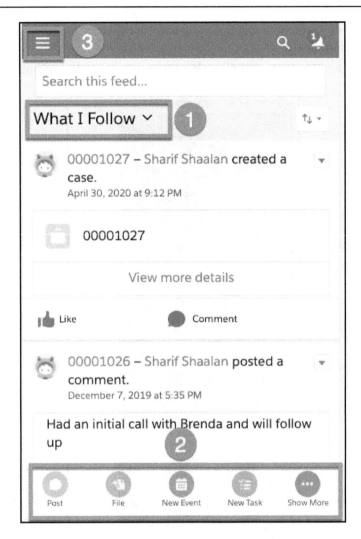

As you can see in the preceding screenshot, there are several sections on the mobile app landing page:

- **What I Follow**: This section shows the latest activity on records you follow in Salesforce through Chatter.

- The actions at the bottom allow you to take the same actions you would in Salesforce desktop.
- Clicking on the menu in the top-left takes you to the following screen:

As you can see, this section allows you to navigate to any of the objects you have access to in Salesforce to access the records on those objects.

Now that we have set up Salesforce Mobile and seen how the screens look, let's summarize what we have learned in this chapter.

Summary

In this chapter, we learned what third-party applications are. We learned that there are two types of applications, managed and unmanaged, and we covered the use cases for using each of these. We gained the skills needed to find an application and install it, and we learned how to uninstall the application if needed.

In this chapter, we also learned that Salesforce provides the Mobile App Quickstart. We learned how to get to the quickstart and explored the different sections included in the quickstart to configure the mobile experience.

This concludes the administration section of this book. Our final section will cover automation starting with workflows in the next chapter!

Questions

You can now answer the following questions:

1. What is a use case for an unmanaged package?
2. What is the benefit of using a managed package?
3. What is the name of the Salesforce marketplace where you can find apps?
4. What are some of the access options you can grant when installing a package?
5. What is an option you have when uninstalling a package?
6. What is the best way to set up Salesforce Mobile for your users?

Further reading

- Understanding packages: `https://help.salesforce.com/articleView?id=sharing_apps.htmtype=5`
- Salesforce AppExchange: `https://AppExchange.salesforce.com/`
- Getting started with the mobile app: `https://trailhead.salesforce.com/en/content/learn/modules/salesforce1_mobile_app/salesforce1_mobile_app_intro`

3
Section 3: Automating Business Processes Using Salesforce

In this section, we will discuss the tools that are available to you to automate business processes. These tools include workflow rules, Process Builder, approvals, assignment rules, flows, and custom development.

This section covers the following chapters:

- Chapter 14, *Understanding the Workflow Rules*
- Chapter 15, *Implementing Process Builder*
- Chapter 16, *Approval Processes*
- Chapter 17, *Assignment Rules*

Understanding the Workflow Rules

14

Business process automation is one of the most important aspects of being a Salesforce system administrator. Taking manual processes and creating automation around those processes saves time and leads to better efficiency all around for your organization. The first type of automation tool we will cover from this chapter onward is workflow rules. Workflow rules allow you to create workflow actions based on a triggering event such as a field update. Workflow actions can be field updates, sending emails, creating tasks, or creating outbound messages.

In this chapter, we will cover the following topics in detail:

- Creating workflow rules
- Setting evaluation and rule criteria
- Creating immediate workflow actions
- Creating time-dependent workflow actions

With the help of these topics, you will be able to understand the business use case for creating workflow rules. You will understand how to create rules, set evaluation and rule criteria, and how to create immediate and time-dependent workflow actions. These skills will help you automate business processes for your organization using workflow rules. Ultimately, this will lead to higher efficiency and fewer errors by your users.

Technical requirements

For this chapter, log in to your development org and follow along as we create a workflow rule from start to finish.

Creating workflow rules

Workflow rules are a great way to execute business logic automatically. Knowing the capabilities of workflows will help you come up with efficient solutions for your users that lead to fewer clicks and cleaner data. Let's take a look at how this is done.

Business use case

You are the Salesforce admin for XYZ Widgets. The sales manager has a use case where, when a sale is closed, a few things are done manually by the sales rep:

1. **Delivery Installation Status** is set to **In progress.**
2. A schedule installation task is created and assigned to an onboarding rep.
3. An email is sent to the sales manager.
4. A task is created for the sales rep to follow up 30 days after the sale closes.

As you analyze the requirements, you determine that all of this can be done within one workflow rule! Let's see how this is built.

Creating workflow rules

To create the workflow rule, we perform the following steps:

1. Navigate to the setup and configuration page **Home** tab (1) | **Workflow Rules** (2) | **New Rule** (3) as you can see in the following screenshot:

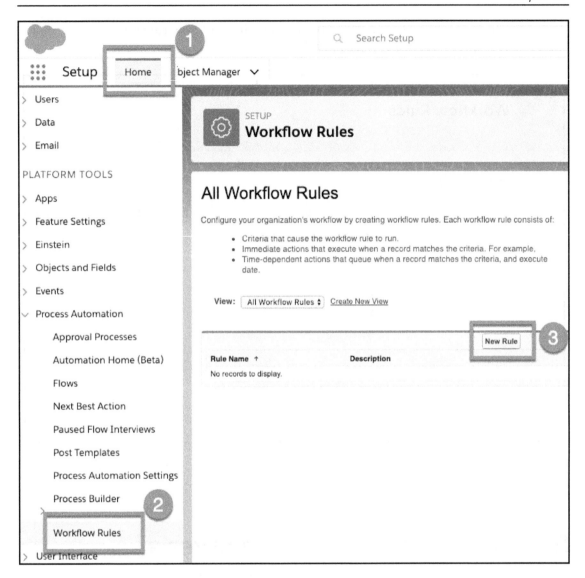

2. The next step is choosing the object where the workflow rule is being built, which is shown in the following screenshot:

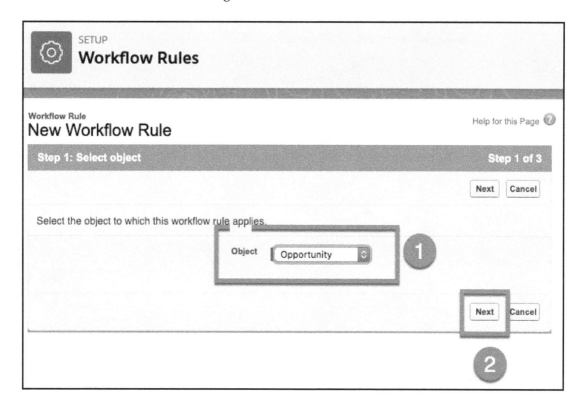

Here, we select the **Opportunity** object (1) and then click on **Next** (2), which takes us to the evaluation and rule criteria section. Let's take a look at what that looks like.

Setting evaluation and rule criteria

The evaluation criteria determine how the rule is to be evaluated in order for it to be triggered. The rule criteria determine the change in the data that will cause the rule to be triggered. Let's look at this in detail.

We navigate to the **Workflow Rules** page, as shown in the following screenshot (which we learned about in the *Creating workflow rules* section):

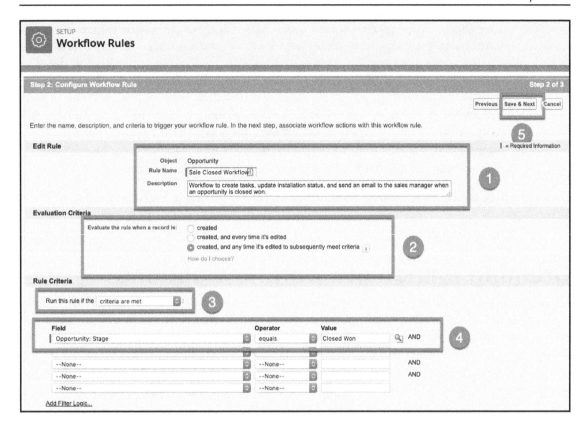

As you can see in the preceding screenshot, there are several sections included on this page:

1. In section (1), we enter **Rule Name** and **Description** based on the business use case.
2. In section (2), we set the evaluation criteria, from the following three options:
   - **created**: This means the rule is evaluated anytime, and only when, a record is created.
   - **created, and every time it's edited**: This means the rule is evaluated anytime a record is created *and* anytime the record is edited thereafter.
   - **created, and any time it's edited to subsequently meet the criteria**: This means the rule is evaluated anytime a record is created *and* if it is updated to meet certain criteria (the rule criteria). For our business use case, we chose this option since we only want it to evaluate if **Opportunity Stage** changes to **Closed Won**.

   The time-dependent workflow would not work if the evaluation criterion was **created, and every time it's edited**.

3. In section (3), you can choose to run the rule if **criteria are met** or if **formula evaluates to true**. The formula option can be used for more complex criteria such as using a formula function. This option uses the API name of the field in the formula. For example, if we were to use a formula for our current example, the formula would be `StageName = "Closed Won"`. The formula option can be used for more complex rule criteria. Since our business use case is only using the change of one field, we will use **criteria are met**.

4. In section (4), the rule criteria are set to meet the business use case. The rule will trigger anytime **Opportunity Stage** is changed to **Closed Won**.

On saving this, we land on the next section, which is for creating immediate workflow actions.

Creating immediate workflow actions

There are several types of workflow actions. In this business use case, we will cover field updates, email alerts, and auto task creation. There is one other action that will not be covered in our use case: outbound messages. Outbound messages are used to send messages with field updates to external systems if a field is changed in Salesforce. Outbound messages are outside of our example use case and more information regarding this action is available in the further reading links at the end of this chapter. Let's continue our use case.

After clicking on **Save & Next** in the previous section, we land on the **Immediate Workflow Actions** screen:

Here, we will create the first action in our use case. For that, click on **New Field Update** (1).

On the **Field Update Edit** screen, we will be editing a few fields to ensure we set the rules as per our use case. Please refer to the following screenshot:

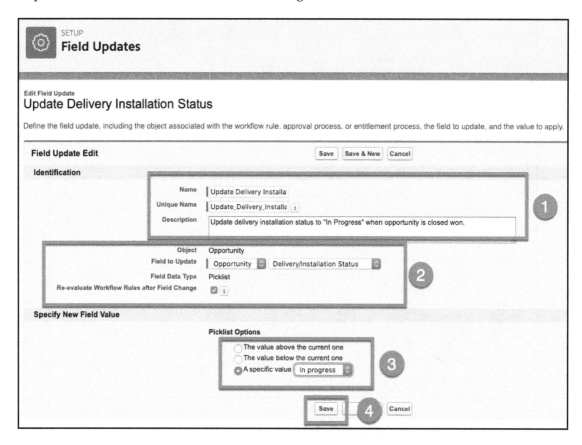

In the preceding screenshot, there are several important sections:

1. In section (1), we set the field update **Name**, **Unique Name**, and **Description**.
2. In section (2), we choose the field to update the **Delivery Installation Status**, and we choose to **Re-evaluate Workflow Rules after Field Change**. This means that if another workflow rule uses the new field value of **Delivery Installation Status** field (**In progress**) as a rule criteria, it will be triggered when this new update is made.
3. In section (3), we set the new value for **Delivery Installation Status** to **In progress**.

Save it to complete the creation of this workflow action. This action will now update **Delivery Installation Status** to **In progress** when **Opportunity Stage** is changed to **Closed Won** on the opportunity object. Let's take a look at the next workflow action.

After clicking **Save** in the previous step, we land back on the **Immediate Workflow Actions** screen:

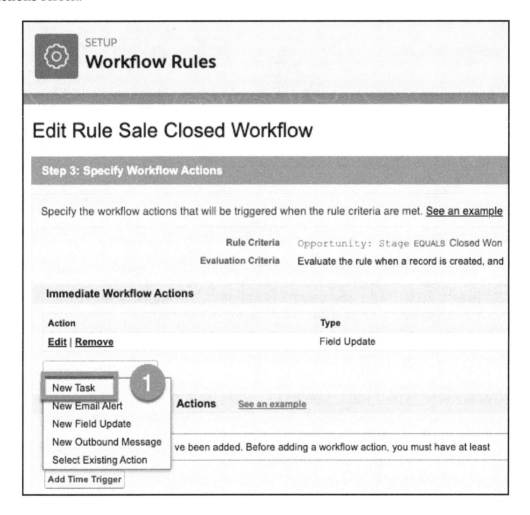

We will now create the second action in our use case. Click on **New Task** (1), which takes you to the **New Task** screen:

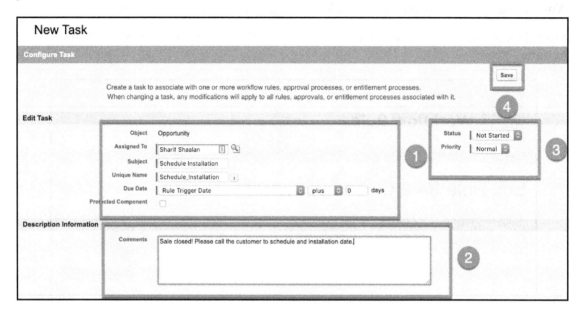

Here, you can see that there are several important sections; let's see what those are:

1. In section (1), we set who the task is **Assigned To**, **Subject**, **Unique Name,** and when we want the task that is auto-created to be due.
2. In section (2), we add the comments we want to show up on the task.
3. In section (3), we can preset **Status** and **Priority,** which have been set as **Not Started** and **Normal** respectively.

Click **Save** to complete the creation of this workflow action. This action will now auto-create a new installation task for the onboarding rep when **Opportunity Stage** is changed to **Closed Won** on the opportunity object.

Next, let's add the email alert action related to our use case.

After clicking on **Save** in the previous step, you can see we are back on the **Immediate Workflow Actions** screen:

We will now create the third action in our use case. Click on **New Email Alert** (1), which will take you to the **Email Alerts** screen, as shown in the following screenshot:

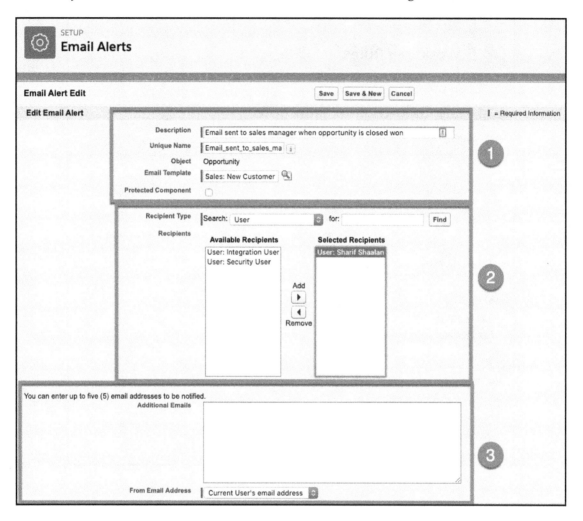

Here, you can see that there are several important sections:

1. In section (1), we set **Description**, **Unique Name**, and **Email Template** used for the email alert.
2. In section (2), we set **Recipient Type** and the selected recipient that will receive this email alert.
3. In section (3), you can add up to five email addresses to be notified as well as **From Email Address**.

Click **Save** to complete the creation of this workflow action. This action will now send an email to the sales manager when **Opportunity Stage** is changed to **Closed Won** on the opportunity object. This concludes our immediate workflow actions. Let's take a look at the final time-dependent action that we need to build for this business use case.

Creating time-dependent workflow actions

Time-dependent workflow actions are the same four types as immediate workflow actions. The difference is time-dependent workflow actions use a defined time trigger to execute in the future. Let's take a look at how this works.

In the following screenshot, you can see that we scrolled down to the **Time-Dependent Workflow Actions** section of the screen:

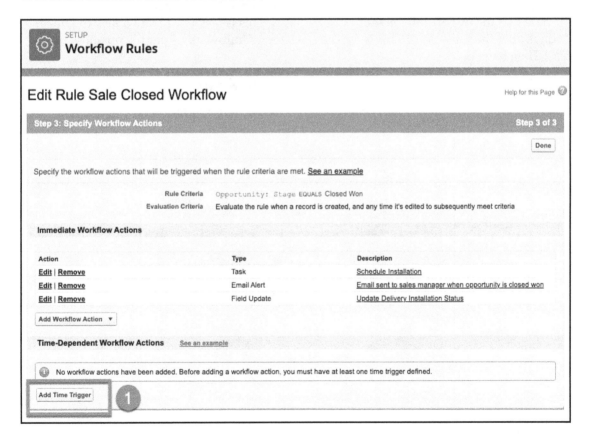

Click on **Add Time Trigger** (1).

The following screenshot shows how to set the time trigger for this workflow action:

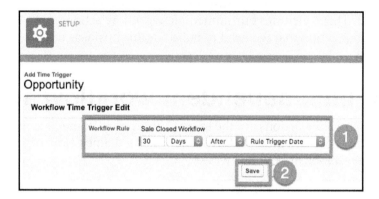

Here, we are setting this time trigger to **30 Days After** the **Rule Trigger Date** (1), which is the date that the opportunity is set to **Closed Won**. This is because I want a task to appear 30 days after the sale closes. This is for the sales rep to follow up as per the business use case. Then **Save** (2) it.

After this, we go back to the **Time-Dependent Workflow Actions** screen:

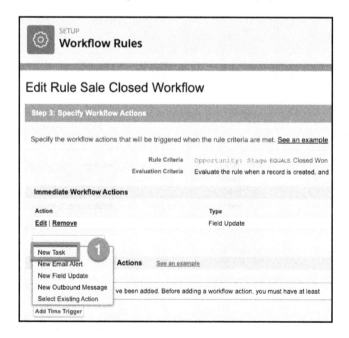

We will now create the final action in our use case. Click on **New Task** (1), which takes you to the **New Task** screen. This is the same screen we walked through when we created a task in the *Immediate Workflow Actions* section:

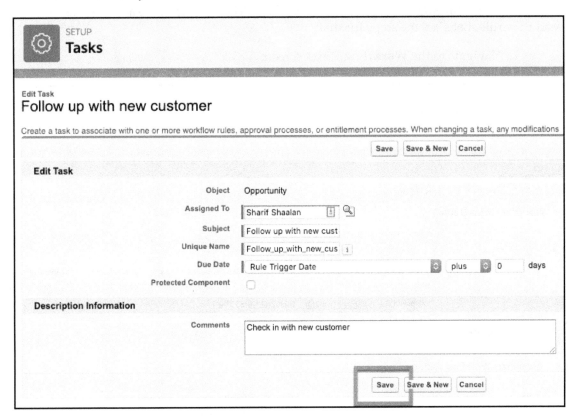

Then we enter all of the information for the sales rep follow-up task and click **Save** to complete the creation of this workflow action. This action will now auto-create a new sales rep follow-up 30 days from the day that **Opportunity Stage** is changed to **Closed Won** on the opportunity object. We are now done creating the rule! Let's activate and test this workflow.

Testing the workflow

Now that we have created the workflow rule to meet the business requirement, let's do an end-to-end walk-through to make sure it is working. The first step is to activate the workflow rule. Let's see the steps for that:

1. Navigate to the **Workflow Rules** screen:

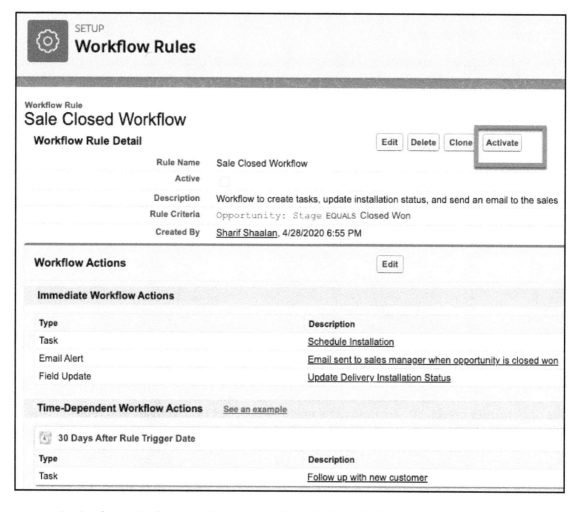

2. As shown in the preceding screenshot, click on **Activate** to make this workflow rule live.
3. Then navigate to the **Burlington Textiles Weaving Plant Generator** opportunity:

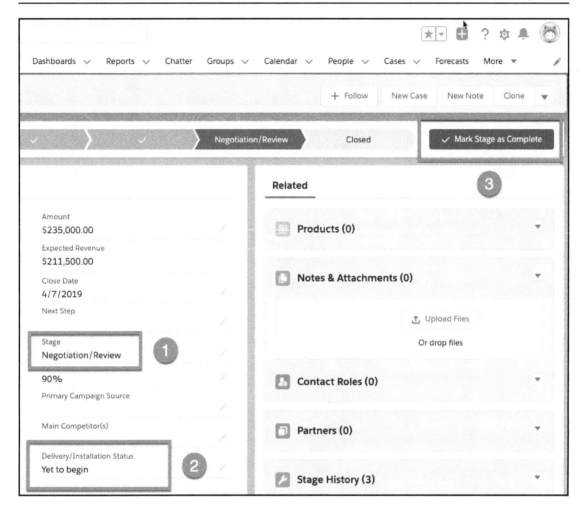

You can observe that **Stage** is **Negotiation/Review** (1) and **Delivery/Installation Status** is **Yet to begin** (2). In order to test this business use case, we should update **Stage** to **Closed Won** since that is the trigger that will run the workflow rule and create all of the actions. Once this is changed to **Closed Won**, we should expect to see the following:

1. **Delivery Installation Status** set to **In progress**
2. A schedule installation task created and assigned to an onboarding rep
3. An email sent to the sales manager
4. A task created for the sales rep to follow up 30 days after the sale closes

Let's change **Stage** to **Closed Won** (3).

In the following screenshot, you can see the popup that comes up when you click on **Mark Stage as Complete**:

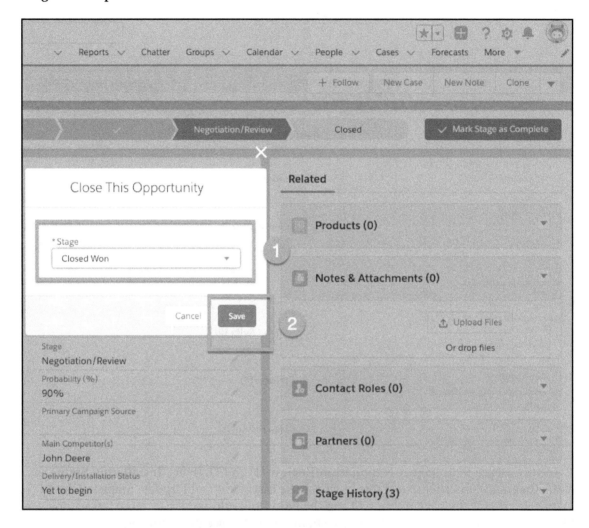

Here, we change **Stage** to **Closed Won** (1) and **Save** the record (2).

In the following screenshot, we can see the opportunity record after it is saved:

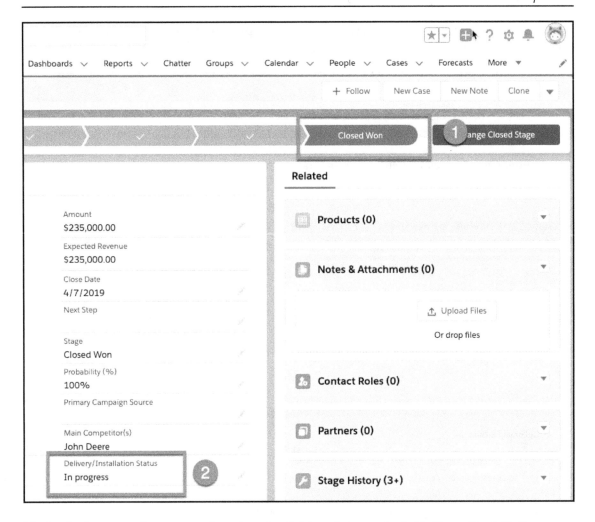

Notice in the preceding screenshot that the field update worked. **Delivery/Installation Status** automatically changed to **In progress**.

Next, let's navigate to the **Activity** (1) section on the opportunity to see whether the schedule installation task was automatically created:

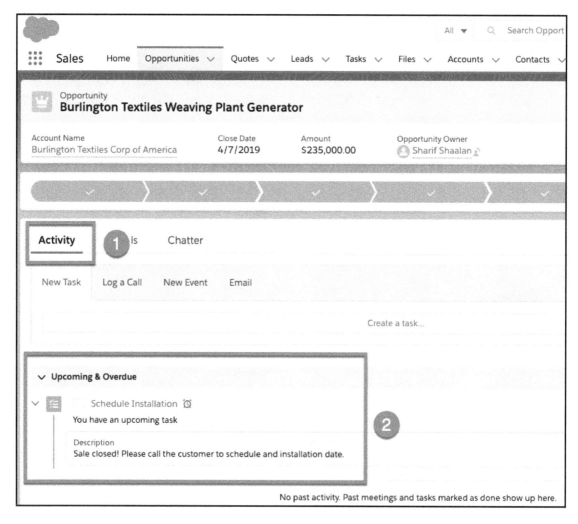

Here, we can see that the **Schedule Installation** task was automatically created (2).

Next, let's check on the time-based task for the sales rep to follow up, which is supposed to be created 30 days from now. How would we do that? Salesforce has a **Time-Based Workflow** monitoring feature. Let's see what that looks like, in the following screenshot:

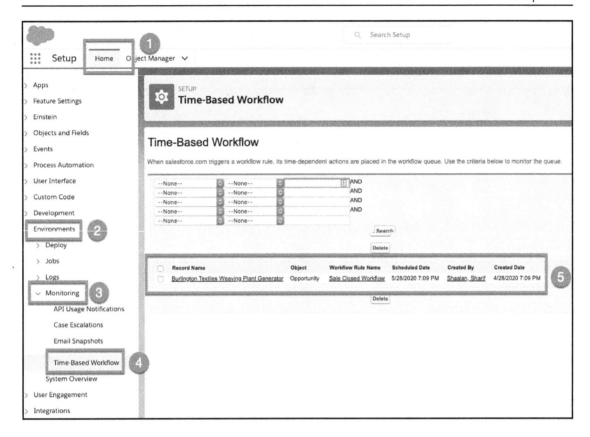

As you can see in the preceding screenshot, under **Setup** and configuration, I went to the
Home tab (1), | **Environments** (2) | **Monitoring** (3) | **Time-Based Workflow** (4). As you
can see, the task is scheduled to be created 30 days from now (5).

Finally, let's see whether the email was automatically sent out to the sales manager. Similar to the time-based workflow, there is an email log file that we can check. Let's see what that looks like, in the following screenshot:

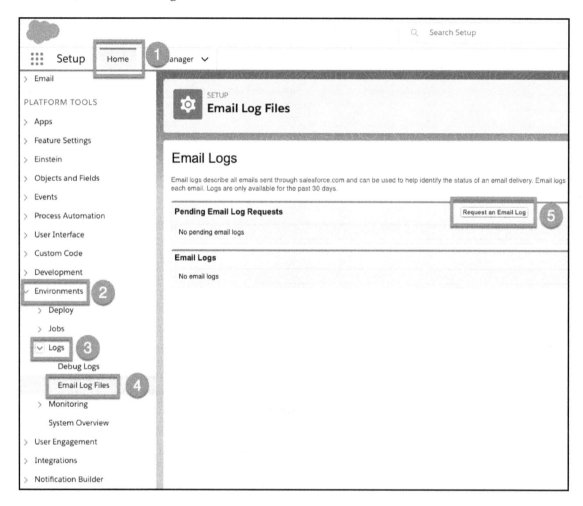

Once again, we navigate to **Home** | **Environments** (2) | **Logs** (3) | **Email Log Files** (4). You can click on **Request an Email Log** (5) to receive a log of all of the emails sent in the period you specify. This will come in the form of a CSV file you can download and check whether the auto email was sent out. This is done by searching for the email address that the email alert was supposed to go to within the spreadsheet.

All four of our actions were successful! This proves that the workflow rules worked well!

Summary

In this chapter, we learned what workflow rules are and the use case for using workflow rules to increase efficiency. We learned how to set rule criteria and evaluation criteria. We gained the skills needed to create immediate and time-based workflow actions including field updates, tasks, and email alerts. We learned what outbound messages are used for. This gives us the skills needed to turn business automation requirements into Salesforce technology solutions.

We also understood how to activate and test our workflow using a combination of checking the records and various log files. With the use of these skills, you will be able to troubleshoot and debug any issues with your workflow rules.

In the next chapter, we will cover process builders, which are similar to workflows but offer other automation features that are not available with workflow rules.

Questions

1. What are the three types of evaluation criteria?
2. What are the two options for adding rule criteria?
3. What are outbound messages used for?
4. On the field update section, what does the **Re-evaluate Workflow Rules after Field Changes** checkbox do?
5. What are time-based workflow actions?
6. How can you check whether a time-based workflow action was created?
7. How can you check whether an email alert was sent?

Further reading

- **Create a Workflow Rule:** `https://help.salesforce.com/articleView?id=workflow_rules_new.htmtype=5`
- **Workflow actions:** `https://help.salesforce.com/articleView?id=creating_workflow_rules_configure_actions.htmtype=5`

Implementing Process Builder

15

Similar to the upgrade from Salesforce Classic to Salesforce Lightning, Salesforce recently added an upgraded automation tool called **Process Builder**. While Salesforce still supports workflow rules, all-new features are being added to Process Builder.

Process Builder is different from workflow rules in several ways. To start, Process Builder allows you to automate more items, such as creating all types of records, as opposed to just creating tasks with workflow rules. Process Builder also allows you to update any related record, as opposed to updating only the record or its parent with workflow rules. It also lets you control the execution order of your criteria, a feature not available with workflow rules.

In this chapter, we will cover the following topics in detail:

- Creating a process
- Adding an object and criteria
- Setting immediate actions
- Adding a second criteria
- Setting scheduled actions
- Process Builder best practice

With the help of these topics, you will be able to understand the business use case for creating a process. You will understand how to create a process using Process Builder, set the object and execution criteria, and how to set immediate and scheduled actions. These skills will help you automate business processes for your organization, leading to higher efficiency and fewer errors being made by your users.

Technical requirements

For this chapter, log into your development organization and follow along as we create a process from start to finish.

Creating a process

Process Builder is a great tool that's used to execute business logic automatically. Knowing the capabilities of Process Builder will help you come up with efficient solutions for your users that lead to fewer clicks and cleaner data. Let's take a look at how this is done.

Business use case

You are the Salesforce Admin for XYZ Widgets. The Sales Manager has a use case where, when a sale is closed, a few things need to happen, listed as follows:

- An open case needs to be created for the installation appointment.
- If the opportunity amount is greater than $200,000, a task needs to be created for the sales representative to follow this up, 30 days after the sale closes.
- If the opportunity amount is greater than $200,000, an email alert needs to go out to the sales manager.

As you analyze the requirements, you determine that all of this can be done within one Process Builder! Let's learn how we can build this.

Creating a process

To create a process, navigate to the **Setup** page, as shown in the following screenshot:

From here, click on the **Home** tab (**1**), then on **Process Builder** (**2**).

This will take you to the next step of creating the process, as shown in the following screenshot:

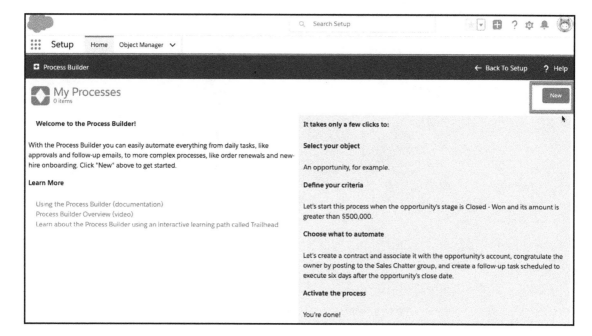

Click on **New** to start creating the process. This leads to the following pop-up opening:

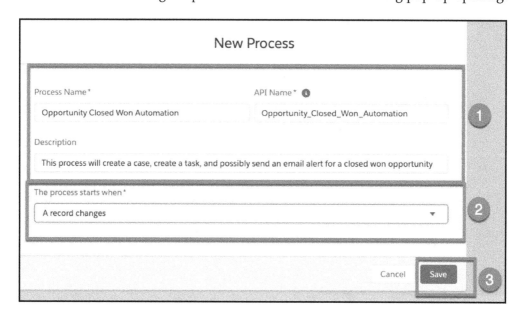

From the preceding screenshot, you can see that we have taken the following actions (the numbers in the following list correlate to the ones provided in the screenshot):

1. We add the **Process Name**, **API Name**, and **Description** for the process.
2. Then, we set the **The process starts when** field to **A record changes**, which means the process will run when a record is edited. In our business use case, this will be when the stage is set to Closed Won.
3. Click on **Save**.

After saving, you will be prompted to add an object and criteria.

Adding an object and criteria

The first step in building the process is adding the primary object that this process will be triggered by. In our business use case, this is the **Opportunity** object since closing a sale will trigger the actions. Consider the following screenshot, which shows how to add an object:

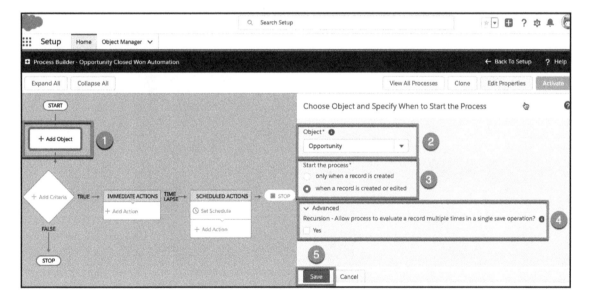

From the preceding screenshot, you can see that we have performed a few actions, as follows (the numbers in the following list correlate to the ones provided in the screenshot):

1. Click on the **+ Add Object** box, which brings up the section on the right.
2. Then, set **Object** to **Opportunity** since we are triggering the process when an **Opportunity** stage is changed to Closed Won.
3. Here, I want to start the process **when a record is created or edited** since a sales representative may set the stage to Closed Won when they create or edit an opportunity. The other available option here is to start the process only **when a record is created**.
4. There is an advanced option here to **Allow the process to evaluate a record multiple times in a single save operation**. This is useful for more complex processes where other automation processes may be executing on the record. We will leave this set to false for our business use case.
5. Click on **Save** to move on to the next step, which is adding criteria.

Next, we need to add the first criteria for this process. Refer to the following screenshot:

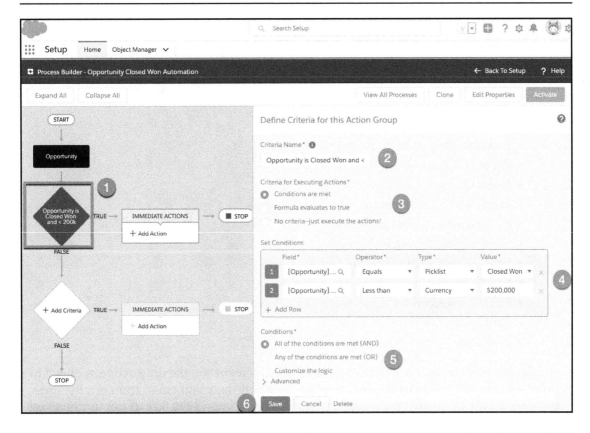

From the preceding screenshot, we can see the following (the numbers in the following list correlate to the ones provided in the screenshot):

1. First, click on **Add Criteria**.
2. I set the criteria name to `Opportunity is Closed Won and < 200k`.
3. I want to execute the criteria only when **Conditions are met**.
4. Next, I set the conditions as per the use case, where the first criteria will be when an opportunity is **Closed Won** and the amount is less than **$200,000**.
5. All of the conditions in *step 3* have to be met for Process Builder to fire.
6. Finally, **Save** it.

Now that we have added the object and the first set of criteria for Process Builder, let's take a look at how to set immediate actions.

Setting immediate actions

Once the object and criteria have been set, the next step is to add immediate actions that will take place if the criteria evaluate to true. The available actions include the ability to do the following:

- Create a Record from a Process
- Invoke a Process from Another Process
- Create a Chatter Post from a Process
- Use a Quick Action from a Process
- Work with Quip Documents from a Process
- Launch a Flow from a Process
- Send an Email from a Process
- Send a Custom Notification from a Process
- Send a Survey Invitation from a Process
- Submit a Record for Approval from a Process
- Update Records from a Process
- Call Apex Code from a Process

Let's see how this works. As shown in the following screenshot, the only action we need to add for our use case is **Create a Case**. This is because the task and email from our business use case will only be created if the sale amount is greater than **$200,000**, as per our business use case. Let's see how the action is configured:

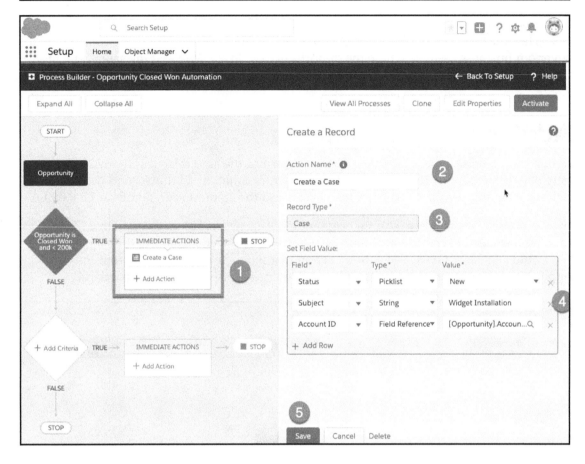

From the preceding screenshot, we can observe the following (the numbers in the following list correlate to the ones shown in the screenshot):

1. First, we click on **Add Action** and choose the **Create a Record** action.
2. Then, we enter the name of the action, which in this case is `Create a Case`.
3. Then, we set the following field values for the case that will be created:
   - **Status** as **New**.
   - **Subject** as **Widget Installation**.
   - **Account ID** will be the same account connected to the opportunity that started our Process Builder.
4. Finally, click on **Save** to complete this step.

Now that we have completed the use case for where the opportunity is Closed Won and the sale is less than $200,000, let's see what it looks like to add a second set of criteria. This will cover our business use case where the opportunity is Closed Won and the sale is greater than $200,000.

Adding a second criteria

In our first use case, where the sale is Closed Won and the amount is less than $200,000, we only had one action, which was to create a case for installation. In this second use case, we will see what happens if the sale is Closed Won and the amount is greater than $200,000.

In this use case, we still have to create an immediate action for case creation. In addition to that, we also need to create a new immediate action for the email alert to the manager, and we would also like to have a scheduled action that will take place 30 days from the opportunity close date. Let's see how the second criteria are added to our process:

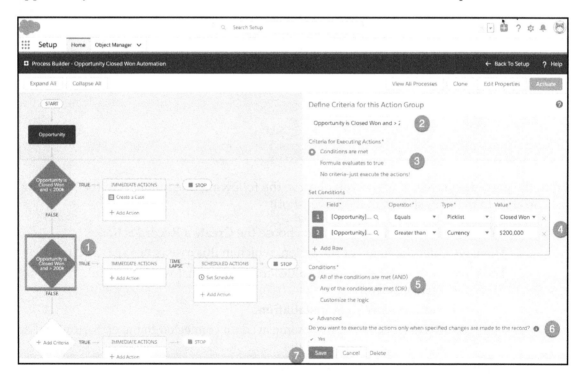

From the preceding screenshot, we can see the following (the numbers in the following list correlate to the ones shown in the screenshot):

1. First, we need to click on **Add Criteria**.
2. Then, we need to set the **Criteria Name** to `Opportunity is Closed Won and > 200k`.
3. I would like to execute the criteria only when **Conditions are met**.
4. As per the business use case, this first condition will be when an opportunity is Closed Won and the amount is greater than $200,000.
5. All of the conditions in *step 3* have to be met in order for Process Builder to fire.
6. I chose to execute the actions only when specified changes are made to the record, not every time the record is edited. *This is a necessary step in order to add scheduled actions to a process.*
7. Finally, we **Save** it.

Now that we have added our second criteria, let's see what it looks like to add the scheduled action needed for this business use case.

Setting scheduled actions

Our second criteria, where the sale is Closed Won and the amount is greater than $200,000, requires an action that takes place 30 days from the opportunity closed date, as per our business use case. In this section, we will learn how to do this.

First, navigate to **Scheduled Actions** on the second criteria, as shown in the following screenshot:

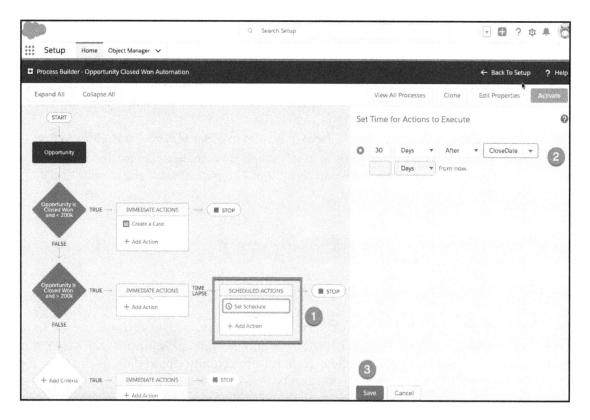

From the preceding screenshot, we can see the following (the following numbers correlate to the ones shown in the screenshot):

1. First, we click on **Set Schedule**.
2. We choose **30 Days After** the opportunity **CloseDate** since that is when these actions need to happen.
3. Click on **Save** to move on to the next step.

Now, let's take a look at how to create the scheduled action, that is, creating a task for the Sales representative to follow up, 30 days after the opportunity close date. Refer to the following screenshot:

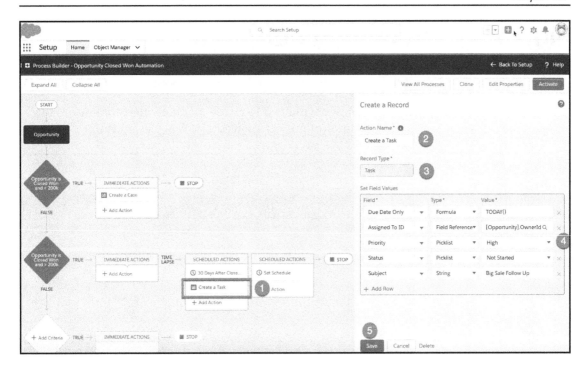

From the preceding screenshot, we can observe the following (the following numbers correlate to the ones shown in the screenshot):

1. First, we click on **Add Action** and choose the **Create a Record** action.
2. Then, we name the action `Create a Task`.
3. Next, we set the type of record to be created to **Task**.
4. Then, we set the field values for the task that will be created, as follows:
    - **Due Date Only** as **TODAY**
    - **Assigned to ID** as the owner of the opportunity that closed
    - **Priority** as **High**
    - **Status** as **Not Started**
    - **Subject** as **Big Sale Follow Up**
5. Finally, we **Save** to continue building the process.

Now that we have added the scheduled action, let's finish up this process by adding the two immediate actions for the second criteria, that is, activating and testing the process.

Finishing and testing our process

Let's finish up this process and test it. For the second set of criteria, we have two remaining immediate actions that need to be created. Let's learn how to go about that.

As shown in the following screenshot, we will need to create an email alert that needs to go to the manager when a sale with an amount greater than $200,000 is Closed Won:

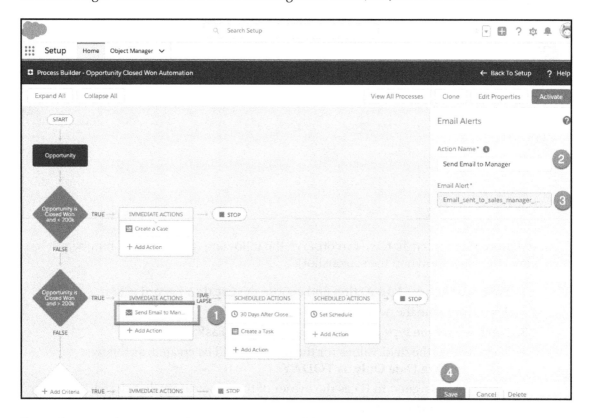

From the preceding screenshot, we can see the following (the numbers in the following list correlate to the ones shown in the screenshot):

1. First, we click on **Add Action** and choose the **Email Alerts** action.
2. Next, we name the action **Send Email to Manager**.
3. Then, we choose the email template for the email alert.
4. Finally, we **Save** to continue.

Now, let's create the final immediate action, that is, the case for widget installation, and then activate our process:

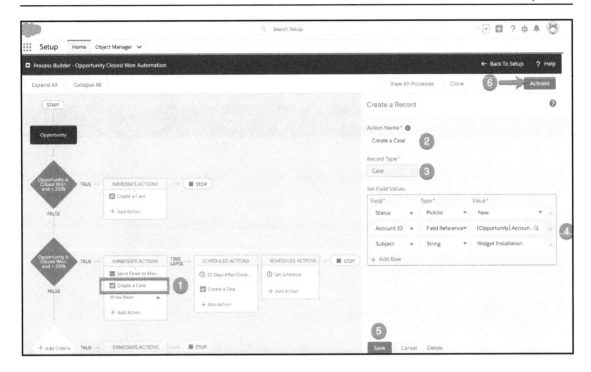

From the preceding screenshot, we can see the following (the numbers in the following list correlate to the ones shown in the screenshot):

1. Click on **Add Action** and choose the **Create a Record** action.
2. Set the name of the action to **Create a Case**.
3. Enter the type of record to be created as **Case**.
4. Set the field values for the case that will be created, as follows:
   - **Status** as **New**.
   - **Account ID** will be the same account that's connected to the opportunity that started our Process Builder.
   - **Subject** as **Widget Installation**.
5. **Save** to complete this step.
6. Click on **Activate** to activate the process.

In the following screenshot, you can see the active process:

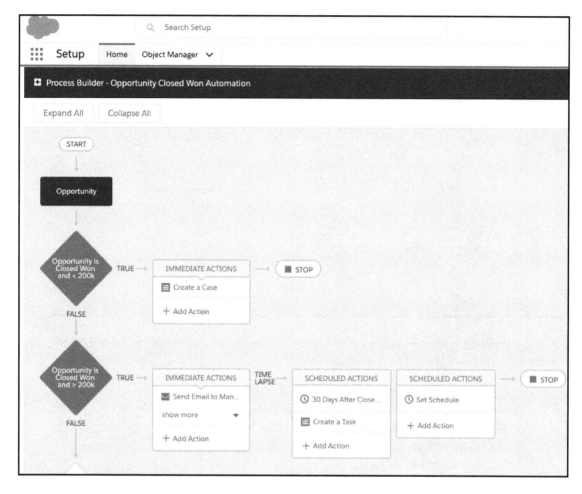

Now that our process has been built and is active, let's test it.

Navigate to the **Opportunities** tab and choose the **Burlington Textiles Weaving Plant Generator** opportunity to test the process:

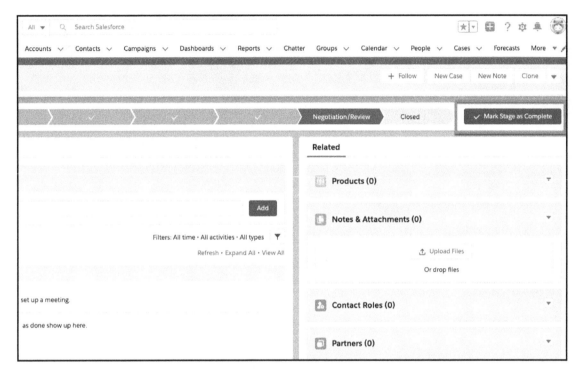

Then, click on **Mark Stage as Complete** to close this opportunity.

In the following screenshot, you can see the Closed Won opportunity:

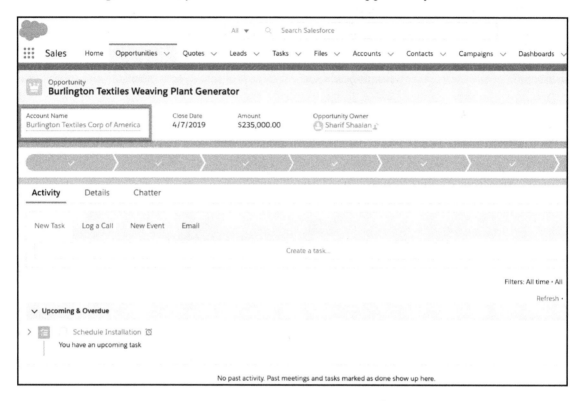

As shown in the preceding screenshot, the opportunity is now Closed Won. Since it is for $235,000, it should fire the second criteria. This means that an email will be sent to the manager, a task will be created 30 days from now, and an installation case will be created. You can check the email alert and the future task creation using the monitoring features we discussed in Chapter 14, *Understanding the Workflow Rules*. In the preceding screenshot, clicking on the **Burlington Textiles Corp of America Account** option checks if the installation case has been auto-created:

As shown in the preceding screenshot, the case is present! Next, let's take a look at one of the Process Builder best practices and how to apply it.

Process Builder best practice

It is important to note that the best practice when working with Process Builder is to build only one process per object. Let's suppose that, in the future, we get another requirement to add automation to the **Opportunity** object, so instead of creating a new process, we would come back to the process we built in the preceding sections and update it. We would do this by creating a new version of our process and activating it. Let's see how this is done:

1. In the following screenshot, I navigated back to the active process we previously built:

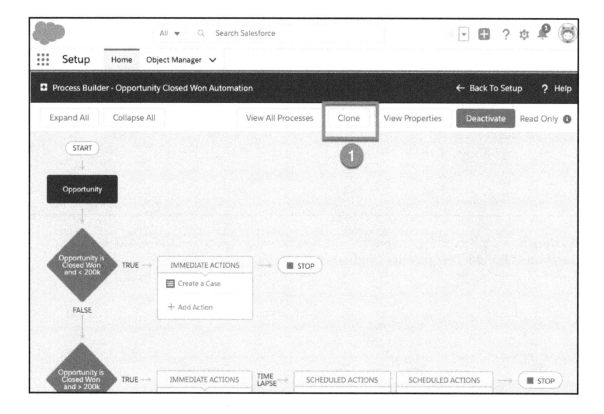

2. As you can see, instead of clicking on **Deactivate**, which would deactivate the current process, I clicked on **Clone** (1), which brought me to the following screen:

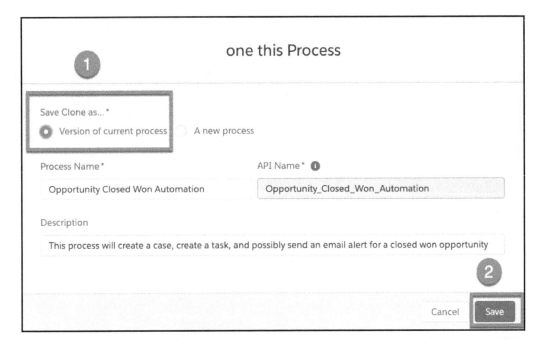

3. Then, I set **Save Clone as...** to **Version of current process** (1) and clicked **Save** (2). What this did is give me a new editable version of my process where I can add my new requirements.

4. Once I'd finished updating the new version of the process, I clicked on **Activate** on the new version, as follows:

5. From the preceding screenshot, you can see I clicked on **Activate** (**1**) and then **Confirm** (**2**) to activate the new version of the process.

6. When the new version is activated, the old version is automatically set to **Inactive**, as shown in the following screenshot:

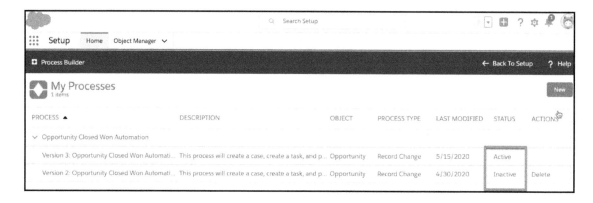

Here, you can see that there are now two processes, one active and one inactive. It is important to note that once a Process Builder is active, it cannot be edited again, so to make any changes to it, you would need to create a new version and activate the new version.

Now that we have created a process to cover our business use case and reviewed how to create a new version of the process, let's go over what we have learned.

Summary

In this chapter, we learned what Process Builder is and how it is different from a workflow rule. We learned how to create a process and define the object that the process will fire off of. We learned how to add multiple criteria to a process, thus allowing us to capture multiple use cases within one process.

Next, we understood how to add immediate and scheduled actions to a process in order to meet business requirements. Finally, we learned how to activate and test the process to make sure it is working and meeting our business use case.

With these skills, you should be able to come up with technical solutions for the business process automation requirements that come from your users. In the next chapter, we will cover a few basics of approval processes.

Questions

1. What are some actions available with Process Builders that are not available with workflow rules?
2. What are the two options we can use to start a process on the add object step?
3. What are the three options for **Criteria for Executing Actions** on the add criteria step?
4. What checkbox must be checked on the criteria screen to allow scheduled actions for those criteria?
5. What is the first step when it comes to creating scheduled actions?
6. How do you activate a process?

Further reading

- Lightning Process Builder: `https://help.salesforce.com/articleView?id=process_overview.htmtype=5`

- Automating Simple Business Processes with Process Builder: `https://trailhead.salesforce.com/en/content/learn/modules/business_process_automation/process_builder`
- Best Practices for Designing
  Processes: `https://help.salesforce.com/articleView?id=process_considerations_design_bestpractices.htm&type=5`
- Troubleshooting
  Processes: `https://help.salesforce.com/articleView?id=process_troubleshoot.htm&type=5`

16
Approval Processes

Approval processes are a type of automation that allows users to submit Salesforce records so that they can be approved in order to continue a specific business process. The approval process has the option of sending the record to one or multiple approvers, as well as the ability to add submission, approval, rejection, and recall actions. Having these checks and balances on business processes allows for a more streamlined and efficient workflow. Creating and maintaining approvals is a vital part of a Salesforce admin's day-to-day work.

In this chapter, we will cover the following topics in detail:

- Creating an approval process
- Adding entry criteria and approver selection
- Adding actions and viewing the approval steps
- Enabling email approvals
- The business use case in action

With the help of these topics, you will be able to understand the business use case for creating an approval process. You will understand how to create an approval process, how to add entry criteria, how to select approver(s), how to add actions, and how to add approval steps. These skills will help you automate business processes for your organization, leading to higher efficiency and fewer errors being made by your users.

Technical requirements

For this chapter, log into your development organization and follow along as we create an approval process from start to finish.

Creating an approval process

An approval process is a great tool that's used to execute business logic automatically based on a Salesforce record being submitted for approval, and then approved or rejected by another user. Knowing the capabilities of approval processes will help you come up with efficient workflows that lead to fewer clicks and cleaner data. Let's see how this is done.

Business use case

You are the Salesforce Admin for XYZ Widgets. The Sales Manager has a use case where all closed sales that are $200,000 or higher and are in the negotiation/review stage need to be submitted to them for final approval. Once the deal is approved, the opportunity stage should automatically update to Closed Won. Let's build this approval!

Creating an approval process

To create the approval process, perform the following steps:

1. Navigate to the **Setup** page | the **Home** tab (1)| **Approval Processes** (2), as shown in the following screenshot:

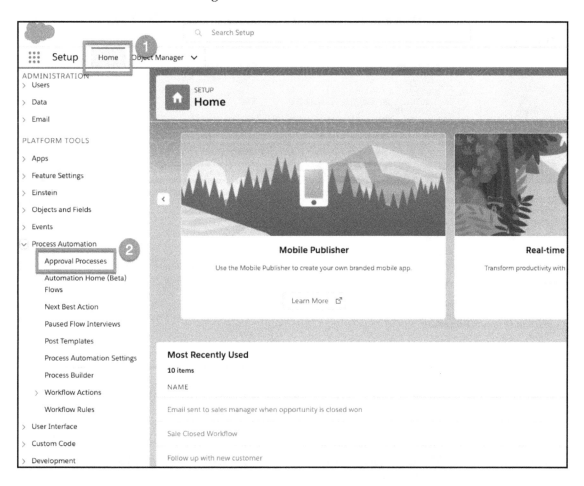

2. This will take you to the next step of creating the approval process, as shown in the following screenshot:

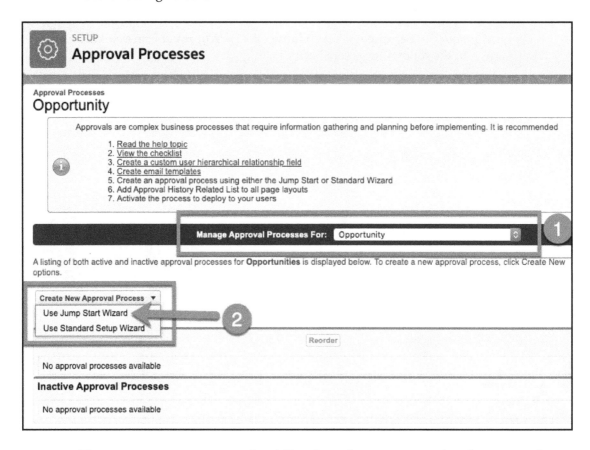

There are two steps you need to follow in order to start creating the approval process, as shown in the preceding screenshot:

1. Choosing the object that the approval process will be applied to. In our case, this is the **Opportunity** object since we are approving sales greater than $200,000.

2. Starting the approval process' creation by either choosing **Use Jump Start Wizard** or the standard **Use Business Setup Wizard**. We will use the Jump Start Wizard as it condenses the steps into two pages as opposed to six pages for the initial creation of the approval process.

Next, let's take a look at adding entry criteria and approver selection.

Adding entry criteria and approver selection

Now, we need to add the basic approval process information, specify the entry criteria for the approval, and select the approver(s) for the approval process. Refer to the following screenshot for more details:

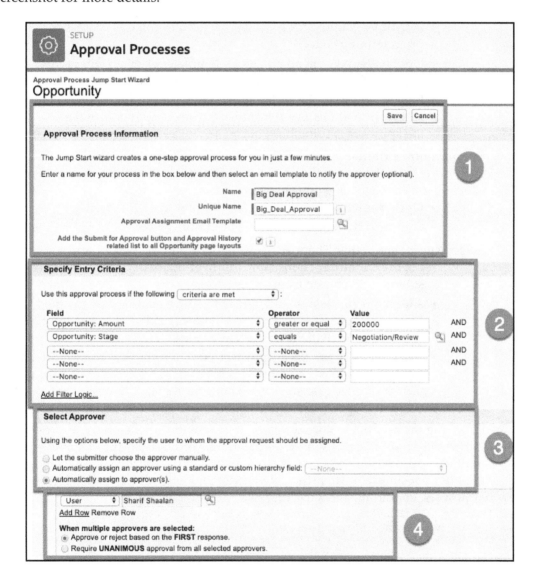

From the preceding screenshot, you can see there are four main sections, each of which has specific settings for the approval process. Let's look at these settings in detail:

1. **Approval Process Information**: This section allows you to add the following:
   - A **Name** for the process. This is a label that shows up when you look at the list of all approval processes.
   - A **Unique Name**. This is used if we need to call this process through programming code.
   - Optionally, you can add an email template for when you request approval from a user. This will let you word the email as needed.
   - Finally, you have the ability to **Add the Submit for Approval** button and **Approval History**-related list to the page layouts of the object that the approval is being built on.

2. **Specify Entry Criteria**: This section, similar to workflow rules, allows you to enter the criteria that allow the record to enter into this approval process. For our business use case, we have two criteria:
   - **Opportunity Amount** is **greater or equal** to $200,000
   - **Opportunity Stage equals Negotiation/Review**

3. **Select Approver** options: There are three options for selecting an approver:
   - **Let the submitter choose the approver manually**: This allows the submitter to choose from all Salesforce users.
   - **Automatically assign an approver using a standard or custom hierarchy field**: This can be the **Manager** field on the user record or a custom hierarchy field on the user record.
   - **Automatically assign to approver (s)**: This option allows you to assign the approval to one or more specific users. This is the option we will use for our use case since it is a specific manager that we need to assign the approval to.

4. **Choosing the approver**: Since we chose to automatically assign the approver in the preceding step, in this step, we will add one or multiple approvers. If multiple approvers are selected, there is an option to **Approve or reject based on the FIRST response** or **Require UNANIMOUS approval from all selected approvers**. For our business use case, we will add one approver.

After saving, we will see the following screen:

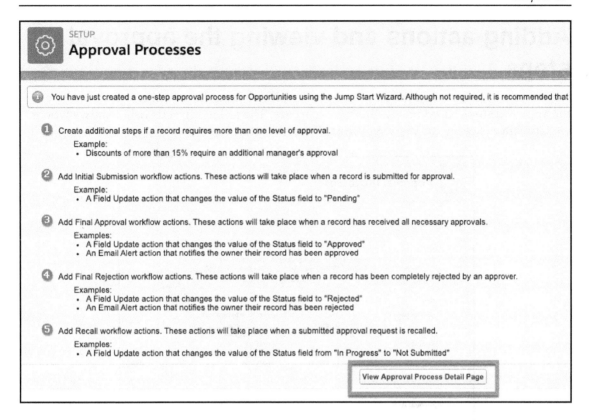

As you can see, the preceding screenshot suggests that we finish setting up this approval by adding additional actions. Let's click on **View Approval Process Detail Page** to proceed.

Now, we can start adding actions and viewing the approval steps.

Adding actions and viewing the approval steps

Now that we have created the approval process, let's look at how to add actions and view the approval steps based on our business use case. The following screenshot shows where we land after clicking on **View Approval Process Detail Page**:

As shown in the preceding screenshot, there are multiple sections to consider:

1. **Initial Submission Actions**: The default action when a user submits a record for approval is to lock the record from being edited. In addition to this, you can add one of the four additional actions, that is, create a task, create an email alert, update a field, or send an outbound message. These are the same four actions we covered in Chapter 14, *Understanding the Workflow Rules*. For our business use case, there are no additional actions to create upon submitting an approval.

2. **Approval steps**: This section shows the steps needed to complete this approval. Had we added multiple approvers and the need for unanimous approval, we would see each approver here as a step. Since our business use case only has one approver, you can see this as *step 1* under approval steps.

Now, let's look at the final approval actions:

For the final approval actions, we do need to add one action. Since our business use case says we want **Opportunity Stage** to automatically update to **Closed Won** when the record is approved, we will need to add a field update. From the **Add New** drop-down, select **Field Updates**, which will take us to the following screen:

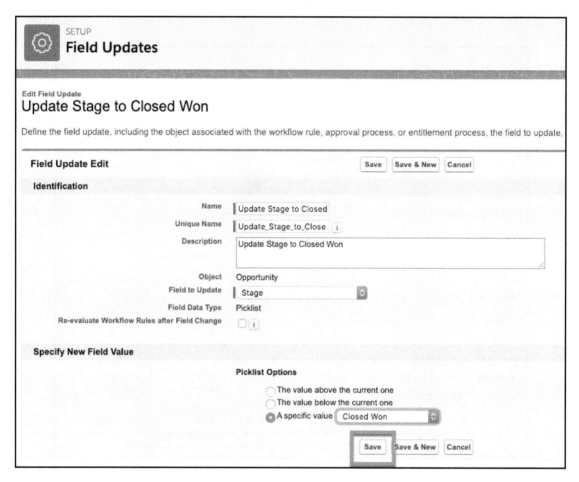

This is the same field update functionality we covered in Chapter 14, *Understanding the Workflow Rules*. After adding the required information here for the field update, save it. This has been set up so that when the approver approves the record, this field update will occur and the Opportunity stage will automatically change to Closed Won. After doing this, we will be sent back to the following screen:

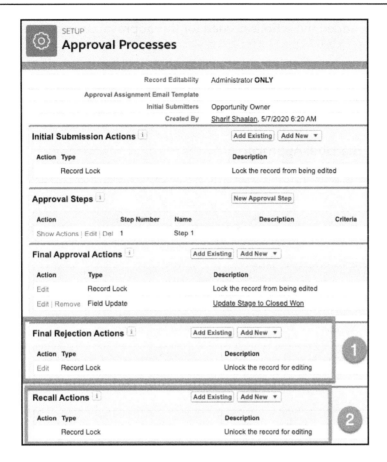

As shown in the preceding screenshot, there are two more sections to cover on this page:

1. **Final Rejection Actions**: The default rejection action is to unlock the record for editing. Along with unlocking the record, you can optionally add one of the four previously mentioned actions (**Create a Task**, **Email Alert**, **Field Update**, or **Outbound Message**). For our business use case, there are no additional actions needed for a rejection, so we will leave this as is.

2. **Recall Actions**: This section defines what happens if the user that submitted the record for approval decides to recall the submission. The default action is to unlock the record for editing, thus allowing the user to make changes as needed and resubmit the record for approval. Along with unlocking the record, you can optionally add one of the four previously mentioned actions (**Create a Task**, **Email Alert**, **Field Update**, or **Outbound Message**). For our business use case, there are no additional actions needed for recalling a record, so we will leave this as is.

Now that we have added the actions needed for this approval process, let's learn how to activate them:

As you can see, I have clicked on the **Activate** button. The approval process is now complete – one more step and we can test this approval process out.

Enabling email approvals

Although the approver(s) will get a notification and can approve the record right from inside Salesforce, we want to add an extra option to make it a little easier for our executives on the move. This option is to allow the approver to approve a record by replying to the approval request email with APPROVE or REJECT.

In the following screenshot, I navigated to **Process Automation Settings** to enable this feature:

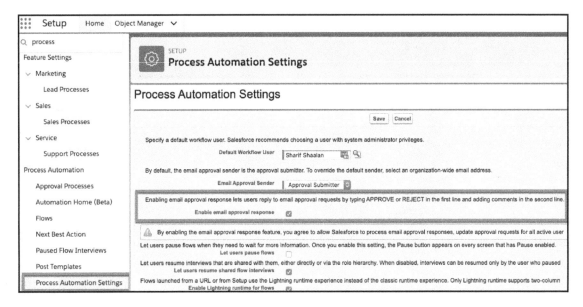

As you can see, I ticked the **Enable email approval response** checkbox. This will now give our approver(s) another option to approve the record.

Now that we have set up the approval process and enabled the option for an approver to approve via email, let's test it out!

The business use case in action

Now that we have built the approval process, let's test it out to see if it meets our business requirements. As a recap, the Sales Manager wants all closed sales that are $200,000 or higher and are in the negotiation/review stage to be submitted to them for final approval. Once the deal has been approved, the opportunity stage should automatically update to **Closed Won**. Let's see how this works:

1. Navigate to the **Burlington Textiles Weaving Plant Generator** opportunity, as follows:

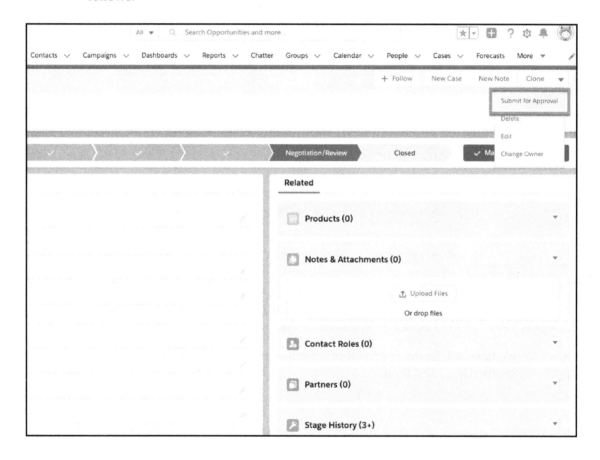

Here, we can see that this opportunity has an amount that is greater than $200,000 and is in the **Negotiation/Review** stage, so it meets the criteria for being submitted for approval.

2. From the drop-down arrow on the upper-right corner, we can access and click on the **Submit for Approval** button. The following popup will appear:

3. The popup in the preceding screenshot allows the submitter to add a comment for the approver to see. Add a comment and click on **Submit**.

The opportunity has now been submitted. The following screenshot shows the **Approval History**-related list on the opportunity:

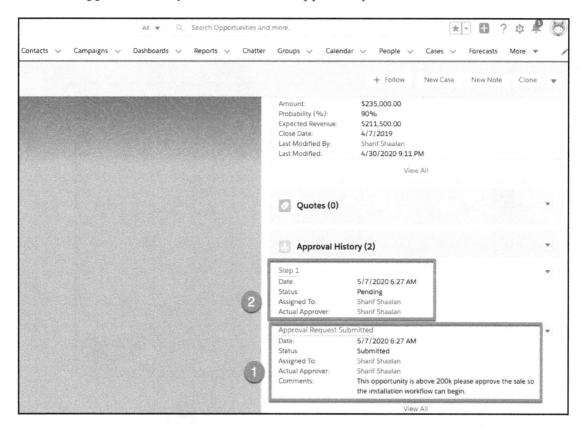

4. As you can see, there are now two entries in the **Approval History** section:
   1. **Approval Request Submitted**: This is an audit trail of the submission that shows when this record was submitted for approval.
   2. **Step 1**: This shows the pending step for the approval and who the approval is assigned to.

5. Next, let's take a look at what the approver will see:

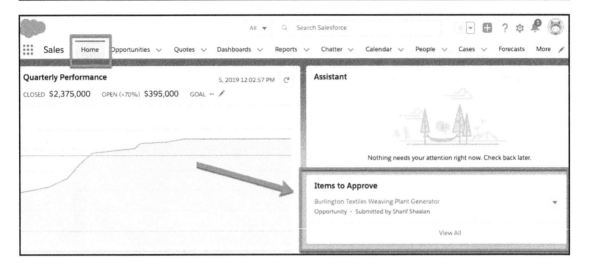

As you can see, the Sales Manager would have to log into Salesforce.

6. On the home page, there is an **Items to Approve** section. The following screenshot shows the screen that comes up when the Sales Manager clicks on the record to approve it:

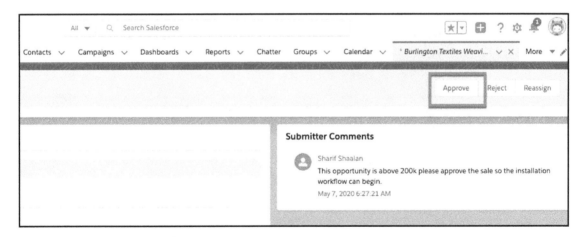

In the preceding screenshot, you can see all of the approval details. The Sales Manager has the option to **Approve**, **Reject**, or **Reassign** the record for approval.

7. When the Sales Manager clicks on **Approve**, the following popup will appear:

This popup allows the approver to add any comments to the approval. The Sales Manager will click on **Approve** and be brought to the following screen:

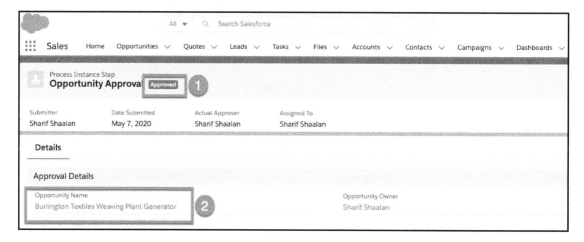

From the preceding screenshot, we can see that the opportunity has been approved (**1**).

8. Let's click on **Opportunity Name** (2) to see if the field update has worked. As we can see, we have been navigated back to the opportunity:

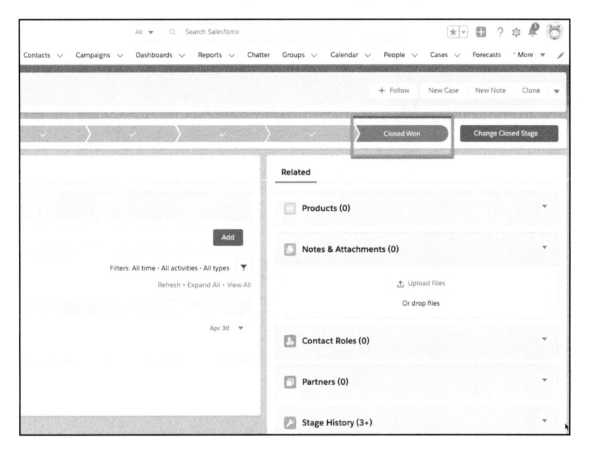

The opportunity automatically changed to Closed Won when it was approved by the Sales Manager.

9. Finally, let's scroll down to see the approval history one more time, as shown here:

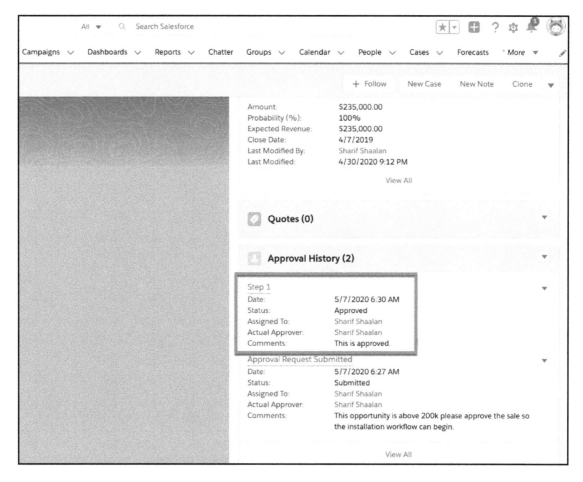

As you can see, **Step 1** has now changed from **Pending** to **Approved**.

Now that we have tested the business use case successfully, let's go over what we have learned in this chapter.

Summary

In this chapter, we learned what approval processes are and the use cases for building approvals into our business processes. We learned how to create an approval process and define the entry criteria and select an approver. We also learned how to view approval steps, as well as add various actions based on submitting, approving, rejecting, and recalling the record.

With the use of these skills, you should be able to come up with checks and balances that control various aspects of the business process flow, as well as apply technical solutions for the approval-related requirements that come from your users. In the next chapter, we will cover assignment rules for various use cases.

Questions

1. What is the difference between the Jump Start Wizard and the standard Setup Wizard?
2. Are you able to have more than one approver on an approval process?
3. Why does the record lock for editing when a user submits it for approval?
4. How are the approval process and workflow rule actions similar?
5. What happens to the editability of a record if a user recalls it from an approval?
6. What is the last step needed for an approval process to be live and working?
7. Where can an approver see all items needing approval that have been assigned to them?

Further reading

- Setting up an Approval Process: `https://help.salesforce.com/articleView?id=approvals_getting_started.htmtype=5`
- Submitting a Record for Approval from a Process: `https://help.salesforce.com/articleView?id=process_action_submit.htmtype=5`

17
Assignment Rules

The final automation feature we want to highlight is assignment rules. Assignment rules allow you to automate your lead generation and support processes by helping you control the record's assignment. Typically, in Salesforce, a lead or case record will be assigned to the person creating the record or to a default user if the lead or case is being created through something such as Web to Lead or Web to Case. Assignment is important since the owner of the record is the person that will work on the specific lead or case to move it along in the process. Assignment rules allow you to set rules that will assign a new lead or case to a specific user or queue based on criteria.

In this chapter, we will cover the following topics in detail:

- Creating lead assignment rules
- Creating a queue
- Creating case assignment rules
- Assignment rules in action

With the help of these topics, you will be able to understand the business use case for creating assignment rules, as well as how to create an assignment rule and the rule entries for a *specific* assignment rule. You will also learn how to create a queue in order to be able to use assignment rules to assign a record to a queue rather than a user. These skills will help you automate business processes for your organization, leading to higher efficiency and fewer errors being made by your users.

Technical requirements

For this chapter, log into your development organization and follow along as we create lead and case assignment rules.

Creating lead assignment rules

Lead assignment rules are a great tool for assigning lead records automatically. Knowing the capabilities of lead assignment rules will lead to fewer clicks for your users and quicker business process execution when working with leads. Lead assignment rules are created in the **Setup** section of Salesforce. Let's learn how to create a lead assignment rule.

Business use case

You are the Salesforce Admin for XYZ Widgets. The Sales Manager has a use case where any new lead created in Salesforce needs to be assigned to a specific user based on the **State/Province** field of the lead. Leads with a State/Province of **New York** will be assigned to a user, while leads with a State/Province of **New Jersey** will be assigned to another user. Let's learn how to build this.

Creating lead assignment rules

To create a lead assignment rule, we need to perform a few steps:

1. Navigate to the **Setup** page | the **Home** tab | **Feature Settings** | **Lead Assignment Rules**, as shown in the following screenshot:

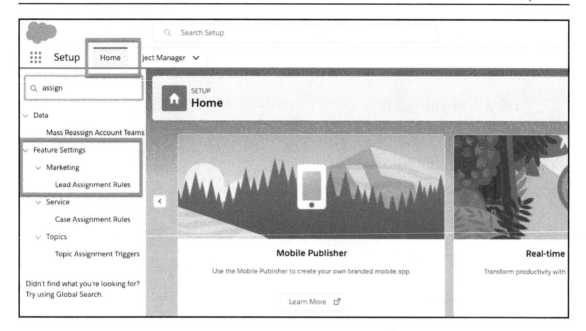

2. This will take you to the next step in creating the lead assignment rule. Click on **New**:

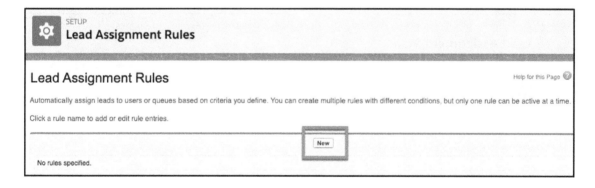

3. This takes us to the following page, where we check the **Active** checkbox (**1**) to mark this rule as **Active**, enter the **Rule Name** (**2**), and click on **Save** (**3**):

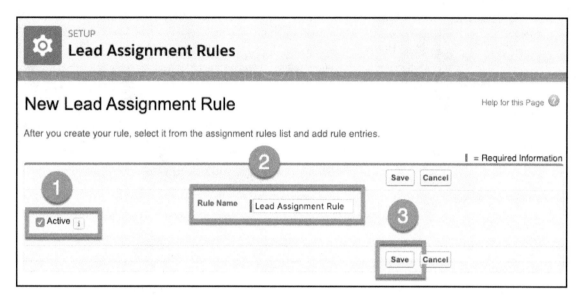

After doing this, we will be sent to the following page:

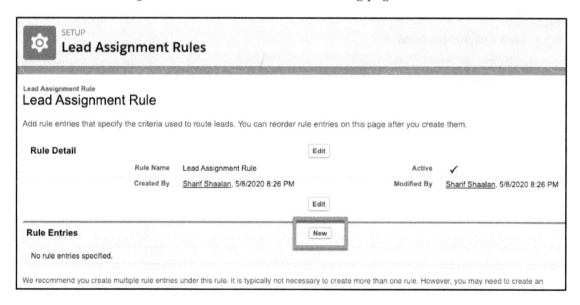

Here, you can see that our **Lead Assignment Rule** has been created.

4. The next step is to add two rule entries for our two business use cases so that we can assign New York and New Jersey leads. Clicking on **New** takes us to the following screen:

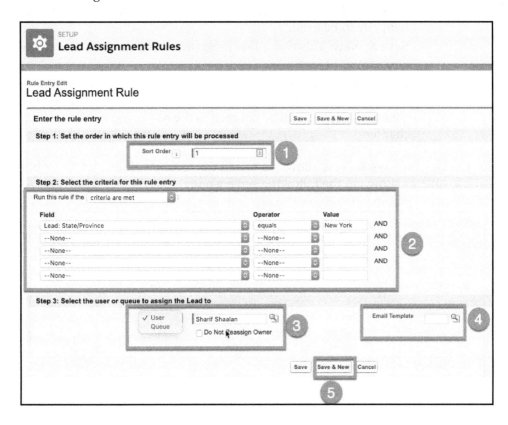

There are a few steps in the preceding rule entry screen to discuss:

1. **Sort Order**: Salesforce evaluates all of the entries on an assignment rule in this sort order. Once a match is found, the lead is assigned and the evaluation process stops. This field allows you to determine the order the rule entries are evaluated in.

2. **Select the criteria for this rule entry**: For our business use case, the criteria for this rule is any lead where **State/Province** is **New York**. Any lead that meets this criterion will trigger this assignment rule.

3. **Email Template**: Here, you can choose to include a custom email template for the email that goes out to the user when a lead is assigned to them. If no template is chosen, a default lead assignment email will go out. I will leave this blank for our use case and allow the default template to be used.

4. **Save & New**: This will allow us to save this rule entry and create the next one right away.

5. **User/Queue Selection**: Here, we have the option to assign this lead to a user or a queue. For our business use case, we will assign it to a user. Creating a queue will be covered in the following section of this chapter.

5. Clicking on **Save & New** allows us to add the second rule entry for our business use case, as shown in the following screenshot:

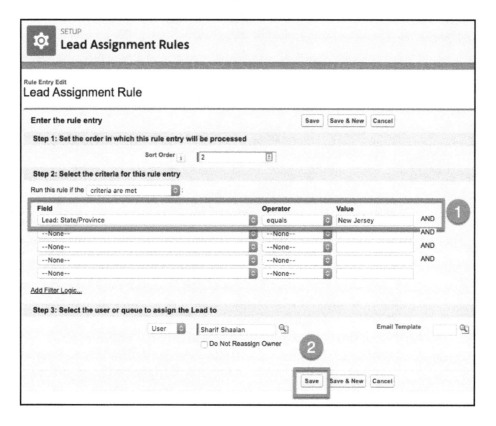

This rule entry has a sort order of **2** since it is the second entry on this assignment rule. For the criteria, I set **State/Province** to **New Jersey (1)**. Clicking on **Save (2)** takes us to the following screen:

As you can see, the assignment rule has been created and is now active. It also has two rule entries to assign any new leads that come in with a New York or New Jersey state to the appropriate user. Our business use case has two entries, but you can add many more entries based on the complexity of your use case.

Now that we have created a lead assignment rule, let's take a look at how to create a queue. We will need this to demonstrate our case assignment rule business use case.

Creating a queue

In Salesforce, every record has to be owned by a user or a queue. A *queue* is a group of users who can own records.

From a business perspective, one example is where new leads are placed in a lead queue. Users who are assigned to it can go into the lead queue list view and reassign leads to themselves that they wish to pursue. It can also be the use case where a group of support users is assigned to a case queue. From there these support users can actively go into the case queue list view to reassign cases to themselves. They will then be the owners of any reassigned cases and are responsible for working on these cases.

Business use case

You are the Salesforce Admin for XYZ Widgets. The Support Manager has a use case where a New York Cases queue needs to be created for the New York region support representatives. This queue will be used in the next section as part of our case assignment rules business use case. Let's learn how to create a case queue.

Creating a queue

To create a queue, we need to perform a few steps:

1. First, we need to navigate to the **Setup** page | the **Home** tab (1) | **Queues** (2) | **New** (3) to create a new queue, as shown in the following screenshot:

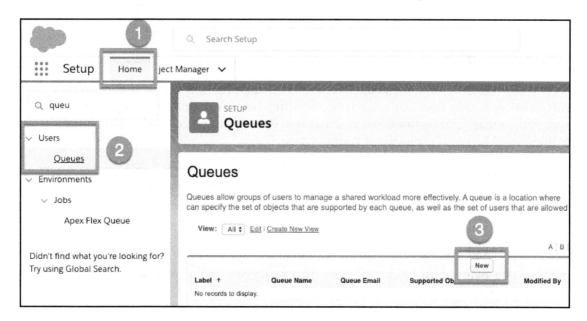

This brings us to the following screen:

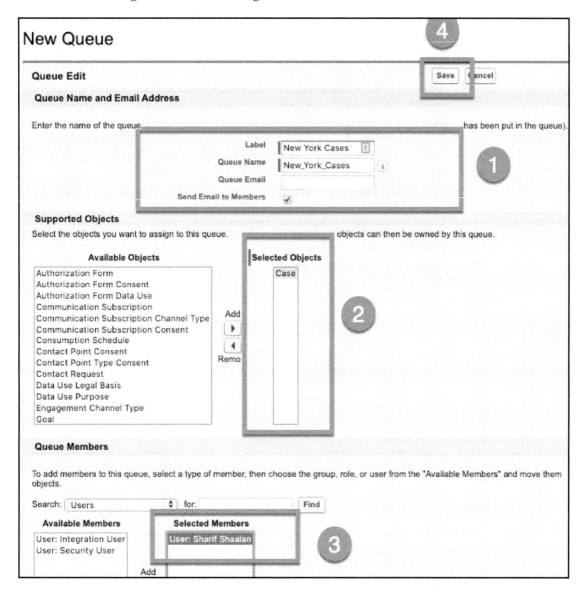

From the preceding screenshot, we can see that we carried out the following steps:

1. **Queue Name** and **Queue Email**: Here, I entered **New York Cases** as the queue label and the queue API name (used to reference the queue throughout the code). Optionally, you can add a queue email address, which will send the assignment email to this address rather than sending individual emails to everyone in the queue when a record is assigned to the queue. Finally, you can check the **Send Email to Members** checkbox, which allows you to send individual emails to everyone in the queue when a record is assigned. This checkbox is typically checked if you don't add a queued email.

2. **Supported Objects**: Here, we add the case object since this will be a case queue.

3. **Selected Members**: Here, we can add all of the users that will be part of this queue.

4. **Save**: Finally, save the queue.

Saving the queue brings us to the following page:

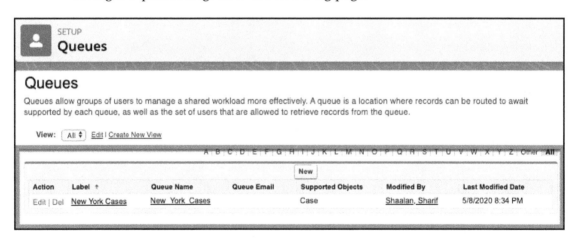

As you can see, the **New York Cases** queue has now been created. Let's move on to creating case assignment rules, where we will use this case queue as part of our business use case.

Creating case assignment rules

Case assignment rules are a great tool for assigning case records automatically. Knowing the capabilities of case assignment rules will lead to fewer clicks for your users and quicker business process execution when working with cases. Case assignment rules are created in the **Setup** section of Salesforce. Let's learn how to create a case assignment rule.

Business use case

You are the Salesforce Admin for XYZ Widgets. The Support Manager has the following use cases for you:

1. Any new case with a **State/Province** of New York will be assigned to the **New York Cases** queue.
2. Any new case with a **State/Province** of New Jersey will be assigned to a user.

Let's learn how to build these.

Creating case assignment rules

To create a case assignment rule, we need to perform the following steps:

1. First, we need to navigate to the **Setup** page | the **Home** tab | **Service** | **Case Assignment Rules**, as shown in the following screenshot:

2. This will take you to the next step in creating the case assignment rule, where we click on **New**:

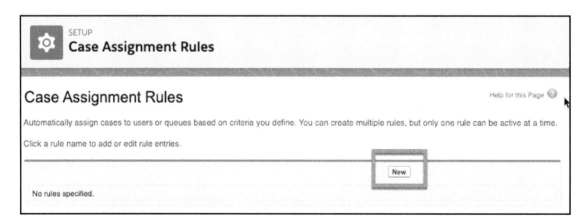

On creating a new assignment, we land on the following screen:

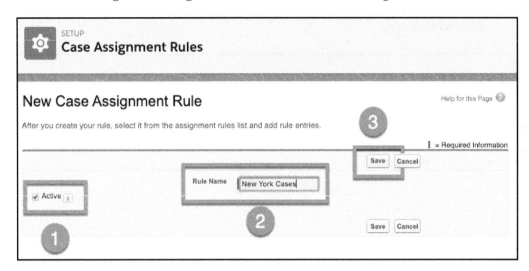

3. Here, we check the **Active** checkbox (**1**) to mark this rule as active, enter the **Rule Name** (**2**), and click on **Save** (**3**), which takes us to the following screen:

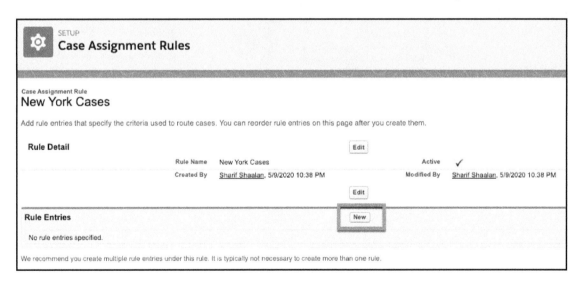

Here, you can see that the case assignment rule has been created.

4. The next step is to add two rule entries for our two business use cases so that we can assign New York and New Jersey cases. Clicking on **New** takes us to the following screen:

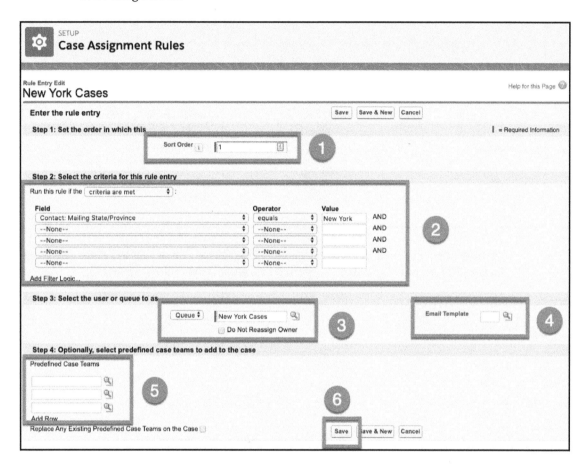

There are a few steps we need to discuss regarding the **Case Assignment Rules** screen:

1. **Sort Order**: Salesforce evaluates all of the entries on an assignment rule in this sort order. Once a match is found, the case is assigned and the evaluation stops. This field allows you to determine the order the rule entries are evaluated in.

2. **Select the criteria for this rule entry**: For our business use case, the criteria for this rule is any case where **State/Province** is New York. Any case that meets this criterion will trigger this assignment rule.

3. **User/Queue Selection**: Here, we have the option to assign this case to a user or a queue. For our business use case, we will assign it to the queue we created previously, that is, the **New York Cases** queue.

4. **Email Template:** Here, you can choose to include a custom email template for the email that goes out to the queue or queue members when a case is assigned to the queue. If no template is chosen, a default case assignment email will go out. I will leave this blank for our use case and allow the default template to be used.

5. **Case Teams:** Optionally, you can add predefined case teams to this case. We will leave this blank for our use case.

6. **Save**: This will allow us to save this rule entry.

5. Next, we will add the second rule, as follows:

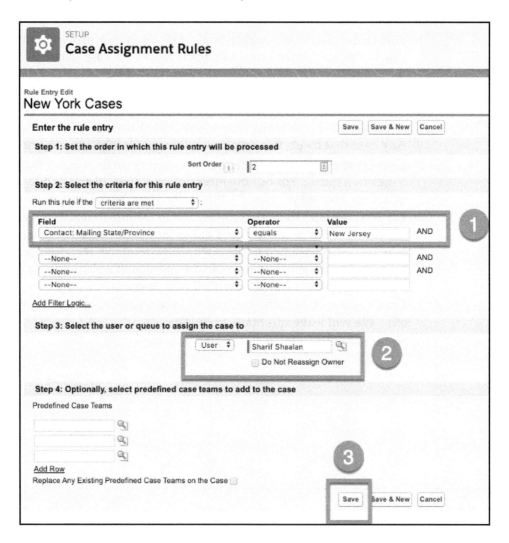

As you can see, this rule entry has a sort order of **2** since it is the second entry on this assignment rule. For the criteria, I entered **State/Province** as New Jersey (**1**). I chose the user that will be assigned the **New Jersey Leads** (**2**) and clicked on **Save** (**3**). Clicking on **Save** takes us to the following screen:

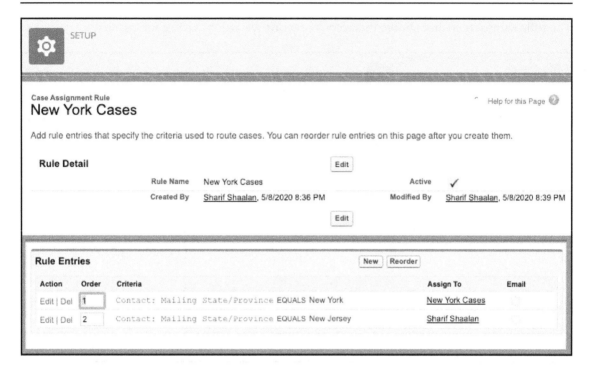

As you can see, the assignment rule has been created and is now active. It also has two rule entries that we can assign to any new leads that come in from New York or New Jersey to the appropriate queue and user. Our business use case has two entries, but you can add many more entries based on the complexity of your use case.

Now that we have created a lead assignment rule, a queue, and a case assignment rule, let's see these assignment rules in action.

Assignment rules in action

Now that we have created a lead and a case assignment rule, let's see how this looks in action. The assignment functionality works the same way for leads and cases, but we will use cases for our example since the case assignment rule allows us to assign to both a user and a queue. Any case that is created automatically through Web to Case or Email to Case will trigger the assignment rules. In our examples, we will create the cases directly in Salesforce.

The following screenshot shows the account record we will be using for our test:

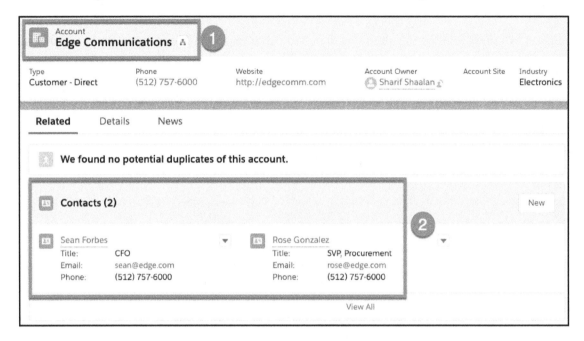

As you can see, we will use the **Edge Communications** account (**1**). We will create cases using the two existing contacts, **Sean Forbes** and **Rose Gonzalez** (**2**). I made sure to update **Mailing State/Province** for **Sean Forbes** to New Jersey and **Mailing State/Province** for **Rose Gonzalez** to New York. These are the criteria the assignment rules will check so that it can assign them to the correct user or queue.

Next, navigate to the **Cases** tab and click on **New**. This brings us to the following screen:

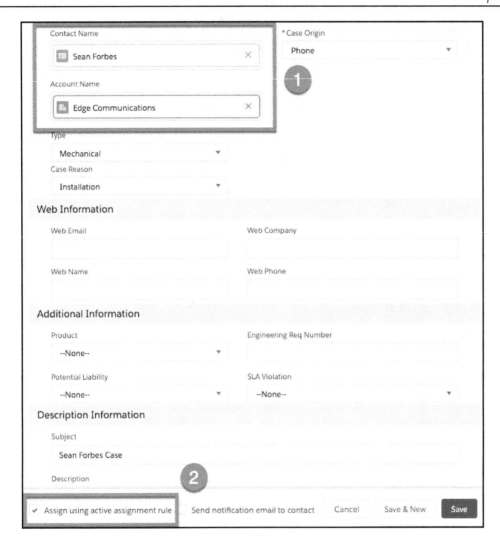

In the preceding screenshot, I filled out the information for a new case, as follows:

1. I added **Sean Forbes** as the contact and **Edge Communications** as the account.
2. I checked the **Assign using active assignment rule** checkbox. This is what makes sure that this new case will be evaluated and assigned appropriately. If I didn't check this box, the case would automatically be assigned to the person creating it.

Upon clicking **Save**, the case should be assigned to the **Sharif Shaalan** user, as per our assignment rule, since **Sean Forbes** has a **Mailing State/Province** of New Jersey on his contact record. In the following screenshot, I navigated back to the **Cases** tab to check on the assignment:

As shown in the preceding screenshot, I took several steps to check this:

1. I went to the **Recently Viewed** view.
2. I searched for the subject of my recently created **Case**.
3. Here, I could see that the case owner alias is **SShaa**, which is the alias for **Sharif Shaalan**. This shows that the test passed.

Next, I want to test the assignment to the New York queue. From the **Cases** tab, I clicked on **New**, which brought me to the following screen:

In the preceding screenshot, I filled out the information for a new case, as follows:

1. I added **Rose Gonzalez** as the contact and **Edge Communications** as the account.
2. I checked the **Assign using active assignment rule** checkbox. This is what makes sure that this new case will be evaluated and assigned appropriately. If I didn't check this box, the case would automatically be assigned to the person creating it.

Upon clicking **Save**, the case should be assigned to the **New York Cases** queue, as per our assignment rule, since **Rose Gonzalez** has a **Mailing State/Province** of New York on her contact record. In the following screenshot, you can see that I navigated back to the **Cases** tab to check on the assignment:

As you can see, I took several steps to check this:

1. I went to the

1. **New York Cases** view. This view was automatically created when we created our queue earlier in this chapter.
2. I searched for the subject of my recently created **Case**.
3. Here, I could see the case owner alias is **New York Cases**, which is the queue that we created. This shows that the test passed.

Now that we have created assignment rules, created a queue, and tested the case assignment rule, let's go over what we have learned in this chapter.

Summary

In this chapter, we learned what an assignment rule is and how to create a lead and a case assignment rule. We learned what queues are and how to assign records to queues using assignment rules. We also understood what rule entries are and how to create multiple rule entries for a single assignment rule. Then, we applied these skills to real-life use cases to help you understand how assignment rules are used within the context of a business.

With the use of these skills, you should be able to come up with technical solutions for the record assignment requirements that come from your users. This brings the automation section of this book to a close.

With this final chapter, we have completed this book and tried to cover as many use cases and examples as possible. I hope that this encourages you to continue your journey with Salesforce and experiment with more use cases using your development organization and Trailhead.

Questions

1. Besides a user, what else can a case or lead record be assigned to?
2. How is the sort order used on an assignment rule?
3. What happens if you don't choose an email template for a rule entry?
4. When creating a queue, what is the **Queue Email** field used for?
5. If you leave the **Queue Email** field blank, who gets notified when a record is assigned to a queue?

Further reading

- **Assignment Rules:** `https://help.salesforce.com/articleView?id=customize_leadrules.htmtype=5`
- **Setting up Queues:** `https://help.salesforce.com/articleView?id=setting_up_queues.htmtype=5`

Assessments

Chapter 1

1. What is Salesforce Economy?

- Salesforce Economy predicts the jobs that will be created due to the Salesforce ecosystem. It's been projected that there will be 3.3 million new Salesforce jobs by 2022.

2. What does CRM stand for?

- Customer Relationship Management.

3. What are the two advantages of using Salesforce Lightning?

- It has a modern user interface and utilizes the Lightning Component framework.

4. Are all tabs objects?

- No, there can be tabs for things such as reports and dashboards.

5. What is an app in Salesforce?

- An app is a collection of tabs that can be customized.

6. What does a global search return?

- Any records where the term you searched for has appeared.

7. What is the default list view that appears when you go to a tab for the first time?

- Recently Viewed.

8. What is Salesforce Einstein?

- Einstein is the artificial intelligence feature provided by Salesforce.

9. Which personal setting allows you to grant login access to Salesforce customer service?

- Grant Account Login Access.

Chapter 2

1. What type of activity should be used to set up a reminder to research an account?

- A task.

2. Which activity type should be used to set up an onsite meeting with a client?

- An Event.

3. Is it possible to send an email to a client and copy someone not in the system as a contact?

- Yes.

4. Do tasks appear on your Salesforce calendar?

- No, only Events.

5. Which tab shows all of your open tasks?

- The **Tasks** tab.

6. If you use Gmail but spend most of your time in Salesforce, which integration option should you use?

- Send through Gmail.

7. Can you log activities regarding Opportunities?

- Yes, you can log activities regarding Opportunities that you work on, as well as any other standard object or custom object with activities enabled.

Chapter 3

1. What are some of the ways leads can be captured?

- Conferences, websites, and purchased lists, to name a few.

2. What determines whether a lead should be converted into an Opportunity?

- If the prospect is interested in the product and wants to continue discussing it with you.

3. What happens to a Closed-Not Converted (Unqualified) lead?

- You can filter it out of list views but it stays in the system for reporting purposes.

4. What happens to a converted lead? Where does it go?

- It becomes an Account, Contact, and, optionally, an Opportunity.

5. Where does the company information go when a lead is converted?

- To the Account.

6. What is web-to-lead used for?

- For capturing leads from company websites.

7. Once you have generated the HTML code, what do you do with it?

- Give it to your web team so they can add it to the website.

8. What does the Org-Wide Merge and Delete lead setting allow you to do?

- If your organization-wide default sharing option is set to Public Read/Write/Transfer for leads, checking this box allows users to also merge and delete leads.

Chapter 4

1. What are some use cases for the types of Accounts an organization may want to keep track of in Salesforce?

- Customers, partners, and vendors.

2. Why would you want to create Contacts related to Accounts you are doing business with?

- These are the people you will be contacting and speaking with in the organization.

3. What is a use case for creating a relationship from a Contact to an Account that the Contact does not directly work for?

- This can be an influencer in the organization, such as a board member.

4. What do you do to enable the relationships feature?

- You will need to enable Contacts to Multiple Accounts.

5. How do you remove a relationship?

- Click on **Remove Relationship** in the related contacts list.

Chapter 5

1. How many Opportunities can you have on an Account?

- There is no limit.

2. What is the difference between Opportunity Stages and the Sales Path?

- The Sales Path is a visual representation of the Opportunity Stages.

3. How many Contact Role instances can be added to an Opportunity?

- As many as needed.

4. What happens to the Amount field on the Opportunity when you add Products?

- It is overridden by the price of the products added.

5. Who do you send Quotes to on an Opportunity?

- The contact role or the client on the Opportunity.

6. What are the two types of Closed stages on an Opportunity?

- Closed Won and Closed Lost.

7. What is included in the Best Case Forecast Category?

- Amounts you are likely to close, Closed Won opportunities, and opportunities in the Commit category.

Chapter 6

1. What are the two types of Campaign Members that can be added to a Campaign?

- Leads and Contacts.

2. Why would you want to add a Parent Campaign to your Campaign?

- To group campaigns together. For instance, all of your webinars might be under the Webinar 2020 campaign, thus allowing you to report on all of the child webinars together.

3. What is the name of the section where you can see Campaigns related to Leads and Contacts?

- Campaign History.

4. What field lets us know if a Campaign is Active?

- The **Active** checkbox.

5. Why would you want to use a third-party app with Campaigns?

- To automate some of the manual work of dealing with campaigns, such as updating the campaign member status.

6. What are three examples of types of Campaigns?

- Direct mail, Events, and Email, to name a few.

Chapter 7

1. What is the main use case for Salesforce Cases?

- Cases are used for customer service purposes.

2. Why is Case Status so important?

- The Case status field drives the Case's life cycle. This field allows you to see where the Case is at any point in time.

3. What is an example of when a Case may be escalated?

- An example would be when a technical issue arises that needs to be escalated to a more skilled technician.

4. Why is there an Order field for Case Escalation rule entries?

- This is needed so that we can specify the order in which the entries will execute within the rule.

5. Why do you need to generate HTML code for Web to Case?

- So you can add the case capture form to a web page.

6. What is a use case for using Email to Case?

- Email to Case allows you to set up a specific email address that converts any email sent to that email address into a Case.

7. What happens if you don't set up an On-Demand Service?

- You would need to download and install the Email to Case agent behind your firewall.

8. Why is it important to verify your email address when setting up Email to Case?

- This is the final step to activate Email to Case.

Chapter 8

1. What type of report has no grouping?

- A tabular report.

2. What type of report has only a row grouping?

- A summary report.

3. What type of report has both row and column grouping?

- A matrix report.

4. How do you add a chart to a report?

- Click on the **Add Chart** button.

5. How does a report relate to a dashboard?

- A dashboard contains multiple components, and each component pulls from an underlying report.

6. How many components can you add to a dashboard?

- 20.

7. What does **KPI** stand for?

- Key Performance Indicator.

Chapter 9

1. Which tab is used for nonobject settings?

- The **Home** tab, under setup and configuration.

2. Which tab is used for managing object settings?

- Object Manager.

3. In the Administration section, which subsection allows you to mass delete records?

- The Data subsection.

4. In the Administration section, which subsection allows you to create users?

- The Users subsection.

5. In the Platform Tools section, which subsection allows you to access Process Builder?

- The Process Automation subsection.

6. In the Settings section, which subsection allows you to see your organization ID?

- The Company Settings subsection.

7. On the Object Manager tab, which setting allows you to edit the Lightning page layout?

- Lightning Record Pages.

Chapter 10

1. What is the first decision that must be made when looking at org-wide settings?

- The first decision that needs to be made is whether you want to have an open organization where all the data is visible and can be edited by everyone or whether any data needs to be restricted from being viewed or edited.

2. What does the Grant Access Using Hierarchies checkbox do?

- It allows someone higher up in the hierarchy to inherit the visibility of someone lower in the hierarchy.

3. What are the two types of sharing rules?

- Owner-based and criteria-based sharing rules.

4. Who adds team members to the Account and Sales teams?

- The Account Owner and the Opportunity Owner.

5. Does the Modify All data setting on a profile work if the org-wide setting for an object is private?

- Yes.

6. What is the use case for using permission sets?

- The use case for permission sets is when you have a group of users that all have the same profile but there is one person that may need extra access for a business reason. It wouldn't make sense to create another profile for just one permission. Permission sets allow you to add the one permission to the user record, which lets you bypass creating a whole new profile for one additional setting.

7. Where is a permission set added after it is created?

- To the user record.

Chapter 11

1. What are the four types of sandboxes?

- Developer, Developer Pro, Partial Copy, and Full Copy.

2. Which type of sandbox is commonly used for development?

- Developer.

3. Which type of sandbox is commonly used for data migration testing?

- Full Copy.

4. Why do you need to add a profile to a changeset?

- If you don't add any profiles, your component won't be visible and you will need to adjust the security in the target organization, so adding this here will save a lot of time.

5. Before you upload a changeset, what step must you take?

- Before you can deploy a changeset, you have to set up a deployment connection between the source organization and the target organization.

6. Should the outbound changeset be set up in the source or the target organization?

- The source organization.

7. What is the refresh interval for a Full Copy sandbox?

- 29 days.

Chapter 12

1. Why would you create a Master-Detail relationship as opposed to a Lookup relationship?

- If the child record needs to be deleted when the master record is deleted, then you should create a Master-Detail relationship.

2. What are some of the optional features when creating a custom object?

- Allow reports, allow activities, track field history, and allow in chatter groups.

3. What are the two types of internal relationship fields you can create on an object?

- Master-Detail and Lookup relationships.

4. What part of the page layout shows related items on a record?

- The related lists section.

5. What is a possible use case for using record types?

- Record types are used when you need to show different page layouts, apply different processes, and/or need to show different picklist values based on a business use case.

Chapter 13

1. What is a use case for using an unmanaged package?

- These applications are usually used to move functionality from one Salesforce environment to the other.

2. What is the benefit of using a managed package?

- The package can be published and listed on App Exchange and the package can be upgraded.

3. What is the name of the Salesforce marketplace where you can find apps?

- App Exchange.

4. What are some of the access options you can grant when installing a package?

- Install for Admins Only, Install for All Users, and Install for Specific Profiles.

5. What option do you have when uninstalling a package?

- You can save a copy of the package's data for 48 hours.

6. What is the best way to set up Salesforce Mobile for your users?

- By using Mobile App Quickstart.

Chapter 14

1. What are the three types of evaluation criteria?

- **Created, Created and every time it's edited**, and **Created and any time it's edited to subsequently meet the criteria**.

2. What are the two options for adding rule criteria?

- If the criteria are met or if a formula evaluates to true.

3. What are outbound messages used for?

- Outbound messages are used to send messages with field updates to external systems if a field is changed in Salesforce.

4. On the field update section, what do the **Re-evaluate Workflow Rules after Field Changes** checkbox do?

- If another workflow rule uses the new field value as a rule criterion, it will be triggered when this new field update is made.

5. What are time-based workflow actions?

- Time-dependent workflow actions provide the same four types as immediate workflow actions. The difference is that time-dependent workflow actions use a defined time trigger so that they can execute in the future.

6. How can you check if a time-based workflow action was created?

- From the time-based workflow monitoring feature.

7. How can you check if an email alert was sent?

- By requesting an Email Log.

Chapter 15

1. What are some actions available with Process Builder that are not available with workflow rules?

- Process Builder allows you to automate more items, such as creating all types of records, as opposed to just creating tasks with workflow rules. Process Builder also allows you to update any related record, as opposed to updating only the record or its parent with workflow rules.

2. What are the two options you can use to start a process on the add object step?

- Only when a record is created and when a record is created or edited.

3. What are the three options for Criteria for Executing Actions on the add criteria step?

- Conditions are met, formula evaluates to true, and no criteria—just execute the actions.

4. What checkbox must be checked on the criteria screen to allow scheduled actions for those criteria?

- The execute the actions only when specified changes are made to the record? checkbox.

5. What is the first step in creating scheduled actions?

- The first step is to set the schedule.

6. How do you activate a process?

- Click on the **Activate** button.

Chapter 16

1. What is the difference between the Jump Start Wizard and the standard Setup Wizard?

- The Jump Start Wizard condenses the steps into two pages as opposed to six pages for the initial creation of the approval process.

2. Are you able to have more than one approver on an approval process?

- Yes.

3. Why does the record lock for editing when a user submits it for approval?

- So that no changes can be made to the record that can affect its approval.

4. How are the approval process and workflow rule actions similar?

- They are the same actions.

5. What happens to the edit-ability of a record if a user recalls it from an approval?

- It is unlocked and available for editing.

6. What is the last step needed for an approval process to be live and working?

- The approval process has to be activated.

7. Where can an approver see all the items that have been assigned to him/her that need to be approved?

- On the home page, when logging into Salesforce.

Chapter 17

1. Besides a user, what else can a case or lead record be assigned to?

- A Queue.

2. How is the sort order used on an assignment rule?

- This field allows you to determine the order in which the rule entries are evaluated.

3. What happens if you don't choose an email template for a rule entry?

- The default assignment template is used.

4. When creating a queue, what is the Queue Email field used for?

- The Queue Email field is used when the assignment email is sent rather than to the individual emails of everyone that is a member of the queue.

5. If you leave the Queue Email field blank, who gets notified when a record is assigned to a queue?

- Everyone that is a member of the queue.

Other Books You May Enjoy

If you enjoyed this book, you may be interested in these other books by Packt:

Salesforce CRM - The Definitive Admin Handbook - Fifth Edition
Paul Goodey

ISBN: 9781789619782

- Configure a variety of user interface features in Salesforce CRM
- Understand the capabilities of the Salesforce CRM sharing model
- Explore Einstein Analytics - Salesforce's new wave of advanced reporting
- Get to grips with the Lightning Process Builder workflow
- Set up user profiles, security, and login access mechanisms
- Find out how Apex and Visualforce coding can be used in Salesforce CRM
- Manage the transition from Salesforce Classic to Lightning Experience
- Implement data manipulation features to apply best practices in data management

Salesforce Lightning Platform Enterprise Architecture - Third Edition

Andrew Fawcett

ISBN: 9781789956719

- Create and deploy AppExchange packages and manage upgrades
- Understand Enterprise Application Architecture patterns
- Customize mobile and desktop user experience with Lightning Web Components
- Manage large data volumes with asynchronous processing and big data strategies
- Implement Source Control and Continuous Integration
- Add AI to your application with Einstein
- Use Lightning External Services to integrate external code and data with your Lightning Application

Leave a review - let other readers know what you think

Please share your thoughts on this book with others by leaving a review on the site that you bought it from. If you purchased the book from Amazon, please leave us an honest review on this book's Amazon page. This is vital so that other potential readers can see and use your unbiased opinion to make purchasing decisions, we can understand what our customers think about our products, and our authors can see your feedback on the title that they have worked with Packt to create. It will only take a few minutes of your time, but is valuable to other potential customers, our authors, and Packt. Thank you!

Index